HELLENISTIC CULTURE AND SOCIETY

General Editors: Anthony W. Bulloch, Erich S. Gruen, A. A. Long, and Andrew F. Stewart

I. Alexander to Actium: The Historical Evolution of the Hellenistic Age, by Peter Green
II. Hellenism in the East: The Interaction of Greek and Non-Greek Civilizations from Syria to Central Asia after Alexander, edited by Amélie Kuhrt and Susan Sherwin-White
III. The Question of "Eclecticism": Studies in Later Greek Philosophy, edited by J. M. Dillon and A. A. Long
IV. Antigonos the One-Eyed and the Creation of the Hellenistic State, by Richard A. Billows
V. A History of Macedonia, by Malcolm Errington, translated by Catherine Errington
VI. Attic Letter-Cutters of 229 to 86 B.C., by Stephen V. Tracy

# Attic Letter-Cutters of 229 to 86 B.C.

# Attic Letter-Cutters of 229 to 86 B.C.

*Stephen V. Tracy*

UNIVERSITY OF CALIFORNIA PRESS

Berkeley   Los Angeles   Oxford

PHOTO CREDITS

Agora Excavations, American School of Classical Studies at Athens
  Figures 1, 4, 8, 16, 18, 23, 24, 25, 27, 30, 32, 33
  Plates 1–5, 7, 9–26, 29

Epigraphical Museum, Athens
  Figures 5, 7, 9, 11, 14, 15, 17, 19, 20, 31, 34–36, 38
  Plates 6, 27, 28

Louvre Museum, Paris
  Figure 41

Author's photographs
  Figures 2, 3, 6, 10, 12, 13, 21, 22, 26, 28, 29, 37, 39
  Plate 8

The Publisher wishes to thank
The Ohio State University, College of Humanities,
for its generous contribution toward
the publication of this book.

University of California Press
Berkeley and Los Angeles, California

University of California Press, Ltd.
Oxford, England

© 1990 by
The Regents of the University of California

### Library of Congress Cataloging-in-Publication Data

Tracy, Stephen V., 1941–
  Attic letter-cutters of 229 to 86 B.C. / Stephen V. Tracy.
    p.  cm.—(Hellenistic culture and society : 6)
  Includes bibliographical references.
  ISBN 0-520-06806-8 (alk. paper)
  1. Inscriptions, Greek—Greece—Attikē.  2. Stone-cutters—Greece—Attikē—History.  3. Paleography, Greek.  4. Attic Greek dialect—Writing.  I. Title.  II. Series.
CN380.A8T73   1990                                    89-20286
487'.4—dc20                                              CIP

Printed in the United States of America
1  2  3  4  5  6  7  8  9

The paper used in this publication meets the minimum requirements
of American National Standard for Information Sciences—Permanence
of Paper for Printed Library Materials, ANSI Z39.48-1984. ∞™

*For June*

# Contents

*List of Figures  ix*
*List of Plates  xi*
*List of Abbreviations  xiii*
*Preface  xv*
*Introduction  1*
*List of Inscriptions Studied  7*

The Letter-Cutters of 229 to 86 B.C.  39

    Agora I 787 Cutter, 229–217 B.C.  41
    *IG* II² 1706 Cutter, 229–*ca*. 203 B.C.  44
    *IG* II² 912 Cutter, 226–*ca*. 190 B.C.  55
    Agora I 7181 Cutter, 224–187 B.C.  61
    *IG* II² 1318 Cutter, 212/1 B.C.  68
    *IG* II² 913 Cutter, 210–170 B.C.  71
    *IG* II² 1309 Cutter, 208/7? B.C.  80
    Agora I 656 + 6355 Cutter, 203–163 B.C.  82
    *IG* II² 1131 Cutter, *ca*. 200 B.C.  89
    *IG* II² 1326 Cutter, 199–175 B.C.  92
    *IG* II² 886 Cutter, 194–177 B.C.  96
    Agora I 247 Cutter, 194–147 B.C.  99
    *IG* II² 1324 Cutter, *ca*. 190 B.C.  110
    *IG* II² 897 Cutter, 189–177 B.C.  113
    *IG* II² 892 Cutter, 188–186 B.C.  117
    Agora I 6765 Cutter, 188–180 B.C.  121
    *IG* II² 1329 Cutter, 183–174 B.C.  125
    Agora I 6512 Cutter, *ca*. 180–161 B.C.  128

*IG* II² 903 Cutter, 179–160 B.C.  *132*
*IG* II² 3479 Cutter, 175–*ca.* 135 B.C.  *137*
*IG* II² 783 Cutter, 173–160 B.C.  *143*
Agora I 6006 Cutter, 169–134 B.C.  *146*
Register of Agora I 247 Cutter, 155/4 B.C.  *163*
Agora I 5469 Cutter, 151/0? B.C.  *167*
*FD* III 2 no. 24 Cutter, 138–127 B.C.  *170*
*IG* II² 937 Cutter, *ca.* 135–122 B.C.  *173*
*IG* II² 1028 Cutter, 131–97 B.C.  *181*
Agora I 286 Cutter, 130–116 B.C.  *187*
Agora I 1594 Cutter, 122/1 B.C.  *192*
*IG* II² 1008 Cutter, 118–96 B.C.  *194*
*IG* II² 1009 Cutter, 116–93 B.C.  *197*
Agora I 6108 Cutter, 112–110 B.C.  *201*
*IG* II² 1135 Cutter, 111–97 B.C.  *204*
*IG* II² 2983 Cutter, 111–97 B.C.  *207*
*IG* II² 1011 Cutter, 106/5 B.C.  *209*
*FD* III 2 no. 5 Cutter, 106–95 B.C.  *212*
*IG* II² 1034 Cutter, 103/2 B.C.  *216*
*FD* III 2 no. 26 Cutter, 98/7 B.C.  *220*

Discussion of Letter-Cutting and Cutters 229 to 86 B.C.  *223*
Inscriptions "Not Assigned"  *237*

*Appendix A. Inscriptions Erroneously Attributed to 229 to 86* B.C.  *259*

*Appendix B. Inscriptions Redated*  *261*

*Appendix C. Joins and Associations: A Summary List*  *266*

*Appendix D. A List of State Decrees, or Probable Decrees, Not Assigned*  *268*

*Morphological Index of Characteristic Letters*  *271*

*Index to Greek Texts*  *275*

*Index of Passages Cited*  *279*

*Index of Persons*  *283*

*General Index*  *289*

*Plates (following 291)*

# *Figures*

Figure 1.   Agora I 787 lines 4–25   *42*
Figure 2.   *IG* II² 1706 lines 4–18   *45*
Figure 3.   *IG* II² 912 lines 38–43   *56*
Figure 4.   Agora I 7181 lines 2–24   *62*
Figure 5.   *IG* II² 1318   *69*
Figure 6.   *IG* II² 913 lines 61–68   *72*
Figure 7.   *IG* II² 1309b   *81*
Figure 8.   Agora I 656 + 6355   *83*
Figure 9.   *IG* II² 1131   *90*
Figure 10.  *IG* II² 1326 lines 4–17   *93*
Figure 11.  *IG* II² 886   *97*
Figure 12.  Agora I 247 lines 50–56   *100*
Figure 13.  *IG* II² 1324 lines 6–13   *111*
Figure 14.  *IG* II² 897   *114*
Figure 15.  *IG* II² 892a   *118*
Figure 16.  Agora I 6765   *122*
Figure 17.  *IG* II² 1329 lines 17–28   *126*
Figure 18.  Agora I 6512   *129*
Figure 19.  *IG* II² 903   *133*
Figure 20.  *IG* II² 3479   *138*
Figure 21.  *IG* II² 783   *144*
Figure 22.  Agora I 6006 lines 36–43   *147*
Figure 23.  Agora I 247 lines 97–103   *164*
Figure 24.  Agora I 247 lines 116–121   *164*
Figure 25.  Agora I 5469   *168*
Figure 26.  *FD* III 2 no. 138 (top), no. 24 lines 1–16 (bottom)   *171*

LIST OF FIGURES

Figure 27.  *IG* II² 937 lines 34–46   *174*
Figure 28.  *IG* II² 1028 lines 93–99   *182*
Figure 29.  Agora I 286 lines 8–15   *188*
Figure 30.  Agora I 1594   *193*
Figure 31.  *IG* II² 1008 lines 79–106   *195*
Figure 32.  Agora I 5952 lines 8–14 (part of *IG* II² 1009)   *198*
Figure 33.  Agora I 6108   *202*
Figure 34.  *IG* II² 1135a   *205*
Figure 35.  *IG* II² 2983   *208*
Figure 36.  *IG* II² 1011 lines 35–87   *210*
Figure 37.  *FD* III 2 no. 13 lines 2–20 (continuation of *FD* III 2 no. 5)   *213*
Figure 38.  *IG* II² 1034a + b + c   *217*
Figure 39.  *FD* III 2 no. 26 lines 1–13 (I)   *221*
Figure 40.  Bar graph charting the careers of the cutters of 229–86 B.C.   *224*
Figure 41.  *IG* II² 2857   *229*

## Plates

(following page 291)

Plate 1.  Agora I 1731
Plate 2.  Agora I 5997
Plate 3.  Agora I 5929
Plate 4.  Agora I 6090
Plate 5.  Agora I 918, crown
Plate 6.  *IG* II² 443
Plate 7.  Agora I 5689
Plate 8.  Agora I 6267
Plate 9.  Agora I 1330
Plate 10. Agora I 4615
Plate 11. Agora I 925
Plate 12. Agora I 3954
Plate 13. Agora I 5798
Plate 14. Agora I 4537
Plate 15. Agora I 896
Plate 16. Agora I 968
Plate 17. Agora I 2768
Plate 18. Agora I 4503
Plate 19. Agora I 4886
Plate 20. Join of Agora I 6035 and I 175
Plate 21. Agora I 6459
Plate 22. Agora I 2016
Plate 23. Agora I 6977 + 6980 + 6978
Plate 24. Join of Agora I 6005 and I 6006
Plate 25. Agora I 750

LIST OF PLATES

Plate 26.  Agora I 1912
Plate 27.  Join of EM 5588 and 6062
Plate 28.  Join of *IG* II² 959 and 1014
Plate 29.  Agora I 5782

# Abbreviations

| | |
|---|---|
| ² (used in lists) | *IG* II² |
| II² | *IG* II² |
| Agora XV | B. D. Meritt and J. S. Traill, *The Athenian Agora* XV *Inscriptions, the Athenian Councillors*, Princeton 1974 |
| ArchEph | Ἀρχαιολογικὴ Ἐφημερίς |
| AthMitt | *Mitteilungen des Deutschen Archäologischen Instituts (Athenische Abteilung)* |
| Bull.épigr. | J. and L. Robert, *Bulletin épigraphique* (in *REG*) |
| Clinton, *Sacred Officials* | K. Clinton, *The Sacred Officials of the Eleusinian Mysteries*, Philadelphia 1974 |
| Deltion | Ἀρχαιολογικὸν Δελτίον |
| Dow Studies | *Studies Presented to Sterling Dow on His Eightieth Birthday*, Greek, Roman, and Byzantine Monograph 10, Durham, N.C. 1984 |
| Dow, *Prytaneis* | S. Dow, *Prytaneis*, *Hesperia* Suppl. 1, 1937 |
| *FD* III 2 | *Fouilles de Delphes* III fasc. 2, *Épigraphie, Inscriptions du Trésor des Athéniens*, Paris 1909–1913 |
| H (used in lists) | *Hesperia* |
| Habicht, *Studien* | Ch. Habicht, *Studien zur Geschichte Athens in hellenistischer Zeit*, Hypomnemata 73, Göttingen 1982 |
| Henry, *Prescripts* | A. S. Henry, *The Prescripts of Athenian Decrees*, Mnemosyne 49, 1977 |

## LIST OF ABBREVIATIONS

| | |
|---|---|
| HSCP | Harvard Studies in Classical Philology |
| ICreticae | M. Guarducci, Inscriptiones Creticae I–IV, Rome 1935–1950 |
| ID | Inscriptions de Délos, Paris 1926– |
| Kirchner-Klaffenbach, Imagines | J. Kirchner, Imagines Inscriptionum Atticarum, 2nd ed., G. Klaffenbach, Berlin 1948 |
| Kerameikos III | W. Peek, Kerameikos III, Inschriften, Ostraka, Fluchtafeln, Berlin 1941 |
| Lettering | S. V. Tracy, The Lettering of an Athenian Mason, Hesperia Suppl. 15, 1975 |
| Maier, Gr.Mauerbauinschriften | F. G. Maier, Griechische Mauerbauinschriften, Vestigia 1–2, 1959–1961 |
| NPA | J. Sundwall, Nachträge zur Prosopographia Attica, Helsingfors 1910 |
| Osborne, Naturalization | M. J. Osborne, Naturalization in Athens I–IV, Brussels 1981–1983 |
| PA | J. Kirchner, Prosopographia Attica, Berlin 1901–1903 |
| Peçirka, Enktesis | J. Peçirka, The Formula for the Grant of Enktesis in Attic Inscriptions, Prague 1966 |
| Pouilloux, Rhamnonte | J. Pouilloux, La forteresse de Rhamnonte, Paris 1954 |
| Praktika | Πρακτικὰ τῆς Ἀκαδημίας Ἀθηνῶν |
| Pritchett-Meritt, Chronology | W. K. Pritchett and B. D. Meritt, The Chronology of Hellenistic Athens, Cambridge, Mass. 1940 |
| Ruck, Victors | C. A. P. Ruck, The List of Victors in Comedies at the Dionysia, Leiden 1967 |
| Tracy, IG II² 2336 | S. V. Tracy, IG II² 2336, Contributors of First Fruits for the Pythaïs, Meisenheim 1982 |

# *Preface*

The study which follows is the natural outgrowth of many years studying the hands of individual Attic letter-cutters. When I began my work twenty years ago, it was generally denied that one could identify the work of individual cutters. In successive studies I believe I have shown not only that the work of individuals can be recognized but that the effort has a serious purpose. The study of hands provides a new approach to one of our most important classes of primary evidence. Inscriptions are a vital source for anyone seriously interested in the ancient world. The ability to recognize the work of individuals and to bring that work together gives us a significant new way to date inscriptions, most of which are fragmentary and difficult to date accurately by any other means. If, for example, one can assign a fragment to a known workman, one obviously then also has a date for it of plus or minus twenty years, the length of a man's working career.

I began the present book out of a conviction that it would be useful to extend my work from studies of isolated individual cutters to all of the inscriptions of a closed period. The attempt has been an ambitious one and larger than I had expected. It is, for one thing, daunting to try to deal with every inscription. Still, the results have been gratifying. By comparing the working careers of cutters, it has been possible to show that the accepted dates for the Athenian archons Achaios, Demetrios, and Pleistainos are quite wrong. There is also evidence, I suspect, for a break in the tribal rotation in the 140s B.C. But, on the whole, this study provides independent corroboration for most of the generally accepted archon dates. My only criterion, I emphasize, for the assignment of an inscription to a particular cutter is the lettering. Most archons in the years 229 to 86 seem to be pretty well placed; there will be improvements involving shifts this way or that, but the chronological framework appears reasonably sound.[1] In addition, I have been able to arrange by in-

---

[1] What is badly needed is a fresh, and dispassionate, examination of all the hard evidence for the archon list followed by the publication of a list which clearly and conservatively

dividual workman a high percentage of the surviving inscriptions. Of the 406 decrees or probable decrees of the state belonging to the period, I have been able to assign all but sixty-six (see Appendix D). Many of those that remain unassigned are so small that they barely permit study. Much knowledge has been gained of the individual inscriptions studied and of the way ancient cutters worked. This knowledge of course only has importance to a relatively small group of specialists in any generation, but it has an intrinsic interest these days for a much wider audience, namely all those who want to know something more about the everyday existence of working-class people. I have sought to bring out this aspect of the results in a concluding chapter on the cutters and trends in cutting in the years 229 to 86 B.C.

I have significant debts to acknowledge. The initial collection of the evidence was funded by a large grant from the National Endowment for the Humanities in 1972. I am indebted to the Greek authorities in general and especially to the Ephor of the Epigraphical Museum, Dr. D. Peppa-Delmouzou. The Ohio State University has been generous with travel money and awarded me one quarter's research leave for writing. The final writing and research have been done in the incomparable environment and facilities of the Institute for Advanced Study. I am greatly indebted to the faculty of the Institute for granting me membership for the past academic year. Professor Emeritus Homer A. Thompson has been ever generous in giving me permission to work on epigraphical fragments found in the Athenian Agora. I am finally most indebted to Professor Christian Habicht. His avid interest has kept me going and his keen knowledge, which he has so generously shared in daily discussions, has taught me much. There is not a page of this study which does not bear his imprint. Thomas Loening kindly put the Greek texts on the computer and helped immensely with the editing of the entire manuscript. The dedication cannot repay, but at least recognizes, the understanding, the sacrifice, and the love of the person to whom I owe most.

*The Institute for Advanced Study, June 1988*

---

provides that evidence. Current lists are virtually impossible to assess. One cannot be sure, for instance, whether a certain secretary really belongs with a particular archon or what the real evidence is for the demotic, and so on. Lists should in the future be published in such a way as to make a distinction between those few archons whose dates are truly fixed and those whose dates are much less sure or even arbitrary.

# *Introduction*

***Scope.*** The present study takes as its subject the inscriptions of Attica covering the years 229–86 B.C. This period forms a fairly well-defined unit, for in 229 the Athenians finally rid themselves of Macedonian occupation and in 86 the Roman general Sulla sacked Athens. Both points are marked by sharp breaks in the political order and indications of disruption in the social order. Intriguingly, none of the cutters of this study is known to have worked before 229. A ready explanation is not to be found, but the fact is observable. I have tried to include for study all inscriptions which have been, or can be, assigned to these years, with the important exception of gravestones.[1] For more on this, see The Problem Posed by Large Lettering, p. 5.

***Purpose.*** I have attempted to identify the letter-cutters working in the period and to collect the work of each.[2] In the process, many inscriptions have been dated more accurately (Appendix B) and a number of new joins and associations have been discovered (Appendix C). No doubt others will find more. In addition, this collection with its descriptions and photographs will provide an all but complete guide to Attic lettering of the period. It should enable those who find inscriptions which belong to these years to place them with relative ease.

---

[1] The evidence early on suggested that inscribing long texts with thousands of small letters is work of a different order from inscribing a name, patronymic, and demotic/ethnic on a gravestone. This is the simplest and most common type of grave marker. In the course of this study, I have examined in passing the lettering of many such grave inscriptions. I have found only one which can be assigned to one of the cutters of the present study, Agora I 3337 by the Cutter of *IG* II² 1706. I regard this as the proverbial exception which proves the rule. See also my comments in *GRBS* 11 (1970) 325 and note 35.

[2] To avoid the potential case of there being as many cutters as there are surviving inscriptions, I define a cutter as identified only when at least two separate texts can be assigned to him. For the single survivals and unique pieces see the chapter below on the Inscriptions "Not Assigned."

INTRODUCTION

*Arrangement.* I present the cutters in chronological order, the dates being determined by the archons which are preserved or can be restored with a reasonable degree of certainty. In large measure I follow the archon list as presented by B. D. Meritt in *Historia* 26 (1977) 161–91. Where I do not, I so indicate. In some cases, I offer alternate dates for archons, not out of a desire to be contrary, but rather to remind readers that the archon list is far more uncertain than the published lists can suggest. The inscriptions are listed under each cutter in the following order: *IG* numbers, Agora inventory numbers, and EM numbers and other rubrics as necessary in alphabetical order. Within categories the order is numerical. Readers looking for a particular inscription should consult the List of Inscriptions Studied.

For each cutter I provide dates, a description of his lettering, a list of his inscriptions, reference to *significant* recent discussions and re-editions, *editiones principes* of unpublished fragments from the Athenian Agora, and any new readings, joins, and associations which I have discovered as a result of this study. Where appropriate, I have also endeavored to include discussion of significant historical/prosopographical issues raised by particular inscriptions. My intention has been to create a handlist/sourcebook for Attic inscriptions of this period, the last great period of Athenian democracy.

A word of explanation is in order concerning the first editions of fragments from the Athenian Agora. They are scraps mostly and were not published sooner because little could be said about them. The American Excavations in the Agora and the American School are committed to making as many of these available as possible. It has seemed useful to publish these fragments with a photograph, since I can at least date each with some precision. I have done what I could with them, but I am often reduced to giving a text in capitals and publishing a photograph.[3] Perhaps another scholar will see something I have not or perhaps other inscriptions by these cutters will someday be found to which some of them may be assigned.

*Method.* Two principal assumptions lie at the basis of this study: namely, that the lettering on Attic inscriptions may be treated as a type of handwriting and that cutters normally inscribed their own particular lettering.[4] These assumptions have been tested now over a long period

---

[3] I owe thanks to Professor Homer A. Thompson and the Publications Committee of the School for permission to study and publish them here.
[4] For the reasoning which justifies these assumptions, see S. V. Tracy, "Identifying Epigraphical Hands," *GRBS* 11 (1970) 323–25 and *Lettering,* especially 86–95, 109–19.

of time and have proven their worth. The primary requisite for studying hands is the ability/patience to train one's eye to recognize individual idiosyncrasies in lettering and then to describe them accurately. The goal is to isolate in a given sample of lettering multiple individual peculiarities in the shape and spacing of the letters such that when another inscription reveals these same peculiarities one may feel safe in concluding that the same man inscribed both pieces. An important part of this, it must be stressed, is noting carefully the range of variation that a given cutter allows himself. Lettering does vary; cutters were not, and could not be, absolutely consistent. At the same time, they did tend, our evidence suggests, to cut rapidly and thus in their own style.

The following steps have been used in studying the cutters presented below. 1) For each hand a large, well-preserved and, if possible, securely dated fragment was chosen for intensive study. The writing on this fragment then became the standard in the search for other examples of the lettering. 2) "Learning" the hand was and is the real challenge in achieving any meaningful study of ancient cutters. One does it by repeated study of the lettering on the fragment selected, drawing every letter, sometimes over and over again, and noting every variation. It is a slow, painstaking process requiring weeks and sometimes months; the time varies from cutter to cutter. After considerable study it helps to verbalize, that is to put in writing, the peculiarities of the cutter's style. By slow degrees one gains a familiarity with the lettering until at some point (I do not know exactly how) one comes to "know" the hand just the way one knows the writing of a close acquaintance. The goal is to reach this point. 3) Once one "knows" a hand, then one does a thorough search for other examples of the writing.[5]

It has become obvious that further clarification is required on one fundamental matter. It is not uncommon for epigraphists to invoke the evidence of hands; most do it sparingly. However, one cannot properly speak of the *hand* of a cutter unless he has learned it. Moreover, to study a hand until one knows it and can recognize it intuitively and instantly, the way one does the writing of one's mother—this, as I have just described, is a long, laborious process and is only possible when one has a large enough sample of the lettering to permit study. Several hundred clearly preserved letters ought ideally to be the minimum. I feel constrained to observe that most assignments of inscriptions to "hands" do not rest on such study. They are merely the opinion of the writer in question that the lettering on two fragments is identical or very similar.

---

[5] I have also described the method and criteria which I employ in *GRBS* 11 (1970) 321–28; *Lettering* 1–11, 90–95; and *Dow Studies* 277–79.

Often, in fact, the fragments involved are very small. *Unless there is an adequate sample of the lettering, it is impossible to speak of hands in any meaningful way.*[6]

***Assignment of Inscriptions.*** After years of exhaustive study, I have been able to assign with (I think and hope) a great deal of accuracy the large majority of the texts which have letters a centimeter or less in height.[7] I have exercised caution and refrained from assigning any fragment if I felt doubt about the attribution. I suspect I have at times been overly precise and expected more uniformity of lettering from a cutter than was possible. In short, it may be that here or there I have seen the work of two cutters where there was only one or failed to see that several inscriptions with diverging letter-shapes are by one man. Obviously, I do not know that I have done this, but I suspect it. I have used precision and caution in order to try to avoid mistakes which others will have to undo.

A number of the inscriptions could not be assigned, among them those which are very worn or which have too few letters to enable meaningful study. Those which have letters more than a centimeter in height are difficult to assign with any degree of accuracy (see below). Then there are some which simply defy assignment. Tempting as it may be, I have refrained from forcing these into the *oeuvre* of one of my cutters. Some may be misdated and thus may not belong in the period studied here; others may be unique survivals. Finally there are a few which are highly idiosyncratic in their lettering and can safely be described as unique, at least among the large sample of inscriptions studied repeatedly during the course of this work. All these inscriptions, which are labelled in the List of Inscriptions Studied which follows as "not assigned," are treated below in a separate chapter. In any case, the point has been reached where I have accomplished all that I profitably can. Perhaps someone with a fresh eye will have better success with some of these pieces.

---

[6] I am often asked by colleagues to comment on the hand of a small fragment with twenty-five letters or less, say a dedication or artist's signature. My only reply can be that we can talk about the peculiarities of these particular letters, but that we must not confuse this with talking about the hand. So few letters do not really provide enough evidence for one to learn the hand and its range of peculiarities. One cannot make a hard and fast rule, but several hundred letters well preserved are usually the minimum necessary. Sometimes, if the lettering is very idiosyncratic a smaller sample may suffice; see my discussion below of the Cutter of Agora I 1594. Once one has learned the lettering of a cutter, one can, of course, recognize even very small fragments; see for example Agora I 6005 below.

[7] Of the 406 decrees or probable decrees of the State, for example, 340, a shade under 84 percent, have been attributed to the cutters of this study.

*The Problem Posed by Large Lettering.* Attic cutters inscribing decrees normally had rather long texts to inscribe and perforce engraved them in relatively small letters. These letters range from *ca.* 0.005 to *ca.* 0.01 m. in height. The inscribers cut them with vertically directed, straight-edged chisels in such a way that the length of cutting edge determined the length of letter-stroke. The great majority of decrees were inscribed in this way and all discussions of styles in Attic lettering are based on scholars' perceptions and intuitions about these (small) letters. I suspect also that all dating by letter-style, that is, a great amount of the dating of all Attic inscriptions, is based, more or less consciously, on the succession of styles as perceived in the small lettering.[8] What is not generally realized is that large letters, that is, letters with a height greater than *ca.* 0.012 m., were cut differently and demonstrably do not much resemble their small counterparts. The basic reason for this is that large letters must be cut rather deeply and with a furrowing technique. With such letters it is important not to err, for an error in cutting will probably require that the block be discarded. Thus these large letters were laid out with care and were often done with greater elaboration.[9] The canon for the succession of styles in large letters has not yet been established in more than the most haphazard rule-of-thumb way. J. Kirchner was the master; alas, he never made a statement about the style of these letters and my impression is, when other criteria failed him, he fell back on his knowledge of the small lettering on decrees for dating purposes. Thus, students of inscriptions which usually have large letters, such as dedications, statue bases, horoi, and grave monuments, should be warned that the dates for these, when they are based, as they often are, solely on the style of the lettering, must be regarded as very tentative, indeed little more than guesswork. They may be wide of the mark by a century or more.

The consequences for the present study are significant. It is, generally speaking, not possible to recognize a cutter's large lettering based on knowlege of his small lettering. We possess only a few large letters inscribed by any of the cutters treated in the present study, not enough to learn the hand, that is, his large hand, even roughly. And, in general, inscriptions with large letters tend to be short, hence there are probably not enough letters to permit study of individual hands in any real way. It

---

[8] The best statement of this succession for Attica is by S. Dow, "The Study of Lettering," in *Lettering*, especially pages xvii–xviii. The ready availability of the excellent photographs published by J. Kirchner and then revised by G. Klaffenbach in the successive *Imagines Inscriptionum Atticarum* (1935 and 1948) has exercised a strong influence over all subsequent scholars.

[9] For more on this whole matter, see *Lettering* 86–92.

should be possible, however, to develop a reasonably firm canon of successive styles for inscriptions with large letters through judicious use of the prosopographical evidence. Such a study is greatly needed and I hope someone will undertake it before long.

***Terminology.*** In the descriptions of the lettering which follow I have tried to use plain language and to avoid creating a special jargon. I trust the reader will understand that there are only so many ways to describe lettering and forgive both the inevitable repetition and also my flights of descriptive fancy. Some of these were necessary to preserve my sanity, as well as to make the lettering more personal to me and to my readers. My descriptions in each case are solely of the lettering on the inscription which serves as the standard and after which the cutter is named. The vagueness of my terms, such as "tends," "usually," "occasionally," is deliberate; none of the samples is large enough to allow more. It would be false to imply a mathematical precision where none can exist.

I use "right" and "left" to mean right and left as one looks at the inscribed surface or a photograph of it. "Terminal stroke" simply means a letter stroke which joins no other at its end. The horizontal of tau, for example, is terminal at both ends, the vertical only at the bottom. "Join" is a technically precise term which means that the two pieces which join can be felt to lock in place when brought together. As with pregnancy, there is no such thing as an almost join. An "association" refers to the case when all the evidence of lettering, marble, spacing, physical dimensions, text, and anything else that can be brought to bear strongly point to two pieces being part of the same inscription. The evidence in my view must be compelling. Many pieces *can* go together; the question is, do they?

***Style of, School of.*** I employ these two categories to indicate two degrees of warning to the reader. In the dossiers which follow I use the heading "Inscriptions in the style of" not infrequently and, let me emphasize, very precisely. I apply it to fragments which I feel were inscribed by the cutter in question, but the lettering shows sufficient deviation from the norm that I do not feel that the inscription can be placed in the dossier with no warning. "School of," which I restrict to the list of unassigned inscriptions offered in the chapter dealing with them, implies no more than a general similarity to the hand in question; such inscriptions are not, I am certain, by the master cutter indicated. In fact there is probably no direct relationship at all. I do not mean to imply one.

# List of Inscriptions Studied

*Explanatory comments*

Every effort has been made to study all of the relevant inscriptions. Over the years I have had access to most of the stones thanks to the cooperation of the authorities in the various countries and museums where they are now located. In addition to my own squeezes, I have consulted at various times those of S. Dow and, for the Eleusinian fragments, those of K. Clinton. In bringing the study to completion I have been given full use of the collection of squeezes at the Institute for Advanced Study in Princeton. There are very few Attic fragments which I have not at one stage of this work seen, at least to make a rapid assessment of the lettering. In the final stages of study, however, I have had to rely primarily on squeezes and in some instances on photographs. Photographs, unless exceptionally detailed and clear, are less satisfactory to work with because the shadowing can be deceptive. One cannot control a photograph the way one can when working from the stone or from a squeeze. When a squeeze or good photograph has not been available at this stage, I have marked a stone as "unavailable" even though it is probable that I have seen it at some point in the last twenty years. The inscriptions which fall into this category are largely dedications with lettering over 0.012 m. in height; in cases where the letter-height is published, I have added a slash plus the words "large lettering." There are relatively few inscriptions with letters less than a centimeter in height which I have not been able to study in detail.

A number of stones are either too worn or have too few letters preserved to allow, in my judgment, meaningful study of the hand. These are marked "unassignable/worn" or "unassignable/few."

"Lost" signifies inscriptions which can no longer be located or which are known only in copies, often made by early travellers. Obviously, one cannot say anything about the hand in these cases, unless of course a new fragment of the inscription has been discovered subsequently. This is true, for example, in the case of *IG* II² 937.

The problems with inscriptions which have large lettering, defined as lettering 0.012 m. or taller, are discussed in a special section at the outset of this study. Hands are difficult, if not impossible, to recognize in such texts. The label "large lettering" is simply descriptive. I have not been able to assign the text in question to any hand known to me, but I make no further claim.

All inscriptions marked "not assigned" are treated in a separate chapter at the end of this study; each labelled "style of X Cutter" is discussed with that cutter; all fragments with the indicator "part of" or "joins" should be looked up under the inscription number given.

| Inscr. Number | Assignment, page reference |
|---|---|
| *IG* II | |
| 398 | ²913 Cutter, 73 |
| *IG* II² | |
| 443 | style of ²1706, 49, 52–53 |
| 701 | I 7181 Cutter, 62 |
| 702 | ²913 Cutter, 71, 73 |
| 735 | style of I 787 Cutter, 43 |
| 736 | I 6006 Cutter, 148, 156 n. 10 |
| 783 | ²783 Cutter, 143 |
| 785 | ²913 Cutter, 73 |
| 786 | ²1706 Cutter, 46 |
| 789 | ²913 Cutter, 71, 73 |
| 794 | ²1706 Cutter, 46, 54 |
| 807 | ²1706 Cutter, 46, 54 |
| 814 | style of ²903 Cutter, 134 |
| 820 | ²903 Cutter, 134 |
| 822 | style of ²913 Cutter, 75 |
| 832 | I 787 Cutter, 42 |
| 833 | ²1706 Cutter, 46 |
| 834 | ²1706 Cutter, 46, 52, 53 |
| 835 | style of I 7181 Cutter, 63 |
| 836 | ²1706 Cutter, 46 |
| 837 | not assigned, 239 |
| 838 | style of I 787 Cutter, 43 |
| 839 | ²1706 Cutter, 46 |
| 840 | ²1008 Cutter, 196 |
| 841 | ²912 Cutter, 57 |
| 842 | I 7181 Cutter, 62 |
| 843 | I 787 Cutter, 42 |

## LIST OF INSCRIPTIONS STUDIED

| Inscr. Number | Assignment, page reference |
|---|---|
| 844 | ²913 Cutter, *73, 160* |
| 846 | ²1706 Cutter, *47* |
| 847 | ²1706 Cutter, *47, 54* |
| 848 | ²1318 Cutter, *68, 244* |
| 849 | ²1706 Cutter, *47* |
| 850 | ²886 Cutter, *98* |
| 851 | ²913 Cutter, *73* |
| 852 | ²1706 Cutter, *47, 54* |
| 853 | I 6006 Cutter, *148* |
| 854 | ²913 Cutter, *73* |
| 855 | ²913 Cutter, *73* |
| 856 | ²897 Cutter, *115* |
| 858 | I 787 Cutter, *42* |
| 859 | ²912 Cutter, *57* |
| 861 | ²912 Cutter, *57* |
| 862 | not assigned, *239* |
| 863 | ²1706 Cutter, *47* |
| 864 | ²913 Cutter, *73* |
| 865 | unassignable/few and worn, *239* |
| 866 | unassignable/few |
| 867 | style of I 247 Cutter, *103, 109* |
| 868 | I 6006 Cutter, *148* |
| 869 | ²1706 Cutter, *47* |
| 870 | lost |
| 871 | ²1706 Cutter, *47* |
| 872 | lost |
| 873 | lost |
| 874 | lost |
| 875 | lost |
| 876 | not assigned, *239* |
| 877 | ²1706 Cutter, *47* |
| 878 | ²1706 Cutter, *47* |
| 880 | unassignable/worn |
| 881 | lost |
| 882 | lost |
| 884 | not assigned, *239* |
| 885 | not assigned, *227 n.7, 239* |
| 886 | ²886 Cutter, *96–98* |
| 887 | not assigned, *240* |
| 888 | I 247 Cutter, *101, 107* |
| 889 + 904 | not assigned, *123, 240* |

*9*

| Inscr. Number (IG II² cont.) | Assignment, page reference |
|---|---|
| 890 | lost, see Agora XV no. 174 |
| 891 | I 6765 Cutter, *76, 122, 123* |
| 892 | ²892 Cutter, *117–19* |
| 893a | ²913 Cutter, *60, 73* |
| 893b,c | not assigned, *240* |
| 894 | style of I 7181 Cutter, *63* |
| 895 | I 6006 Cutter, *148* |
| 896 | ²913 Cutter, *73* |
| 897 | ²897 Cutter, *113–14, 115, 235* |
| 898 | ²897 Cutter, *115, 116, 235* |
| 899 | ²913 Cutter, *73* |
| 900 | ²897 Cutter, *115, 116* |
| 901 | I 656 + 6355 Cutter, *84–86* |
| 902 | I 247 Cutter, *101, 107* |
| 903 | ²903 Cutter, *132–34* |
| 904 | joins 889 *q.v.* |
| 905 | lost |
| 906 | unassignable/worn |
| 907 | I 6006 Cutter, *148* |
| 908 | I 247 Cutter, *101* |
| 909 | ²897 Cutter, *115* |
| 910 | I 247 Cutter, *101* |
| 911 | ²903 Cutter, *134, 235* |
| 912 | ²912 Cutter, *55–56, 57* |
| 913 | ²913 Cutter, *71–73* |
| 914 | ²913 Cutter, *73* |
| 915 | I 656 + 6355 Cutter, *84* |
| 916 | ²912 Cutter, *57* |
| 917 | ²1706 Cutter, *47, 239* |
| 918 | I 247 Cutter, *101* |
| 919 | unassignable/worn |
| 920 | I 6765 Cutter, *122, 124* |
| 921 | frag. lost; part of ²977 |
| 922 | not assigned, *227 n.7, 240* |
| 923 | lost |
| 924 | I 6006 Cutter, *148* |
| 925 | ²892 Cutter, *119* |
| 926 | I 6006 Cutter, *148* |
| 927 | ²1706 Cutter, *47* |
| 929 | ²897 Cutter, *115* |
| 930 | I 6006 Cutter, *148* |

## LIST OF INSCRIPTIONS STUDIED

| Inscr. Number | Assignment, page reference |
|---|---|
| 931 | ²912 Cutter, *57* |
| 932 | part of ²1008 |
| 933 | part of I 5469 |
| 934/5 | unassignable/worn, see Habicht, *Studien* 163 |
| 936 | ²886 Cutter, *98* |
| 937 | ²937 Cutter, *173–75* |
| 938 | I 656 + 6355 Cutter, *84* |
| 939 | ²1309 Cutter, *80–81* |
| 940 | ²897 Cutter, *115* |
| 941 | = *IG* XII.v 596B |
| 942 + 944 | ²912 Cutter, *56, 57* |
| 943 | I 7181 Cutter, *62* |
| 944b | joins I 7181 |
| 945 | not assigned, *135, 227 n.7, 240, 252* |
| 946 | I 247 Cutter (lines 4–6), *101* |
| | style of I 247 (lines 1–3, 7–14), *103* |
| 947 | I 656 + 6355 Cutter, *84* |
| 948 | I 656 + 6355 Cutter, *84* |
| 949 | not assigned, *58, 235, 240* |
| 950 | not assigned, *235, 240* |
| 951 | ²903 Cutter, *134* |
| 952 | ²783 Cutter, *144* |
| 953 | I 6006 Cutter, *148* |
| 954 | I 247 Cutter, *101* |
| 955 | I 6006 Cutter, *148* |
| 956 | ²903 Cutter, *134, 185* |
| 957 | not assigned, *185, 240* |
| 958 | not assigned, *140, 161, 185, 241* |
| 959 | style of ²1028 Cutter, *183, 184–85* |
| 960 | I 6006 Cutter, *148* |
| 961 | I 6006 Cutter, *148, 185* |
| 962 | I 6006 Cutter, *148* |
| 963 | lost |
| 964 | not assigned, *241* |
| 965 | lost |
| 966 | I 6006 Cutter, *148* |
| 967 | I 6006 Cutter, *148* |
| 968 | I 6006 Cutter, *140, 148, 161* |
| 969 | lost |
| 970 | I 6006 Cutter, *148* |

ATTIC LETTER-CUTTERS OF 229–86 B.C.

| Inscr. Number (IG II² cont.) | Assignment, page reference |
|---|---|
| 971 | not assigned, *67, 241* |
| 972 | I 247 Cutter, *101, 107* |
| 973 | not assigned, *241* |
| 974 | I 6006 Cutter, *104, 142 n. 6, 148* |
| 975 | I 6108 Cutter, *104, 201* |
| 976 | not assigned, *104, 241* |
| 977 | ²937 Cutter, *175, 177–79* |
| 978 | ²913 Cutter, *73* |
| 979 | I 247 Cutter, *101* |
| 980 | not assigned, *241* |
| 981 | I 6006 Cutter, *149* |
| 982 | not assigned, *241* |
| 983 | I 6006 Cutter, *149* |
| 984 | unavailable |
| 985 | not assigned, *241* |
| 986 | not assigned, *241* |
| 987 | I 6006 Cutter, *149* |
| 988a | I 6006 Cutter, *149* |
| 988b | I 6006 Cutter, *149, 155* |
| 989 | ²1028 Cutter, *182* |
| 990 | I 247 Cutter, *101* |
| 991 | part of I 286 |
| 992 | I 247 Cutter, *101* |
| 993 | ²1706 Cutter, *47, 66* |
| 994 | I 7181 Cutter, *62, 66* |
| 995 | *FD* III 2 no. 26 Cutter, *220* |
| 996 | ²783 Cutter, *144, 235* |
| 997 | I 247 Cutter, *101* |
| 998 | = 867 |
| 1000 | lost |
| 1001 | lost |
| 1002 | unavailable |
| 1003 | not assigned, *241* |
| 1004 | not assigned, *235, 241* |
| 1005 | lost |
| 1006 | not assigned, *235, 242* |
| 1007 | part of I 286 |
| 1008 | ²1008 Cutter, *76, 142 n. 4, 194–96* |
| 1009 | ²1009 Cutter, *197–98* |
| 1010 | lost |
| 1011 | ²1011 Cutter, *76, 185, 209–11* |

LIST OF INSCRIPTIONS STUDIED

| Inscr. Number | Assignment, page reference |
|---|---|
| 1012 | unavailable |
| 1013 | lost |
| 1014 | style of ²1028, *183, 184–85* |
| 1015 | unassignable/few |
| 1016 | unassignable/few |
| 1017 | unavailable |
| 1018 | not assigned, *242* |
| 1019 | not assigned, *142 n. 6, 242* |
| 1020 | unavailable |
| 1021 | unassignable/worn and few |
| 1022 | not assigned, *242* |
| 1023 | ²1028 Cutter, *182* |
| 1024 | I 7181 Cutter, *62, 66* |
| 1026 | lost |
| 1027 | I 6006 Cutter, *130, 149* |
| 1028 | ²1028 Cutter, *181–82, 183, 219 n. 2* |
| 1029 | *FD* III 2 no. 5 Cutter, *213* |
| 1030 | ²1009 Cutter, *198* |
| 1031 | part of 1006 |
| 1032 | part of I 286 |
| 1033 | style of ²1009, *199* |
| 1034 | ²1034 Cutter, *216–19* |
| | col. II bottom unique |
| 1036 | ²1008 Cutter, *196, 219* |
| 1037 | I 5469 Cutter, *169* |
| 1038 | not assigned, *242* |
| 1045 | I 6006 Cutter, *149, 156 n. 10* |
| 1054 | style of ²1008, *196* |
| 1055 | not assigned, *242* |
| 1056/7 | not assigned, *242* |
| 1060 | part of 1036 |
| 1061 | part of 975 |
| 1124 | = 1171 |
| 1130 | not assigned, *242* |
| 1131 | ²1131 Cutter, *89–90, 91* |
| 1132 | style of ²937, *175* |
| 1133 | I 286 Cutter, *189, 191* |
| 1134 | I 286 Cutter, *189, 191* |
| 1135 | ²1135 Cutter, *91, 204–206* |
| 1136 | ²1028 Cutter, *183* |
| 1137 | not assigned, *243* |

## ATTIC LETTER-CUTTERS OF 229–86 B.C.

| Inscr. Number (IG II² cont.) | Assignment, page reference |
|---|---|
| 1170 | not assigned, *243* |
| 1171 | I 286 Cutter, *189* |
| 1220 | I 7181 Cutter, *62, 67* |
| 1221 | ²912 Cutter, *57* |
| 1223 | not assigned, *243* |
| 1224 | I 6006 Cutter, *149, 155* |
| 1227 | ²1028 Cutter, *183* |
| 1228 | ²1028 Cutter, *183* |
| 1235 | ²1706 Cutter, *47, 54* |
| 1236 | ²1326 Cutter, *93, 95* |
| 1243 | ²913 Cutter, *71, 73, 79, 106* |
| 1281 | ²1706 Cutter, *47, 52* |
| 1292 | ²1706 Cutter, *47* |
| 1293 | ²913 Cutter, *73* |
| 1296 | ²913 Cutter, *71, 73* |
| 1300 | not assigned, *52, 228, 243* |
| 1301 | unavailable |
| 1302 | not assigned, *52, 243* |
| 1303 | I 7181 Cutter, *52, 63, 67* |
| 1304 | ²912 Cutter, *52, 57* |
| 1305 | ²1706 Cutter, *47, 52* |
| 1306 | ²1706 Cutter, *47, 52* |
| 1307 | I 7181 Cutter, *52, 63, 67* |
| 1308 | not assigned, *52, 228, 243* |
| 1309 | ²1309 Cutter, *52, 80* |
| 1310 | not assigned, *52, 243* |
| 1311 | not assigned, *243* |
| 1312 | not assigned, *52, 243* |
| 1313 | unassignable/worn, *52* |
| 1314 | ²1706 Cutter, *47* |
| 1315 | ²1706 Cutter, *47* |
| 1318 | ²1318 Cutter, *68* |
| 1319 | ²1706 Cutter, *47* |
| 1320 | ²1706 Cutter, *47* |
| 1321 | not assigned, *243* |
| 1322 | not assigned, *228, 243–44* |
| 1323 | lost |
| 1324 | ²1324 Cutter, *110–11, 112* |
| 1325 | ²1326 Cutter, *93, 95, 112* |
| 1326 | ²1326 Cutter, *92–93, 94, 95, 112* |
| 1327 | ²913 Cutter (lines 1–29), *74, 77, 79* |

*14*

## LIST OF INSCRIPTIONS STUDIED

| *Inscr. Number* | *Assignment, page reference* |
|---|---|
| 1328 | unassignable/few (lines 1–3), *126* |
| | ²1329 Cutter (lines 4–20), *125, 126–27* |
| | unassignable/worn (lines 21–44), *126, 235* |
| 1329 | ²1329 Cutter, *125, 235* |
| 1330 | unavailable, *60* |
| 1331 | ²937 Cutter, *175* |
| 1332 | I 286 Cutter, *189, 191* |
| 1333 | I 286 Cutter, *189* |
| 1335 | ²2983 Cutter (lines 1–24), *207* |
| | not assigned (lines 25–65), *244* |
| 1336 | lost |
| 1337 | not assigned, *244* |
| 1341 | ²1028 Cutter, *183* |
| 1536 | style of ²903 Cutter, *134* |
| 1537/38 | ²1706 Cutter, *47* |
| 1539 | ²912 Cutter, *56, 57* |
| 1552a | *FD* III 2 no. 5 Cutter, *213* |
| 1706 | ²1706 Cutter, *44–46, 47, 53, 229 n. 11* |
| 1707 | part of I 7496 |
| 1708 | style of I 656 + 6355 Cutter, *84, 88* |
| 1709 + 2863 | ²1706 Cutter, *47* |
| 1710 | unavailable |
| 1711 | not assigned, *244* |
| 1712 | not assigned, *244* |
| 1714 | not assigned, *244* |
| 1934 | I 6006 Cutter, *149, 155–56* |
| 1937 | I 6006 Cutter, *149* |
| 1938 | I 247 Cutter, *101, 140* |
| 1939 | I 6006 Cutter, *140, 142 n. 4, 149, 246* |
| 1940 | I 6006 Cutter, *149* |
| 1941 | not assigned, *244* |
| 1942 | ²1028 Cutter, *183, 219* |
| 1943 | ²1034 Cutter, *217–19* |
| 1944, lines 5–9 | not assigned, *244* |
| 1958 | not assigned, *244* |
| 1960 | part of I 286 |
| 2272 | not assigned, *245–46* |
| 2313 | I 7181 Cutter, *63* |
| 2314 | ²913 Cutter (col. I), *74, 77–78, 79, 233 n. 17* |

| Inscr. Number (IG II² cont.) | Assignment, page reference |
|---|---|
| 2314 (cont.) | I 247 Cutter (col. II), *101* |
| | lines 98–103 part of ²13121 |
| 2315 | lost |
| 2316 | lost |
| 2317 | lost |
| 2323 | ²1706 Cutter (lines 97–112), *47, 53* |
| | ²913 Cutter (lines 113–43), *74, 233* |
| | not assigned (lines 144–204), *142 n.5, 246* |
| | I 6006 Cutter (lines 205–52), *149* |
| 2327 | ²1034 Cutter, *217* |
| 2330 | I 6006 Cutter, *149* |
| 2331 | ²913 Cutter, *74* |
| 2332 | I 247 Cutter, *101, 112* |
| 2333a | ²912 Cutter, *57, 112* |
| 2333b,c | unassignable/worn |
| 2334 | I 6006 Cutter, *149, 155, 156* |
| 2335 | not assigned, *246* |
| 2336 | multiple hands, *183, 185–86, 205, 207–8, 213, 226, 229 n.11, 230, 233* |
| 2353 | style of ²1706 Cutter, *49* |
| 2354 | not assigned, *246* |
| 2357 | I 247 Cutter, *101, 105, 107–108* |
| 2358 | unavailable |
| 2359 | not assigned, *246* |
| 2362 | ²913 Cutter, *74* |
| 2363 | unavailable |
| 2392 | = 2404 |
| 2404 | ²903 Cutter, *134* |
| 2435 | I 6006 Cutter, *149, 156* |
| 2436 | I 6006 Cutter, *149, 156–57* |
| 2440 | register of I 247 Cutter, *165* |
| 2442 | lost? |
| 2443 | I 247 Cutter (lines 22–25), *79, 102, 108, 233* |
| | style of ²913 (lines 1–12, 16, 18), *75, 78–79* |
| 2444 | unavailable |
| 2445 | not assigned, *155, 246* |
| 2446 | large lettering |
| 2447 | not assigned, *246–47* |

*16*

LIST OF INSCRIPTIONS STUDIED

| Inscr. Number | Assignment, page reference |
|---|---|
| 2448 | style of ²2983, *208* |
| 2450 | part of 2272 |
| 2451 | not assigned, *247* |
| 2452 | multiple hands, *112, 185, 213, 214–15, 220, 233, 246* |
| 2453 | part of I 286 |
| 2454 | part of 2336 |
| 2455 | not assigned, *247* |
| 2456 | part of 1009 |
| 2457 | part of 1009 |
| 2458 | not assigned, *247* |
| 2459 | ²1009 Cutter, *198, 199* |
| 2460 | not assigned, *247* |
| 2503 | I 7181 Cutter, *63* |
| 2504 | lost |
| 2788 | lost |
| 2798 | unavailable, *156* |
| 2799 | large lettering |
| 2800 | large lettering |
| 2801 | not assigned, *247* |
| 2857 | large lettering, *228* |
| 2858 | ²1326 Cutter, *94, 95* |
| 2859 | lost |
| 2860 | large lettering |
| 2861 | unavailable |
| 2862 | lost |
| 2863 | joins ²1709 |
| 2864a | I 6006 Cutter, *149* |
| 2864b | not assigned, *247* |
| 2864c | not assigned, *247* |
| 2864c' (pub. in commentary *ad. loc.*) | not assigned, *247* |
| 2865 | not assigned, *247* |
| 2866 | large lettering |
| 2867 | unavailable |
| 2868 | large lettering |
| 2869 | unavailable/large lettering |
| 2870 | large lettering |
| 2871 | not assigned, *247* |
| 2872 | unavailable |

*17*

| Inscr. Number (IG II² cont.) | Assignment, page reference |
|---|---|
| 2873 | large lettering |
| 2944 | I 6006 Cutter, *149, 157* |
| 2945 | large lettering |
| 2946 | not assigned, *247–48* |
| 2947 | style of ²1318 Cutter, *70* |
| 2948 | ²1324 Cutter, *111, 112* |
| 2949 | ²937 Cutter, *175* |
| 2950/1 | unavailable |
| 2952 | lost |
| 2978 | lost |
| 2980 | not assigned, *248* |
| 2980a | = I 176 |
| 2981 | not assigned, *248* |
| 2982 | unavailable |
| 2983 | ²2983 Cutter, *207, 208* |
| 2984 | unavailable |
| 2985 | unavailable |
| 2986 | not assigned, *248* |
| 2987 | large lettering |
| 2988 | not assigned, *248* |
| 2989 | not assigned, *248* |
| 2990 | style of ²1008, *196* |
| 2991 | unavailable |
| 2993a | = I 25 |
| 3058 | style of ²3479, *139, 141* |
| 3088 | style of ²3479, *139, 141* |
| 3089 | unavailable |
| 3145 | lost |
| 3146 | lost |
| 3147 | I 286 Cutter, *189* |
| 3148 | style of ²903, *135* |
| 3149 | large lettering |
| 3150 | part of 3147 |
| 3171 | part of I 6135 |
| 3172 | large lettering |
| 3211 | ²913 Cutter, *71, 74, 78, 79* |
| 3215 | I 6006 Cutter, *149* |
| 3216 | not assigned, *248* |
| 3217 | style of ²1011, *211* |
| 3461 | lost |
| 3462 | style of Register I 247 Cutter, *165* |

## LIST OF INSCRIPTIONS STUDIED

| *Inscr. Number* | *Assignment, page reference* |
|---|---|
| 3463 | I 6006 Cutter, *149, 156 n.10, 157* |
| 3467 | unavailable |
| 3468 | large lettering |
| 3469 | ²3479 Cutter, *138, 141* |
| 3470 | large lettering |
| 3471 | unavailable |
| 3472 | unavailable |
| 3473 | style of ²912, *58, 60* |
| 3474 | I 286 Cutter, *189, 191* |
| 3475 = 3570 | part of 3476 |
| 3476 | large lettering, *see* Clinton, *Sacred Officials* 124 |
| 3477 | ²937 Cutter, *141, 175, 179–80* |
| 3478 | large lettering |
| 3479 | ²3479 Cutter, *137–38, 141* |
| 3479a | large lettering |
| 3480 | large lettering |
| 3481 | large lettering |
| 3482 | ²3479 Cutter, *138* |
| 3483 | unavailable/large lettering |
| 3484 | large lettering |
| 3485 | ²1011 Cutter, *211* |
| 3486 | large lettering |
| 3487 | large lettering |
| 3488 | *FD* III 2 no. 5 Cutter, *213* |
| 3570 | = 3475 |
| 3780 | unavailable |
| 3781 | ²3479 Cutter, *138–39, 141* |
| 3782 | lost |
| 3783 | lost |
| 3784 | style of ²937, *175* |
| 3856 | large lettering |
| 3857 | style of ²1706, *49, 54* |
| 3858 | large lettering |
| 3859 | style of I 787, *43* |
| 3863 | large lettering |
| 3864 | unavailable/large lettering |
| 3865 | unavailable |
| 3866 | not assigned, *248* |
| 3867 | ²3479 Cutter, *139, 140, 141, 161* |
| 3868 | large lettering |

| Inscr. Number (IG II² cont.) | Assignment, page reference |
|---|---|
| 3869 | large lettering |
| 3870 | unavailable |
| 3871 | ²3479 Cutter, *139–40, 141* |
| 3872 | large lettering |
| 3873 | unavailable |
| 3874 | style of ²903, *135 and n. 2* |
| 3875 | unavailable |
| 3876 | lost |
| 3877 | unavailable/large lettering |
| 3878 | lost |
| 3879 | not assigned, *248* |
| 3880 | unavailable/large lettering |
| 3881 | large lettering |
| 3882 | unavailable/large lettering |
| 3890 | unavailable/large lettering |
| 4030 | large lettering |
| 4031 | lost |
| 4032 | large lettering |
| 4033 | not assigned, *248* |
| 4034 | style of ²1135, *206* |
| 4035 | large lettering |
| 4099 | unavailable |
| 4100 | large lettering |
| 4101 | large lettering |
| 4102 | unavailable |
| 4103 | large lettering |
| 4256 | large lettering |
| 4257 | large lettering |
| 4276 | not assigned, *248* |
| 4279 | lost |
| 4280 | not assigned, *248* |
| 4281 | lost |
| 4282 | unavailable |
| 4283 | unavailable |
| 4284 | unavailable |
| 4285 | lost |
| 4286 | not assigned, *248* |
| 4287 | lost |
| 4288 | lost |
| 4289 | unavailable |
| 4290 | lost |

## LIST OF INSCRIPTIONS STUDIED

| Inscr. Number | Assignment, page reference |
|---|---|
| 4291 | lost, *191* |
| 4292 | large lettering |
| 4293 | lost |
| 4294 | lost |
| 4295 | style of Agora I 286, *190, 191* |
| 4296 | lost |
| 4297 | unavailable/large lettering |
| 4298 | ²3479 Cutter, *139, 140* |
| 4299 | unavailable/large lettering |
| 4300 | unavailable/large lettering |
| 4301 | large lettering |
| 4302 | unavailable/large lettering |
| 4303 | unavailable |
| 4304 | large lettering |
| 4305 | ²1011 Cutter, *211* |
| 4309 | large lettering |
| 4339a | unavailable/large lettering |
| 4339b | unavailable/large lettering |
| 4340 | unavailable |
| 4441 | ²913 Cutter (lines 1–7), *74* |
| 4453 | large lettering |
| 4454 | ²1324 Cutter, *111, 112* |
| 4455 | unavailable |
| 4456 | large lettering |
| 4457 | unavailable |
| 4458 | unavailable |
| 4459 | ²1324 Cutter, *111, 112* |
| 4460 | unavailable/large lettering |
| 4461 | not assigned, *248* |
| 4462 | not assigned, *249* |
| 4463 | unavailable |
| 4688 | not assigned, *249* |
| 4689 | large lettering |
| 4691 | large lettering |
| 4692 | unassignable/worn and few |
| 4693 | not assigned, *249* |
| 4694 | not assigned, *249* |
| 4695 | large lettering |
| 4696 | not assigned, *249* |
| 4697 | not assigned, *249* |
| 4698 | not assigned, *249* |

| Inscr. Number (IG II² cont.) | Assignment, page reference |
|---|---|
| 4699 | unavailable |
| 4700 | lost |
| 4701 | large lettering |
| 4702 | not assigned, *249* |
| 4703 | unavailable |
| 4931 | large lettering |
| 4931a | = I 171 |
| 4932 | large lettering |
| 4933 | large lettering |
| 4934 | lost |
| 4935 | unavailable |
| 4936 | large lettering |
| 4937 | lost |
| 4986 | large lettering |
| 4987 | large lettering |
| 4988 | lost |
| 4989 | lost? |
| 4991 | ²1028 Cutter (lines 1–3), *183* |
| 4992 | large lettering |
| 5024 | large lettering |
| 5029 | large lettering |
| 5058 | large lettering |
| 5080 | large lettering |
| 6398 | style of ²3479 Cutter, *139, 141, 180* |
| 8494 | I 6006 Cutter, *149, 161–62* |
| 13121 | I 6006 Cutter, *78, 149, 161* |
| 13124 | = I 1466 |

*IG* XII.v

| | |
|---|---|
| 596B | I 6006 Cutter, *149, 157–58* |
| 600 | I 6006 Cutter, *150, 158* |
| 647 | I 7181 Cutter, *63, 66* |

Agora I

| | |
|---|---|
| 25 | style of ²937, *175* |
| 73 | unassignable/worn, *249* |
| 77 | I 247 Cutter, *102* |
| 78 | not assigned, *249* |
| 79 | ²1706 Cutter, *48* |
| 84 | unassignable/few, *see* H3 (1934) 10 |
| 94 | ²903 Cutter, *134* |
| 113 | not assigned, *249* |

## LIST OF INSCRIPTIONS STUDIED

| Inscr. Number | Assignment, page reference |
|---|---|
| 138 | I 286 Cutter, *189* |
| 147 | not assigned, *249* |
| 164 | unassignable/worn, *235, 249* |
| 165 | ²912 Cutter, *57* |
| 166 | ²913 Cutter, *74* |
| 171 | style of ²913, *75* |
| 175 | I 6512 Cutter, *128–30* |
| 176 | not assigned, *249* |
| 178 | style of I 7181, *64, 67* |
| 189 | part of 94 |
| 243 | not assigned, *249–50* |
| 245 | ²1706 Cutter, *48* |
| 247 | I 247 (lines 1–65), *99–101, 102, 233* |
|  | Register I 247 (66–122), *163–66* |
| 260 | unassignable/few, *250* |
| 286 | I 286 Cutter, *187–89, 229 n. 11* |
| 319 | not assigned, *250* |
| 382a–e | part of ²3147 |
| 388 | ²3479 Cutter, *139* |
| 432 | ²1326 Cutter, *94, 244* |
| 453 | = ²3215 |
| 456 | not assigned, *250* |
| 515 | style of ²912, *58* |
| 524 | ²1706 Cutter |
| 535 | part of 138 |
| 560 | not assigned, *235* |
| 582 | part of ²1009 |
| 600 | part of ²910 |
| 605 | I 656 + 6355 Cutter, *84* |
| 626 | ²912 Cutter, *57* |
| 629 | not assigned, *250* |
| 632 | ²912 Cutter, *57* |
| 642 | ²912 Cutter, *57* |
| 647 | part of 94 |
| 656 | I 656 + 6355 Cutter, *84, 86–87* |
| 684a,b | ²903 Cutter, *134* |
| 706 | not assigned, *250* |
| 719 | joins 388 |
| 721 | not assigned, *250* |
| 728 | unassignable/worn, see *Agora* XV no. 223 |

| Inscr. Number (Agora I cont.) | Assignment, page reference |
|---|---|
| 737 | part of 813 |
| 746 | not assigned, *250* |
| 750 | ²937 Cutter, *175, 176* |
| 756 | part of 138 |
| 764 | part of ²915 |
| 787 | I 787 Cutter, *41–42* |
| 813 | not assigned, *250* |
| 819 | part of 813 |
| 834 + 909 | part of 605 |
| 838 | ²783 Cutter, *144, 252* |
| 884 | multiple hands, *150, 158* |
| 896 | I 247 Cutter, *102, 104* |
| 907 | I 6006 Cutter, *150* |
| 918 | ²1706 Cutter, *48, 52–53* |
| 925 | style of I 7181, *64, 65* |
| 933 | not assigned, *251* |
| 958 | part of 286 |
| 968 | I 247 Cutter, *102, 104–105* |
| 973 | part of ²916 |
| 979 | ²897 Cutter, *115, 116* |
| 983 | I 247 (lines 1–29), *102, 108, 206, 233* style of I 6108 (lines 38–40), *202, 206* ²1135 (lines 51–58), *206* |
| 984 | I 6006 Cutter, *150* |
| 989 | part of 286 |
| 992 | part of 286 |
| 999 | ²913 Cutter, *71, 74* |
| 1003 | style of ²1326, *94* |
| 1005 | I 6006 Cutter, *150, 159* |
| 1007 | joins 1005 |
| 1013 | I 7181 Cutter, *63, 66–67* |
| 1015 | part of 979 |
| 1017 | part of 979 |
| 1025 | I 656 + 6355 Cutter, *84* |
| 1028 | not assigned, *251* |
| 1029 | I 656 + 6355 Cutter, *84, 86–87* |
| 1033 | style of ²913, *75, 79* |
| 1036 | ²912 Cutter, *57* |
| 1049 | unassignable/few, *see* H16 (1947) *160–61* |
| 1057 | style of I 6006, *151* |

24

LIST OF INSCRIPTIONS STUDIED

| Inscr. Number | Assignment, page reference |
|---|---|
| 1080 | unassignable/few, see H16 (1947) 164 |
| 1106 | part of 746 |
| 1125 | = ²702 |
| 1126 | joins ²1709 |
| 1220 | not assigned, *251* |
| 1250 | not assigned, *251* |
| 1299 | not assigned, *251* |
| 1312 | style of I 6006, *151* |
| 1315 | part of ²3147 |
| 1318 | style of I 656 + 6355, *84* |
| 1325 | I 247 Cutter, *102* |
| 1330 | I 7181 Cutter, *63, 64* |
| 1331 | I 7181 Cutter, *63, 67* |
| 1419 | I 247 Cutter, *102* |
| 1422 | ²913 Cutter, *74* |
| 1423b | ²1706 Cutter, *48* |
| 1460 | not assigned, *251* |
| 1462 | part of ²920 |
| 1466 | not assigned, *251* |
| 1518a,b | part of 1013 |
| 1553 | ²913 Cutter, *74* |
| 1559 | not assigned, *251* |
| 1561 | unassignable/worn, see Agora XV no. 154 |
| 1572 | I 247 Cutter, *102, 105* |
| 1582 | I 247 Cutter, *102* |
| 1594 | I 1594 Cutter, *192–93* |
| 1640 | ²1706 Cutter, *48* |
| 1655 | style of ²1706, *49* |
| 1659 | I 6006 Cutter, *150* |
| 1679 | style of I 787, *43* |
| 1680 | I 6006 Cutter, *150* |
| 1690 | ²912 Cutter, *57* |
| 1692 | ²1706 Cutter, *48* |
| 1712 | I 7181 Cutter, *63* |
| 1720 | I 6006 Cutter, *150* |
| 1731 | ²1706 Cutter, *48, 50* |
| 1773a | ²1028 Cutter, *183* |
| 1773b,c | part of ²989 |
| 1813 | I 7181 Cutter, *63* |
| 1857 | large lettering, see H16 (1947) 162 |

| Inscr. Number (Agora I cont.) | Assignment, page reference |
|---|---|
| 1860 | ²1706 Cutter, *48* |
| 1871 | ²897 Cutter, *115* |
| 1886 | I 656 + 6355 Cutter, *84* |
| 1912 | ²937 Cutter, *175, 177* |
| 1916 | part of 1712 |
| 1920 | ²1706 Cutter, *48* |
| 1921 | not assigned, *251* |
| 1938 | style of ²783, *144* |
| 1939 | part of 1938 |
| 1943 | part of 1938 |
| 1948 | part of 1938 |
| 1966 | ²913 Cutter, *74* |
| 2010 | I 6006 Cutter, *150, 156* |
| 2016 | I 6006 Cutter, *150, 151–52* |
| 2105 | part of ²954 |
| 2115 | I 247 Cutter, *102* |
| 2145 | I 6006 Cutter, *150* |
| 2155 | ²892 Cutter, *119–20* |
| 2165 | not assigned, *251* |
| 2184 | ²903 Cutter, *134* |
| 2211 | unassignable/worn, see H10 (1941) 60 |
| 2264 | style of I 6006, *151* |
| 2309 | part of 1005 |
| 2334 | ²913 Cutter, *74* |
| 2361 | ²1706 Cutter, *48* |
| 2373 | not assigned, *252* |
| 2451 | joins 1860 |
| 2453 | not assigned, *252* |
| 2497 | ²1131 Cutter, *90* |
| 2498 | style of ²1706, *49, 53* |
| 2499 | part of 6982 |
| 2527 | ²913 Cutter, *74* |
| 2539 | I 656 + 6355 Cutter, *84* |
| 2665 | ²913 Cutter, *74* |
| 2701 | not assigned, *252* |
| 2716 | part of 2539 |
| 2768 | I 247 Cutter, *102, 105–6* |
| 2861 | I 656 + 6355 Cutter, *84–86* |
| 2897 | ²1706 Cutter, *48* |
| 2913 | I 247 Cutter, *102* |
| 2943 | style of I 6006, *151* |

## LIST OF INSCRIPTIONS STUDIED

| Inscr. Number | Assignment, page reference |
|---|---|
| 2944 | ²1706 Cutter, *48, 54* |
| 2945 | ²1028 Cutter, *183* |
| 2965 | part of 432 |
| 2967 | ²903 Cutter, *134* |
| 2987 | ²912 Cutter, *57* |
| 3028 | I 656 + 6355 Cutter, *84* |
| 3046 | part of 138 |
| 3054 | I 6006 Cutter, *150* |
| 3087 | joins 5424 |
| 3142 | ²913 Cutter, *71, 74* |
| 3318 | part of ²2336 |
| 3320 | part of ²2336 |
| 3321 | part of ²2336 |
| 3323 | part of ²2336 |
| 3337 | ²1706 Cutter, *1 n.1, 48* |
| 3360 | style of I 656 + 6355, *84* |
| 3365 | style of I 656 + 6355, *84* |
| 3425 | part of ²917 |
| 3456 | part of ²2336 |
| 3457 | part of 286 |
| 3527 | ²3479 Cutter, *139, 140, 141* |
| 3601 | joins 3527 |
| 3642 | style of I 6765, *123* |
| 3658 | ²1706 Cutter, *48, 54* |
| 3668 | ²937 Cutter, *175* |
| 3675 | ²913 Cutter, *71, 74* |
| 3676 | part of ²916 |
| 3684 | ²912 Cutter, *57* |
| 3687 | part of 2701 |
| 3699 | style of ²937, *175, 180* |
| 3717 | I 247 Cutter, *102* |
| 3755 | style of ²783, *145* |
| 3777 | I 247 Cutter, *102* |
| 3782 | ²913 Cutter, *74* |
| 3783 | I 247 Cutter, *102* |
| 3785 | I 656 + 6355 Cutter, *84* |
| 3791 | I 6006 Cutter, *150* |
| 3804a | style of ²937, *176* |
| 3804b | not assigned, *252* |
| 3810 | part of ²1028 |
| 3871a | ²1028 Cutter, *183* |

27

| Inscr. Number (Agora I cont.) | Assignment, page reference |
|---|---|
| 3871b | ²1028 Cutter, *183* |
| 3939 | I 286 Cutter, *190* |
| 3941 | not assigned (lines 1–2) |
| | style of ²783 (lines 3–6), *145* |
| 3951 | joins ²1705 |
| 3954 | ²913 Cutter, *74, 75–76* |
| 3988 | ²1326 Cutter, *94, 95* |
| 3989 | not assigned, *252* |
| 4003 | style of ²913, *75* |
| 4018 | not assigned, *252* |
| 4026 | joins 3871b |
| 4033 | joins ²917 |
| 4037 | part of ²2336 |
| 4076 | joins ²1706 |
| 4115 | part of 746 |
| 4121 | part of 1857 |
| 4143 | not assigned, *252* |
| 4144 | I 656 + 6355 Cutter, *84* |
| 4146 | part of ²912 |
| 4171 | ²1706 Cutter, *48, 54* |
| 4176 | part of ²989 |
| 4187 | not assigned, *252* |
| 4221 | style of ²1318, *70* |
| 4234 | I 6006 Cutter, *150* |
| 4241 | I 247 Cutter, *102, 108* |
| 4246 | ²3479 Cutter, *139* |
| 4250 | I 247 Cutter, *102* |
| 4253 | I 247 Cutter, *102* |
| 4260 | ²912 Cutter, *57* |
| 4267 | style of I 247, *104* |
| 4342 | part of ²1537/38 |
| 4343 | not assigned, *252* |
| 4363 | not assigned, *252* |
| 4377 | not assigned, *252* |
| 4389 | I 6006 Cutter, *150, 155* |
| 4427 | ²913 Cutter, *74* |
| 4441 | not assigned, *252–53* |
| 4462 | I 247 Cutter, *102, 142* |
| 4476 | part of ²977 |
| 4500 | part of 2539 |
| 4503 | I 247 Cutter, *102, 105, 106* |

LIST OF INSCRIPTIONS STUDIED

| Inscr. Number | Assignment, page reference |
|---|---|
| 4512 | part of ²1006 |
| 4522 | part of ²937 |
| 4537 | style of ²913, *75, 77* |
| 4541 | ²1706 Cutter, *48, 54* |
| 4547 | I 286 Cutter, *190* |
| 4594 | unassignable/worn, *see Agora* XV no. 227 |
| 4597 | ²1131 Cutter, *90* |
| 4605 | ²912 Cutter, *57* |
| 4608 | unassignable/worn, *253* |
| 4609 | not assigned, *253* |
| 4615 | I 7181 Cutter, *63, 64–65* |
| 4673 | style of I 6765, *123* |
| 4678 | style of ²1706, *49* |
| 4683 | style of I 247, *104* |
| 4685 | joins 4441 |
| 4758 | style of ²937, *176* |
| 4791 | not assigned, *253* |
| 4798 | part of ²937 |
| 4803 | not assigned, *253* |
| 4811 | ²937 Cutter, *175* |
| 4875 | *FD* III 2 no. 26 Cutter, *220* |
| 4886 | I 247 Cutter, *102, 107* |
| 4900 | I 247 Cutter, *102* |
| 4908 | style of I 1594, *193* |
| 4915 | I 247 Cutter, *102* |
| 4917 | I 247 Cutter, *102* |
| 4920 | part of ²937 |
| 4933 | I 247 Cutter (lines 1–4), *103, 233* ²886 Cutter (lines 5–8), *98* |
| 4966 | ²1326 Cutter, *94* |
| 4991 | not assigned, *253* |
| 4992 | part of 4171 |
| 5016 | style of ²1706, *49* |
| 5031 | part of ²917 |
| 5032 | style of ²783, *145* |
| 5044 | part of ²2336 |
| 5045 | part of ²2336 |
| 5090 | ²1706 Cutter, *48* |
| 5131 | not assigned, *253* |
| 5143 | ²897 Cutter, *115* |

| Inscr. Number (Agora I cont.) | Assignment, page reference |
|---|---|
| 5165 | not assigned, 253 |
| 5175 | part of 4171 |
| 5224 | ²913 Cutter, 74 |
| 5225 | part of ²1023 |
| 5238 | style of I 286, 190 |
| 5302 | ²913 Cutter, 74, 78 |
| 5310 | unassignable/worn, H29 (1960) 54 |
| 5322 | part of 4260 |
| 5344 | I 6765 Cutter, 122, 124 |
| 5348 | I 247 Cutter, 103 |
| 5395 | part of ²916 |
| 5400 | not assigned, 253 |
| 5412 | not assigned, 253 |
| 5414 | style of I 6006, 151 |
| 5424 | ²897 Cutter, 115 |
| 5424a | joins 3087 |
| 5427 | I 6006 Cutter, 150 |
| 5446 | ²1706 Cutter, 48 |
| 5458 | I 7181 Cutter, 63 |
| 5469 | I 5469 Cutter, 167–69 |
| 5486 | not assigned, 254 |
| 5547 | part of 4683 |
| 5556 | part of 4389 |
| 5573 | part of ²864 |
| 5589 | ²912 Cutter, 57 |
| 5601 | ²1706 Cutter, 48, 54 |
| 5617 | ²1706 Cutter, 48 |
| 5651 | style of ²1326, 94 |
| 5679 | part of ²1133 |
| 5689 | ²912 Cutter, 58–59 |
| 5691 | ²1706 Cutter, 48 |
| 5708 | part of ²1934 |
| 5715 | part of 4363 |
| 5722 | ²913 Cutter, 74–75 |
| 5734 | part of ²2336 |
| 5761 | I 247 Cutter, 103, 235 |
| 5782 | I 286 Cutter, 190 |
| 5787 | ²912 Cutter, 58 |
| 5798 | ²913 Cutter, 75, 76–77 |
| 5800 | ²897 Cutter, 115, 116 |
| 5871 | joins ²851 |

LIST OF INSCRIPTIONS STUDIED

| Inscr. Number | Assignment, page reference |
|---|---|
| 5887 | not assigned, *254* |
| 5912 | ²903 Cutter, *134, 135* |
| 5916 | part of 1005 |
| 5918 | style of ²1706, *49* |
| 5919 | ²1028 Cutter, *183* |
| 5929 | style of ²1706, *49, 51* |
| 5952 | part of ²1009 |
| 5953 | part of ²1006 |
| 5968 | unassignable/few, see H17 (1948) 39 |
| 5982 | I 247 Cutter, *103, 108* |
| 5988 | style of I 6006, *151, 161* |
| 5993 | ²912 Cutter, *58, 60* |
| 5996 | ²1706 Cutter, *48* |
| 5997 | ²1706 Cutter, *48, 50* |
| 6003 | I 6006 Cutter, *150* |
| 6004 | I 6006 Cutter, *150* |
| 6005 | I 6006 Cutter, *150, 159* |
| 6006 | I 6006 Cutter, *146–48, 150* |
| 6020 | not assigned, *254* |
| 6035 | I 6512 Cutter, *128–130* |
| 6041 | unassignable/few, see *Agora* XV no. 237 |
| 6053 | I 6006 Cutter, *150, 159–60* |
| 6057 | ²913 Cutter, *75, 78* |
| 6060 | part of ²915 |
| 6065 | ²912 Cutter, *58* |
| 6081 | ²903 Cutter, *134* |
| 6086 | I 1594 Cutter, *193* |
| 6090 | style of ²1706, *50, 51* |
| 6097 | ²1131 Cutter, *90* |
| 6099 | joins 6097 |
| 6100 | ²1326 Cutter, *94, 95, 161* |
| 6103 | style of ²903, *135* |
| 6108 | I 6108 Cutter, *201* |
| 6115 | part of 1871 |
| 6126 | large lettering, see H30 (1961) 269 |
| 6127 | part of 560 |
| 6135 | style of ²3479, *139, 141* |
| 6140 | I 6006 Cutter, *150, 156 n. 10* |
| 6155 | not assigned, *254* |
| 6156 | unassignable/worn, see H26 (1957) 31 |
| 6161 | ²903 Cutter, *134* |

*31*

| Inscr. Number (Agora I cont.) | Assignment, page reference |
|---|---|
| 6162 | I 247 Cutter, *103* |
| 6163 | I 7181 (lines 1–6), *63, 233* |
| | style of ²1706 (7–50), *50* |
| 6165 | I 247 Cutter, *103* |
| 6166 | ²903 Cutter, *134* |
| 6169 | part of ²989 |
| 6171 | part of ²989 |
| 6178 | not assigned, *254* |
| 6190 | I 247 Cutter, *103* |
| 6197 | part of ²899 |
| 6200 | ²3479 Cutter, *139, 141* |
| 6218 | part of ²915 |
| 6231 | I 286 Cutter, *190, 191* |
| 6234 | ²1131 Cutter, *90, 91* |
| 6244 | style of ²892, *119* |
| 6253 | not assigned, *254* |
| 6256 | ²1706 Cutter, *48* |
| 6257 | style of I 247, *104* |
| 6258 | ²1706 Cutter, *48, 67* |
| 6261 | part of ²915 |
| 6267 | ²912 Cutter, *58, 59–60* |
| 6271 | unassignable/worn, see *Agora* XV no. 207 |
| 6275 | unassignable/few and worn, see H30 (1961) 223 |
| 6282 | I 6108 Cutter, *202* |
| 6295 | part of 2145 |
| 6299 | not assigned, *254* |
| 6310 | joins ²1006 |
| 6319 | part of ²1008 |
| 6329 | ²913 Cutter, *75* |
| 6333 | I 6006 (lines 1–3), *150, 214, 233* |
| | *FD* III 2 no. 5 (lines 5–8), *213, 214* |
| 6341 | ²913 Cutter, *75* |
| 6355 | joins 656 |
| 6367 | ²903 Cutter, *134, 135–36, 252* |
| 6372 | not assigned, *254* |
| 6413 | not assigned, *254* |
| 6420 | ²913 Cutter, *75* |
| 6422 | I 286 Cutter, *190* |
| 6459 | joins 5912 |

LIST OF INSCRIPTIONS STUDIED

| Inscr. Number | Assignment, page reference |
|---|---|
| 6461 | ²1706 Cutter, *48* |
| 6471 | part of 286 |
| 6512 | I 6512 Cutter, *128, 130* |
| 6529 | not assigned, *254* |
| 6530 | I 7181 Cutter, *63, 67* |
| 6545 | I 6512 Cutter, *128, 130–31* |
| 6546 | style of ²897, *115* |
| 6563 | ²1706 Cutter, *49* |
| 6575 | not assigned, *255* |
| 6589 | ²913 Cutter, *75* |
| 6592 | style of ²913 Cutter, *75* |
| 6595 | not assigned, *255* |
| 6605 | unassignable/few, see H32 (1963) 47 |
| 6625 | ²912 Cutter, *58* |
| 6648 | part of ²989 |
| 6668 | style of I 656 + 6355, *84, 88* |
| 6671 | I 247 Cutter, *103* |
| 6675 | ²903 Cutter, *134* |
| 6676 | ²886 Cutter, *75, 98* |
| 6695 | part of ²1008 |
| 6700 | part of 984 |
| 6701 | ²912 Cutter, *58* |
| 6726 | unassignable/few, see H51 (1982) 207 |
| 6750 | I 247 Cutter, *103* |
| 6756 | ²1706 Cutter, *49* |
| 6765 | I 6765 Cutter, *121–22, 124* |
| 6771 | ²886 Cutter, *98* |
| 6819 | I 7181 Cutter, *63* |
| 6827 | ²1318 Cutter, *68* |
| 6843 | I 247 Cutter, *103* |
| 6885 | *FD* III 2 no. 5 Cutter, *213* |
| 6906 | not assigned, *255* |
| 6909 | not assigned, *255* |
| 6934 | not assigned, *255* |
| 6965 | not assigned, *255* |
| 6977 | I 6006 Cutter, *150–51, 152–54* |
| 6978 | part of 6977 |
| 6979 | ²1706 Cutter, *49* |
| 6980 | part of 6977 |
| 6982 | ²913 Cutter, *75* |
| 6983 | large lettering, see H41 (1972) 280–81 |

| Inscr. Number (Agora I cont.) | Assignment, page reference |
|---|---|
| 6986 | ²903 Cutter, *134* |
| 6989 | unassignable/few, see H37 (1968) 271 |
| 6995 | not assigned, *255* |
| 7014 | part of 6819 |
| 7030 | not assigned, *255* |
| 7042 | not assigned, *255* |
| 7111 | not assigned, *255* |
| 7138 | style of I 656 + 6355, *84* |
| 7148 | ²1706 Cutter, *49* |
| 7156 | I 286 Cutter, *190, 191* |
| 7181 | I 7181 Cutter, *61–62, 63* |
| 7182 | ²1706 Cutter, *49* |
| 7186 | ²3479 Cutter, *139, 140, 141, 161* |
| 7188 | I 247 Cutter, *103, 142* |
| 7191 | ²1326 Cutter, *94* |
| 7197 + 7199 | part of ²898 |
| 7203 | ²1009 Cutter, *198, 200* |
| 7226 | ²897 Cutter, *115* |
| 7235 | I 247 Cutter, *103* |
| 7254 | I 7181 Cutter, *63* |
| 7286 | I 247 Cutter, *103* |
| 7287 | ²1706 Cutter, *49* |
| 7304 | part of 4363 |
| 7345 | not assigned, *256* |
| 7361 | part of ²2336 |
| 7375 | unassignable/few, see H53 (1984) 369 |
| 7401 | I 247 Cutter, *103* |
| 7421 | I 6006 Cutter, *151* |
| 7449 | ²1706 Cutter, *49* |
| 7453 | ²897 Cutter, *115* |
| 7478 | part of 138 |
| 7482 | ²1706 Cutter, *49* |
| 7484 | I 7181 Cutter, *63* |
| 7486 | style of ²1326, *94* |
| 7492 | part of 984 |
| 7496 | I 6765 Cutter, *122, 124* |
| 7510 | I 6006 Cutter, *151* |
| 7529 | I 247 Cutter, *103* |

*Agora* XV
| no. 251 | not assigned, *256* |

## LIST OF INSCRIPTIONS STUDIED

| *Inscr. Number* | *Assignment, page reference* |
|---|---|
| ArchEph | |
| 1896 35 no. 18 | I 247 Cutter, *103* |
| 1897 45 no. 14 | I 7181 Cutter, *63, 67* |
| 1960 (1963) 38–42 | unavailable, *see* H35 (1966) 242–43; *Bull. épigr.* 1966 137, 1967 187 |
| 1971 127–28 no. 22 | ²1706 Cutter, *49, 54* |
| AthMitt | |
| 62 (1937) 3–5 no. 2 | I 6006 Cutter, *151* |
| 62 (1937) 5–6 no. 3 | I 6006 Cutter, *151* |
| 66 (1941) 228 no. 4 | I 6006 Cutter, *151* |
| 67 (1942) 22 no. 25 | ²1706 Cutter, *49* |
| BCH | |
| 90 (1966) 727–31 | ²1326 Cutter, *94, 95* |
| Corinth VIII.1 | |
| 5 | I 247 Cutter, *103, 108–9* |
| Deltion | |
| 24B (1969) 89–90 | not assigned, *256* |
| EM | |
| 454 | style of I 247, *104* |
| 649 | ²1028 Cutter, *183* |
| 2282 | I 247 Cutter, *103* |
| 2388 | style of ²913, *75* |
| 2402 | part of ²937 |
| 2404 | part of ²937 |
| 2543 | ²1706 Cutter, *49* |
| 2857 | FD III 2 no. 24 Cutter, *172* |
| 3191 | FD III 2 no. 5 Cutter, *214* |
| 4691 | ²1706 Cutter, *49* |
| 4694 | not assigned, *256* |
| 4697 | part of ²975 |
| 4699 | I 6006 Cutter, *151* |
| 4722 | part of ²1009 |
| 5182 | part of ²968 |
| 5228 | ²1028 Cutter, *183* |
| 5560 | ²912 Cutter, *58* |
| 5581 | ²1028 Cutter, *183* |
| 5588 | ²937 Cutter, *175, 177–79* |
| 6062 | ²937 Cutter, *175, 177–79* |

| Inscr. Number (EM cont.) | Assignment, page reference |
|---|---|
| 12379 | I 247 Cutter, *103* |
| 12694 | not assigned, *228, 243, 256* |
| 12714 | ²1706 Cutter, *49* |
| 12727 + 13408 | I 247 Cutter, *103* |
| 12763 | I 247 Cutter, *103* |
| 12873 | ²913 Cutter, *75* |
| 13099 | not assigned, *256* |
| 13100 | not assigned, *256* |
| 13101 | not assigned, *256* |
| 13235 | I 7181 Cutter, *63* |

*FD* III 2

| | |
|---|---|
| 2 | ²1028 Cutter, *183* |
| 3 | *FD* III 2 no. 24 Cutter, *172* |
| 4 | *FD* III 2 no. 5 Cutter, *214* |
| 5 | *FD* III 2 no. 5 Cutter, *214* |
| 6 | ²1028 Cutter, *183* |
| 7 | *FD* III 2 no. 24 Cutter, *172, 180* |
| 8 | *FD* III 2 no. 24 Cutter, *172, 246* |
| 9 | *FD* III 2 no. 5 Cutter, *214* |
| 10 | ²1028 Cutter, *183* |
| 11 | *FD* III 2 no. 24 Cutter, *172, 180* |
| 12 | not assigned, *257* |
| 13 | *FD* III 2 no. 5 Cutter, *214* |
| 14 | *FD* III 2 no. 5 Cutter, *214* |
| 15 | *FD* III 2 no. 5 Cutter, *214* |
| 16 | ²1028 Cutter, *183* |
| 17 | ²1028 Cutter, *183, 221* |
| 23 | *FD* III 2 no. 24 Cutter, *172, 180* |
| 24 | *FD* III 2 no. 24 Cutter, *170–72* |
| 25 | *FD* III 2 no. 5 Cutter, *214, 246* |
| 26 lines 1–24 (I) | *FD* III 2 no. 26 (I) Cutter, *221* |
| lines 3–10 (II) | *FD* III 2 no. 26 (I) Cutter, *221* |
| lines 11(II)–end | ²1028 Cutter, *183* |
| 27 | *FD* III 2 no. 24 Cutter, *172* |
| 28 | *FD* III 2 no. 5 Cutter, *214* |
| 29 | *FD* III 2 no. 24 Cutter, *172, 180* |
| 30 | *FD* III 2 no. 5 Cutter, *214* |
| 31 | ²1028 Cutter, *183* |
| 32 | lost |
| 33 | *FD* III 2 no. 24 Cutter, *172* |

## LIST OF INSCRIPTIONS STUDIED

| *Inscr. Number* | *Assignment, page reference* |
|---|---|
| 34–42 | *FD* III 2 no. 24 Cutter, *172* |
| 43 | *FD* III 2 no. 5 Cutter, *214* |
| 44 | *FD* III 2 no. 5 Cutter, *214* |
| 45 | ²1028 Cutter, *183* |
| 46 | *FD* III 2 no. 24 Cutter, *172* |
| 47 | *FD* III 2 no. 24 Cutter, *172* |
| 48 lines 1–27, 39–43 | ²1028 Cutter, *183* |
|    lines 28–38, 44–61 | *FD* III 2 no. 26 (I) Cutter, *221* |
| 49 | *FD* III 2 no. 5 Cutter, *214* |
| 50 | *FD* III 2 no. 24 Cutter, *172* |
| 52 | *FD* III 2 no. 24 Cutter, *172* |
| 56a | *FD* III 2 no. 24 Cutter, *172* |
| 137 | *FD* III 2 no. 24 Cutter, *172* |
| 138 | *FD* III 2 no. 24 Cutter, *172* |

*Hesperia*
28 (1959) 186     I 6006 Cutter, *151*

Kerameikos I
1     I 6006 Cutter, *151, 160–61*
  10 lines 1–18     I 6006 Cutter, *151*
    lines 19–21     style of I 6006, *151, 161*
    lines 22–28     multiple hands, *161*
    lines 29–31     I 286 Cutter, *161, 190*

*Kerameikos* III
  A2     not assigned, *257*
  A3     not assigned, *235, 257*
  A5     ²1028 Cutter, *183*
  A6     I 286 Cutter, *190, 191*
  A7     not assigned, *257*

Pnyx I 33 + 36     part of ²13121

*Praktika*
1958 29–30 pl. 27     not assigned, *257*

Wilhelm, *SAWW* 179.6 (1915)
21–23     unavailable

# The Letter-Cutters of 229 to 86 B.C.

In the following dossiers a plus sign (⁺) before an inscription number indicates that that text receives discussion in the comments which follow. In the case of cutters who have been published in preliminary fashion before, an asterisk (*) signifies inscriptions new to the dossier.

# The Cutter of Agora I 787

### Dates: 229/8–218/7

## *General characteristics of the lettering* (fig. 1)

This cutter inscribed plain letters which reveal on close examination a good deal of variation. The individual strokes are placed quite precisely so that the lettering has a neat appearance. The letters tend to be spaced out liberally on the surface of the stone.

## *Peculiarities of individual letters*

| | |
|---|---|
| *Alpha* | This letter, as well as its counterparts, delta and lambda, is wide. The crossbar, straight and usually horizontal, occurs about 90 percent of the time slightly below the mid-point of the letter. |
| *Beta* | This letter shows a surprising amount of variation. The lower loop begins not at the vertical, but rather extends down from the upper loop in an awkward way. It is sometimes smaller than the upper loop and sometimes larger. Once the cutter made the letter with two curves which meet each other at the vertical mid-point of the letter, without coming in contact with the vertical or even close to it. |
| *Epsilon* | The top and bottom horizontals are as long as the vertical making this a wide letter. The central horizontal is shorter, at times very short. |
| *Zeta* | This letter and xi, similarly, are short, about two-thirds the height of the other letters, and "hang," as it were, from the top of the letter-space. |
| *Omikron* | This letter is quite round and varies in size. It is often rather small and occurs in the upper part of the space. |
| *Sigma* | The upper half of this letter tends to be larger; the |

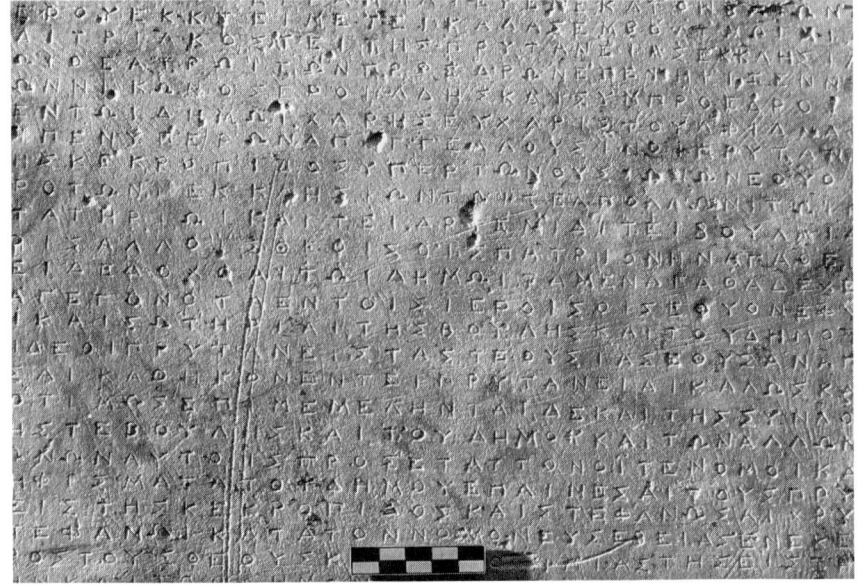

*Figure 1.* Agora I 787 lines 4–25.

|  |  |
|---|---|
| | lowest stroke often breaks the line of the letter-space at the bottom. |
| *Phi* | This letter is about the same height as the others. The variation in the loop is remarkable. Once it is simply a straight line. Normally there are two distinct rather flattened ovals, the one on the right being larger. |
| *Omega* | This letter is open with finials which vary from horizontal to slanting upwards. Again the variation is surprising. |

## *List of Inscriptions*

| | |
|---|---|
| *IG* II² 832 | Archon Heliodoros (229/8). Osborne, *Naturalization* no. D90. |
| *IG* II² 843 | Archon [Kalli___] (218/7). See Wilhelm, *Pragm.Ak. Athenon* 4 (1936) 29–30. |
| *IG* II² 858 | Wilhelm, "Att. Urk. III," *SAWW* 202 (1925) 56–58. |
| Agora I 787 | Archon Leochares (228/7). *Agora* XV no. 120. |

## Inscriptions in the style of

| | |
|---|---|
| ⁺ *IG* II² 735 | The date in *IG* appears to be about 50 years too early. |
| ⁺ *IG* II² 838 | Archon Er[gochares] (226/5). |
| *IG* II² 3859 | |
| Agora I 1679 | *Agora* XV no. 116. |

## Adnotatiunculae

### IG II² 735

Line 3. The first letter, which Kirchner read as rho, should at least be dotted. I do not think in fact that rho can be correct. The only stroke discernible is the lower half of a hasta at the far right side of the letter-space—the letters at this point are virtually *stoichedon*. This stroke slants very slightly. Dotted mu (or possibly pi) appears to be a preferable reading.

Line 19. The last three letters have been erased and awkwardly remade. Kirchner notes "*littera septima fortasse* Σ *est.*" An initially inscribed epsilon has been, it seems, made into a sigma. The third letter *in rasura* has the following shape ⊟. The cutter apparently began to inscribe epsilon and then realized that eta was the letter needed. The name, as corrected, then began ΣTH.

### IG II² 838

Line 6. In the final preserved letter-space appears the vertical and upper slanting stroke of kappa, thus confirming Ch. Habicht's restoration of the name Ktesias; see *Studien* 202–3. See also J. Labarbe, *Thorikos: les Testimonia* (Gent 1977) 77 no. 65, who reads lines 6 and 7 as Ι[ . . ]σιας Θορί[κιος].

# The Cutter of *IG* II² 1706

## Dates: 229/8 – ca. 203

### General characteristics of the lettering (fig. 2)

This cutter[1] inscribed lettering which is plain and rather sloppy. Letterstrokes often do not meet precisely and are frequently not aligned in relation to each other. Vertical strokes are not vertical, horizontals are not horizontal. The cutter tended to render "round" letters with one or more straight strokes and habitually left a gap at the top of alpha, delta, and lambda. It was also his normal practice to leave interlines equal to or larger than the height of the letters; this practice sets him apart from most cutters. The overall impression is of lettering done in haste.

### Peculiarities of individual letters

*Alpha*      In addition to the prominent gap at the top, the left hasta is usually shorter than the right and inclines more or, to put the converse, the right tends to be longer and is more nearly vertical. The crossbar usually slants and often bisects the right vertical. The gap at the top is sometimes so large that it is difficult to distinguish alpha from eta.

*Beta*      This letter appears to be an epsilon converted. It usually has an awkward appearance and is at times difficult to distinguish from theta and omikron.

*Delta*      See the comments on alpha. The horizontal often slants downwards from right to left. In addition, the cutter sometimes failed to place it at the bottom of the letter, with the result that alpha and delta are not always easily distinguishable.

---

[1] Published in *Hesperia* 47 (1978) 247–55; additions to the list there published are here asterisked. A. Wilhelm (*Urkunden dramatischer Aufführungen in Athen* [Wien 1906] 63–64)

*Figure 2.* IG II² 1706 lines 4–18.

| | |
|---|---|
| *Kappa* | The slanting strokes tend to be as long as or longer than the vertical, making this a relatively wide letter. |
| *Lambda* | See the comments on alpha. |
| *Xi* | This letter is never made with a central vertical; the central horizontal tends to be shorter than the other two. |
| *Rho* | The loop tends to be misshapen. Very often it is flat and thin with one or more sides made with straight strokes. |
| *Tau* | The crossbar is placed off-center, usually to the left; the vertical tends to lean to the left. |
| *Phi* | The central section is usually rendered by a straight horizontal surmounted by an arc. The letter is approximately the same height as the other letters. |
| *Omega* | Inverted-v serifs occur at the bottom; the upper part of the letter tends to be fairly round. The placement and size of the serifs varies greatly. |

## *List of Inscriptions*

A "D" in parentheses indicates inscriptions which Dow assigned; a "W" those which Wilhelm cited in first identifying this hand.

| | |
|---|---|
| *IG* II² 786 (W) | See Peçirka, *Enktesis* 106–10. |
| *IG* II² 794 (D) | Archon Hagnias (216/5). *HSCP* 48 (1937) 108–9. |
| \**IG* II² 807 | This text should be dated *ca. a.* 215 *a.* |
| *IG* II² 833 (WD) | Archon Heliodoros (229/8). Kirchner-Klaffenbach, *Imagines* no. 92.² |
| *IG* II² 834 (WD) | Maier, *Gr. Mauerbauinschriften* 76–80. Kirchner-Klaffenbach, *Imagines* no. 93. See Habicht's important discussion of this text in *Studien* 118–27. |
| *IG* II² 836 (D) | |
| *IG* II² 839 (WD) | Archon Thrasyphon (221/0). Kirchner-Klaffenbach, *Imagines* no. 94. For a general discussion of the contents and layout of this inscription, see S. Dow in *BASP* 22 (1985) 33–47. |

---

first described this hand and listed seven inscriptions as characteristic. S. Dow (*AJA* 40 [1936] 58–60) expanded this list to 26.

²On the king referred to in line 11, see Habicht, *Studien* 104 note 114.

| | |
|---|---|
| *IG* II² 846 (D) | Archon [Diokle]s (215/4). *HSCP* 48 (1937) 117. |
| *IG* II² 847 (WD) | Archon Diokles (215/4). |
| \**IG* II² 849 (D) | Archon Kallistratos (207/6 BDM or 208/7 ChH).³ |
| *IG* II² 852 | *Hesperia* 32 (1963) 364–65. |
| *IG* II² 863 (D) | |
| *IG* II² 869 (D) | *Hesperia* 47 (1978) 253–54. |
| *IG* II² 871 (D) | |
| *IG* II² 877 (D) | |
| *IG* II² 878 (D) | *Hesperia* 47 (1978) 254–55. |
| *IG* II² 917 (D) | *Agora* XV no. 128 + Agora I 4033 (*Hesperia* 47 [1978] 251–52). |
| *IG* II² 927 (D) | |
| *IG* II² 993 (D) | *HSCP* 48 (1937) 120–21. |
| *IG* II² 1235 (D) | |
| ⁺*\*IG* II² 1281 | Maier, *Gr.Mauerbauinschriften* 116–17. |
| *IG* II² 1292 (D) | *HThR* 30 (1937) 188–90. |
| \**IG* II² 1305 | |
| \**IG* II² 1306 | |
| *IG* II² 1314 (D) | Archon Herakleitos (213/2). Kirchner-Klaffenbach, *Imagines* no. 95. |
| *IG* II² 1315 (D) | Archon Aischron (211/0). Kirchner-Klaffenbach, *Imagines* no. 96. |
| *IG* II² 1319 (D) | |
| *IG* II² 1320 (D) | |
| *IG* II² 1537/38 (D) | For a new text and join of Agora I 4342, see S. T. Edmunds, *Hesperia* 47 (1978) 266–68. |
| *IG* II² 1706 (WD) | Archon Herakleito[s] (213/2). *Hesperia* 2 (1933) 418–46 + *Hesperia* 23 (1954) 244 (Agora I 4076). |
| *IG* II² 1709 + 2863 (D) | Archon So[stratos] (210/09). For a new text and join of Agora I 1126, see *Hesperia* 41 (1972) 43–46. |
| *IG* II² 2323, lines 97–112 (WD) | Ruck, *Victors* 12, lines 81–96. |

---

³"BDM" indicates Meritt's date in *Historia* 26 (1977) 161–91; "ChH" Habicht's in *Studien* 176–77.

| | |
|---|---|
| Agora I 79 (D) | Archon Chairephon (219/8). *Hesperia* 11 (1942) 298–99. |
| Agora I 245 | *Agora* XV no. 133. |
| Agora I 524 | *Hesperia* 15 (1946) 214–15. |
| +*Agora I 918 | Archon Ergochares (226/5). *Hesperia* 4 (1935) 525–29. See *SEG* 25 no. 106. |
| Agora I 1423b | *Agora* XV no. 142. |
| Agora I 1640 | *Agora* XV no. 127. |
| Agora I 1692 | *Hesperia* 47 (1978) 250–51. |
| *Agora I 1731 | Published below. |
| Agora I 1860 + 2451 | *Agora* XV no. 132. |
| Agora I 1920 | *Hesperia* 47 (1978) 251. |
| Agora I 2361 | *Hesperia* 13 (1944) 251–54. |
| *Agora I 2897 | *Agora* XV no. 134. |
| *Agora I 2944 | *Hesperia* 29 (1960) 53–54. |
| *Agora I 3337 | *Hesperia* 23 (1954) 270. |
| Agora I 3658 | *Hesperia* 23 (1954) 235–36. |
| Agora I 4171 | Archon [M]enekrates (220/19). *Hesperia* 15 (1946) 190–93. |
| Agora I 4541 | *Hesperia* 26 (1957) 57–58. |
| Agora I 5090 | A. G. Woodhead in *Dow Studies* 315–18. |
| Agora I 5446 | *Hesperia* 47 (1978) 252–53. |
| *Agora I 5601 | *Hesperia* 30 (1961) 218. |
| *Agora I 5617 | *Hesperia* 30 (1961) 259. |
| *Agora I 5691 | *Hesperia* 30 (1961) 228. |
| Agora I 5996 | *Agora* XV no. 145. |
| *Agora I 5997 | Published below. |
| Agora I 6256 | *Agora* XV no. 151. J. S. Traill, *Demos and Trittys* (Toronto 1986) 20–26 associates this fragment with Agora I 1860+2451. |
| *Agora I 6258 | *Agora* XV no. 98; this text should be dated to about 215. |
| Agora I 6461 | *Agora* XV no. 203. This fragment is to be dated well before 200. |

| | |
|---|---|
| Agora I 6563 | *Agora* XV no. 146. |
| Agora I 6756 | *Agora* XV no. 117. |
| Agora I 6979 | *Hesperia* 47 (1978) 253. |
| *Agora I 7148 | *Hesperia* 51 (1982) 203. |
| *Agora I 7182 | Osborne, *Naturalization* no. D95. On the date of this decree, which must be *ca.* 203, see also Ch. Habicht, "Der Archon Philaitolos von Delphi," *ZPE* 69 (1987) 87–89. |
| *Agora I 7287 | *Hesperia* 51 (1982) 57–58. |
| *Agora I 7449 | *Hesperia* 53 (1984) 369–70. |
| *Agora I 7482 | *Hesperia* 47 (1978) 283. |
| ArchEph 1971 127–28 no. 22 | |
| AthMitt 67 (1942) 22 no. 25 | |
| *EM 2543 | Unpublished. |
| *EM 4691 | Unpublished. |
| *EM 12714 | Unpublished. |

## *Inscriptions in the style of* [4]

| | |
|---|---|
| +*IG* II² 443 | |
| *IG* II² 2353 | This text dates to *ca. a.* 215 *a.* |
| *IG* II² 3857 | |
| Agora I 1655 | *Agora* XV no. 139. |
| +Agora I 2498 | Archon Ankylos (197/6 BDM, 195/4? ChH, or ?). *Agora* XV no. 165. |
| Agora I 4678 | *Agora* XV no. 148. |
| Agora I 5016 | *Hesperia* 28 (1959) 274. |
| Agora I 5918 | *Agora* XV no. 124. |
| Agora I 5929 | Published below. |

---

[4] The reader is reminded that this is a new category which I have introduced to take account of those inscriptions which I believe to be by the cutter but whose lettering differs enough that I feel they should be placed in a subsidiary category. Since the category is new, obviously all of these texts are new to this cutter's published dossier.

Agora I 6090    Published below.
Agora I 6163,   *Agora* XV no. 141. For corrections to the readings in
lines 7–50      lines 28 and 31, see *ZPE* 41 (1981) 101–2.

## *Preliminary publication of fragments from the Athenian Agora*

**1** (pl. 1). Fragment of white marble, inscribed face alone preserved, found in a second to third century A.D. context under the floor of a Byzantine building east of the Stoa of Zeus (J 6) on March 28, 1934.

H. 0.092 m.; W. 0.085 m.; Th. 0.033 m.; LH. 0.006 m.

Inv. No. I 1731

*ca. a.* 215 a.       NON-STOICH.

1 [ ＿＿＿ ] ΒΟΥΛ[Η ＿＿＿ ]
[ ＿＿＿ ]ΡΙΣΟΤΙ[ ＿＿＿＿ ]
3 [ ＿＿＿ ]ΑΙΔΙΕ[ ＿＿＿＿ ]
[ ＿＿＿ ]Υ[ ＿＿＿＿＿ ]

Line 2. Just the top right of the loop of dotted rho is preserved at the break; dotted beta is also possible.

Line 3. The apex of dotted alpha is clear; lambda and delta are also possible.

**2** (pl. 2). Fragment of white marble, inscribed face alone preserved, found in a late Roman context over the civic offices (I 12) on June 9, 1947.

H. 0.05 m.; W. 0.095 m.; Th. 0.041 m.; LH. 0.006 m.

Inv. No. I 5997

*ca. a.* 215 a.       NON-STOICH.

1 [ ＿＿＿＿＿ ]ΘΟΙ[ ＿＿＿＿ ]
[ ＿＿＿ Α]ΡΙΣΤΟ[ ＿＿＿＿ ]
*vacat*
4 [ ＿＿ ]ΑΡΧ[ ＿＿＿＿＿＿ ]

Line 1. The left side of omikron is a straight line. Iota was inscribed initially and then changed to omikron.

The remains are too fragmentary to allow any certain restorations. Line 1 may well contain part of the demotic, Perithoides.

**3** (pl. 3). Fragment of white marble, inscribed face alone preserved, brought in from the marble dump west of the Odeion on July 29, 1946.

H. 0.042 m.; W. 0.075 m.; Th. 0.082 m.; LH. 0.006 m.

Inv. No. I 5929

        *ca. a.* 215 *a.*        NON-STOICH.

        1 [_____]Φ[____]

        [__ Φ]ιλωτ[άδης __]

        3 [___]ΣΚΑ[____]

Line 2. The vertical of dotted iota can be discerned along the edge of the break.

Line 3. Dotted alpha could also be delta or lambda.

**4** (pl. 4). Fragment of gray marble, right side preserved, found in a Byzantine wall southwest of the market square and east of the great drain (E 17) on March 26, 1948.

H. 0.105 m.; W. 0.21 m.; Th. 0.15 m.; LH. lines 1-4 0.01 m., lines 5-8 0.005 m.

Inv. No. I 6090

    *ca. a.* 215 *a.*        NON-STOICH.

    1 [_____]ρος      5  Θησέ-

    [____]ωνος       α ῾Αρμα-

    [____] ιεύς        τίδου

    4 [___]ΝΑΙ        8  Τ[ήι]ον

Line 4. Of dotted nu there is just a tip of the vertical at the break; iota is also possible.

Line 7. Only a single small curving segment from the bottom of dotted omikron is preserved.

Lines 5–8 are inscribed in smaller letters and are very worn. Their disposition and the proximity of the right edge suggest that they are a citation. The difference in letter-height is puzzling. I have examined the stone closely and can find no evidence of erasure. The two texts seem to be contemporaneous.

The person or persons named in lines 1-4 honor Theseus of Teos. Presumably a balancing citation is lost to the left. Neither the *nomen* nor the patronymic is known in the inscriptions from Teos. The name Harmatides is attested twice at Thespiae (Herodotos 7.227 and Aelian *Var. Hist.* 6.2).

## Adnotatiunculae

### IG II² 1281

This inscription has been dated on the basis of the lettering in the first half of the third century B.C., specifically to sometime before 263. We are now in a position to know that the repair to the fortification walls at Sounion referred to in lines 7 and 8 took place in the years after 229 B.C. This accords well with the policy of Mikion and Eurykleides to safeguard Athens and Attica (see especially *IG* II² 834, lines 7–15). This fragmentary text becomes part of the ensemble of evidence from the last quarter of the third century which reveals activity at the border forts, namely Sounion and the Paralia (*IG* II² 1300, 1302, 1308, 1309), Eleusis, Panakton, and Phyle (II² 1303, 1304, 1305, 1306, 1307), and Rhamnous (II² 1310, 1312, 1313;[5] *SEG* 31 112, 120).[6] It is much to be regretted that the name of the hoplite general honored has not survived.

### IG II² 443 and Agora I 918

The crown preserved at the bottom of Agora I 918 (pl. 5) and that published as *IG* II² 443 (pl. 6) are identical in lettering and design. The letters in the crowns, large and few, do differ from this cutter's small lettering, but it is the natural assumption that he cut them. It is, of course, possible that a different workman executed the crowns and the lettering within them. However that may be, the workmanship of the crowns is all but identical; this fact may be seen clearly at the top center. The ends of the band to which the gold leaves are attached are joined by a cross, apparently representing ties. These then hang down into the crown in single wavy lines. Moreover, the first leaf to the right in each of these crowns leans to the right and crosses over a leaf which projects up on the other side of it; more generally, the leaves are rendered in identical fashion.

The conclusion must be either that there was more than one copy of Agora I 918 (but the language of I 918 in lines 45–49 suggests only one) or that there was another closely contemporaneous decree honoring Prytanis inscribed by this cutter. The latter alternative seems the more likely, especially in view of Prytanis' attested activities as a roving ambassador and law-giver. In addition to the mission to Antigonos on be-

---

[5] These last inscriptions are numbers 16, 21, 22 in Pouilloux, *Rhamnonte*. Pouilloux no. 18 also apparently belongs to this period. As a caution, I must observe that the inscriptions at Rhamnous all appear to be of local workmanship and are very difficult to date.

[6] On this point, see also Habicht, *Studien* 127–42, especially 128.

half of Athens referred to in Agora I 918, Antigonos sent Prytanis from Athens to establish a law code for Megalopolis in the late 220s.[7] Prytanis, moreover, was a prominent member of the Lyceum[8]; *IG* II² 443 (now to be dated to about 226/5) provides further evidence both of his activity on behalf of his adopted city and of the city's appreciation.

**Agora I 2498**

Though the lettering of this text is unusually sloppy—the strokes are very imprecisely placed in relation to one another—the shapes conform entirely to this cutter's hand. If this text is correctly attributed to him, I think it unlikely that the archon Ankylos, in view of the clustering of this man's other work in the years 229 to about 203, dates after 200. Dow, *Prytaneis* 86–88, also noted the closeness of the lettering to this hand and consequently dated this text to either 210/09 or 208/7.

This workman was one of the major cutters of his day; in fact, his dossier, numbering in excess of eighty items, qualifies him as the most prolific cutter so far known. His work is not known before 229, although his lettering shows some striking similarities in shape to that of the Cutter of *IG* II² 788, another major cutter, whose work belongs to the generation before 230, that is, to the period of Macedonian control.[9] The II² 1706 Cutter was perhaps an apprentice of the II² 788 Cutter. He came into his own only with the new democratic regime and inscribed a number of important texts, not least of which are the great archon list, *IG* II² 1706, and the continuation of the list of victors in comedies at the Dionysia, *IG* II² 2323. The former begins with the archons of 230/29, the latter probably began about the same time, that is, as a record of performances under the renewed democracy. These texts reveal the democracy keeping new records and marking their ascendance as a new beginning. It appears a significant indicator of the importance of this cutter that he was chosen to inscribe them. He also cut *IG* II² 834, the text honoring Eurykleides, one of the two primary leaders of the democratic movement, for his role in reestablishing Athenian freedom. Two other

---

[7] Polybios 5.93.8.
[8] See the note by R. Kassel, "Der Peripatetiker Prytanis," *ZPE* 60 (1985) 23–24 and the references collected there, to which add Dow's and Edson's remarks on Prytanis in *HSCP* 48 (1937) 168–72, 179.
[9] On him, see *Hesperia* 57 (1988) 311–22.

aspects of his output seem to suggest a city free of the Macedonians and striving to revive important institutions: these are the prominence of texts related on the one hand to Eleusis and the mysteries, *viz. IG* II² 807, 847, 852, 1235, 3857, Agora I 4541, and *ArchEph* 1971 127–28, and on the other to the ephebeia, *viz. IG* II² 794, Agora I 2944, 3658, 4171, and 5601.[10]

---

[10] He also inscribed about fifteen known texts honoring the prytaneis. Prytany inscriptions, as published and dated in *Agora* XV, appear with roughly equal frequency in the years 260–230 and 229–200. There is, perhaps, a small increase in the number after 229 but nothing dramatic. The activity of the council and assembly appears to have remained quite consistent throughout the period, at least to judge from this particular class of inscriptions.

# The Cutter of *IG* II² 912

## *Dates: 226/5 – ca. 190*

### *General characteristics of the lettering* (fig. 3)

The letter-strokes of this cutter[1] are thin; the letters themselves are very plain and evenly spaced out. The effect *in toto* is one of grace, simplicity, and economy of style. An important element of this is this cutter's habit of curving the horizontal strokes of epsilon, xi and sigma.

### *Peculiarities of individual letters*

| | |
|---|---|
| *Alpha* | The slanting strokes often do not meet at the apex; the crossbar varies between a straight line and a curve, the former occurring more frequently. |
| *Beta* | Relative to the other letters, the beta (and, similarly, rho) tends to be thin; the two spheres are not differentiated in size. |
| *Epsilon* | The top and bottom horizontals normally curve outwards to such an extent that one might describe them as flaring; the central horizontal is straight and disproportionately short, only half as long or less than the others. |
| *Xi* | The top and bottom horizontals curve; there is never a central vertical stroke. |
| *Omikron* | This letter tends to be small and to occur in the upper part of the letter-space; it is often composed of two semicircles which do not meet precisely. |
| *Pi* | This is the cutter's most idiosyncratic letter, for here |

---

[1] This cutter was first published in *GRBS* 11 (1970) 328–30, pls. 25–26. Asterisks mark inscriptions added to his dossier.

*Figure 3.* IG II² 912 lines 38–43.

alone, at the bottom of the right vertical, he places a serif with some regularity. (He occasionally also places a serif on the bottom horizontal of epsilon and in two cases, *IG* II² 942 + 944 and 1539, used serifs apparently—the texts are fragmentary—throughout inscriptions.) In addition, the horizontal of pi often begins to the left of the first vertical and terminates at the second.

*Sigma*      The top and bottom strokes curve dramatically; often the bottom stroke is short, only slightly curved, and meets part way up the stroke which it joins to form the lower part of the letter.

*Upsilon*      The upsilon is composed of three separate strokes; the vertical frequently does not meet perfectly at the v formed by the other strokes.

*Omega*      It is never a complete circle. V-shaped serifs turned on their sides are placed on each side; the one on the left is usually larger and therefore more distinct.

## List of Inscriptions

| | |
|---|---|
| IG II² 841 | |
| IG II² 859 | |
| IG II² 861 | |
| IG II² 912 | *Agora* XV no. 138. |
| IG II² 916 | Archon Diodotos after Phanarchides (192/1). *Agora* XV no. 187. |
| IG II² 931 | |
| *IG II² 942 + 944 | *Deltion* 33 (1978 [1985]) 5–6. |
| IG II² 1221² | |
| IG II² 1304 | Archon Aischron (211/0). |
| IG II² 1539 | Archon Diokles (215/4). |
| *IG II² 2333a | Fragments *b* and *c* do not seem to be by this hand but they are so worn as to preclude certainty. |
| *Agora I 165 | Archon Achaios (*ca. a.* 190 *a.*).³ *Agora* XV no. 216. |
| Agora I 626 | *Hesperia* 15 (1946) 187–88. |
| Agora I 632 | *Agora* XV no. 176. |
| Agora I 642 | *Agora* XV no. 188. |
| Agora I 1036 | *Hesperia* 39 (1970) 308. |
| Agora I 1690 | *Agora* XV no. 187 frg. *g*. |
| Agora I 2987 | *Agora* XV no. 160. |
| Agora I 3684 | Archon Ergochares (226/5). *Agora* XV no. 121. |
| Agora I 4260 and 5322 | Osborne, *Naturalization* no. D119. |
| Agora I 4605 | *Hesperia* 29 (1960) 10–11, where the date assigned to it, *ca. a.* 267/6 *a.*, is too early; C. G. Higgins and W. K. Pritchett, "Engraving Techniques in Attic Epigraphy," *AJA* 69 (1965) 367–71, discuss this fragment on p. 370 and refer to it as plate 98B-E. |
| Agora I 5589 | *Hesperia* 13 (1944) 249–51. |

---

²On the speaker, see Habicht, *Studien* 172, 203.
³On the date of Achaios, see S. Tracy, "The Date of the Athenian Archon Achaios," *AJAH* 9 (1984) [1988] 43–47. Please note that plate I in this article was printed upside down.

| *Agora I 5689 | Published below. |
|---|---|
| Agora I 5787 | *Hesperia* 30 (1961) 268. |
| +*Agora I 5993 | *Agora* XV no. 177. |
| *Agora I 6065 | Unpublished. |
| *Agora I 6267 | Published below. |
| Agora I 6625 | Archon [Euphil]etos (214/3). *Agora* XV no. 135. |
| *Agora I 6701 | *Hesperia* 32 (1963) 46. |
| *EM 5560 | Unpublished. |

## Inscriptions in the style of

+*IG* II² 3473

Agora I 515   *Agora* XV no. 149. The very thin beta and characteristic pi (here without a serif) all but guarantee the attribution.

## Preliminary publication of fragments from the Athenian Agora

**1** (pl. 7). Fragment of white marble, face only preserved, found in a marble pile in the area southwest of the Eleusinion on March 2, 1939.

H. 0.075 m.; W. 0.092 m.; Th. 0.038 m.; LH. 0.006 m.

Inv. No. I 5689

ca. a. 210 a.      NON-STOICH.

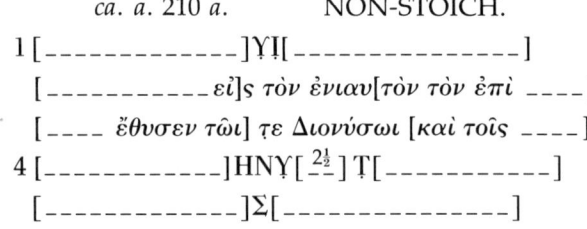

This fragment appears to be from an honorary decree; see *IG* II² 949, lines 31–32 for wording similar to that of lines 2 and 3; see also II² 780, lines 6–8.

Line 1. Directly above the first nu in line 2 appears the lower half of a vertical. Since the space to the right is preserved uninscribed, this stroke must be part of gamma, tau, or upsilon. The tip of a vertical stroke is visible above and to the left of the epsilon in line 2; this is the basis for dotted iota.

Line 3. Of dotted tau, only the right tip of the horizontal is preserved.

Line 4. Only the top half of dotted upsilon is preserved. What appears as a central vertical in the photograph seems to be a scratch and not a stroke. The only other certain letter-stroke to the right is the horizontal which appears under the space between the omega and sigma of line 3. It appears to be joined by a vertical, thus my reading of dotted tau.

**2** (pl. 8). Fragment of white marble, face only preserved, found in a late Roman wall east of the Panathenaic Way (N–P 7–12) in January 1950.

H. 0.031 m.; W. 0.143 m.; Th. 0.127 m.; LH. 0.007 m.

Inv. No. I 6267

ca. a. 210 a.       NON-STOICH.

```
 1 [_____πρυ]τανεία[ς_____]
   [_____Με]νεκράτου [_____]
   [_____]ν Φίλωνο̣[ς_____]
 4 [_____]σ̣ιάδος Π̣[_____]
   [_____]ν ὑπάρχ[ει?_____]
   [_____]Ο[ . . . ]Ι[_____]
 7 [_____] ΗΣ̣ΑΠΕΡ[_____]
   [_____]ΕΔ[_____]
   [_____]Ο̣[_____]
10 [_____]Ε[_____]
   [_____]Τ[_____]
   [_____]Ε[_____]
```

*Illegible traces of at least eight more lines are visible.*

This text is much abraded and very difficult to read. Only a few odd letters can be made out below the seventh line.

Line 2. Just the left top of dotted upsilon is visible.

Line 3. The upper left half of dotted omikron is legible at the break.

Line 4. The only certain trace of dotted sigma is the tip of the upper slanting stroke. Kappa is also possible and perhaps epsilon. The left vertical and part of the horizontal of dotted pi are preserved.

Line 7. The bottom of dotted sigma is very worn. In some lighting conditions the remains resemble an upsilon.

Line 9. Dotted omikron could also be theta.

The first three lines of this text seem to form part of an honorary decree and may be restored *exempli gratia* as follows:

NON-STOICH. ca. 56

[ _ _ _ _ day date _ _ _ τῆς πρυ]τανεία[ς· ἐκκλησία ἐν τῶι θεάτρωι· τῶν]
[προέδρων ἐπεψήφιζεν nomen Με]νεκράτου [demotic καὶ συμπρόεδροι·]
[ἔδοξεν τῆι βουλῆι καὶ τῶι δήμωι _ _ _ ]ν Φίλωνο[ς demotic εἶπεν· ἐπειδὴ]

Line 4 probably contains part of the ethnic or place of origin of the honoree. I can, however, suggest no probable name with this ending in the genitive. However tempting, the reading of the tribe [Δημητρ]ιάδος does not seem possible.

Line 5. One might restore a phrase such as [ _ _ εὔνους τῶι δήμωι τῶι Ἀθηναίω]ν ὑπάρχ[ει _ _ _ ]; see, for example, IG II² 1330, line 71.

## Adnotatiunculae

### Agora I 5993

Meritt suggests *ad loc.* in *Agora* XV that this decree was passed on the same day as IG II² 893a and, thus, restores it and dates it to 188/7. This piece is desperately worn. There is no certain trace of the tau read at the end of line 3. I do not think the synchronism is very likely.

### IG II² 3473

The letters of this text are considerably larger than those which this cutter normally inscribes, *viz.* 0.013 as opposed to 0.006 m. in height. Except for omega, which does not have the crow's-foot serif but rather ones of the straight-line variety, the lettering is completely characteristic and I am of the opinion that this inscription is his work. If so, it must be dated to about 210 and the stemma published by Kirchner in *IG* will have to be adjusted somewhat.

It seems notable that eleven of this cutter's thirty-two extant inscriptions are prytany decrees.

# The Cutter of Agora I 7181

*Dates: 224/3–188/7*

## General characteristics of the lettering (fig. 4)

This cutter is one of the earliest to employ serifs. He tends to space out his letters liberally as though under the influence of the checquer in *stoichedon*. The serifs occur regularly, but not invariably, on terminal letter-strokes; they are small, made probably with the corner of the straight-bladed chisel.

## Peculiarities of individual letters

| | |
|---|---|
| *Alpha* | This letter varies in width from quite thin to quite wide. The crossbar is usually straight, but occasionally it curves slightly. The position of the crossbar in the letter varies from well above the mid-point to well below. |
| *Gamma* | The horizontal stroke tends to be longer than the vertical making this a rather wide letter. |
| *Epsilon* | The central horizontal tends to be very short and rarely has a serif. The bottom horizontal usually has a serif and sometimes curves perceptibly. |
| *Mu* | This letter is quite wide, with the right half of the letter tending to be larger than the left. The central v does not normally reach down to the bottom of the letter. Sometimes the outer strokes clearly slant and sometimes they are virtually straight. |
| *Nu* | The second vertical does not ordinarily extend down to the base of the letter. |
| *Rho* | The loop is occasionally rather small but ordinarily it is quite large. |
| *Sigma* | The top and bottom strokes always slant. |

*Figure 4.* Agora I 7181 lines 2–24.

Tau	The crossbar is usually longer than the vertical; it often curves noticeably and is not centered on the vertical.

Upsilon	This letter is composed of three strokes which vary in size. The vertical tends to be fairly long, never less than half the height of the letter. At times the v at the top of the letter is so shallow that it is difficult to distinguish this letter from tau.

## List of Inscriptions

IG II² 701	The date in *IG* must be lowered about 70 years.
IG II² 842	Archon Antiphilos (224/3).
IG II² 943
⁺IG II² 994	The date in *IG* is approximately 50 years too late.
⁺IG II² 1024
IG II² 1220

| | |
|---|---|
| *IG* II² 1303 | Archon [K]alli[ _ _ _ ] (218/7). *Hesperia* 2 (1933) 447–49. |
| *IG* II² 1307 | |
| *IG* II² 2313 | This inscription has been rediscovered in Italy; see M. Lazzarini, "Una Collezione Epigrafica di Pesaro," *RFIC* 113 (1985) 35–36.[1] |
| *IG* II² 2503 | |
| ⁺*IG* XII.v 647 = *SIG*³ no. 958 | |
| ⁺Agora I 1013 and 1518 | *Hesperia* 30 (1961) 18–19. |
| Agora I 1330 | Published below. |
| ⁺Agora I 1331 | *Hesperia* 16 (1947) 168–69. |
| Agora I 1712 | *Agora* XV no. 192. |
| Agora I 1813 | *Agora* XV no. 191. |
| Agora I 4615 | Published below. |
| Agora I 5458 | Archon [Chai]rephon (219/8). *Hesperia* 29 (1960) 76. |
| Agora I 6163, lines 1–6 | *Agora* XV no. 141. Lines 7–50 are in the style of the II² 1706 Cutter, *q.v.* |
| ⁺Agora I 6530 | *Agora* XV no. 99. |
| Agora I 6819 + 7014 | *Agora* XV no. 259. On the date, see *BCH* 100 (1976) 443–47. |
| Agora I 7181 + *IG* II² 944b | Archon Diodotos (205/4). *Hesperia* Suppl. 19 157–60 and *Hesperia* 45 (1976) 296–303. For some restorations, see P. Gauthier, *Chiron* 15 (1985) 150–55. |
| Agora I 7254 | Osborne, *Naturalization* no. D92. |
| Agora I 7484 | Archon Euphiletos (214/3). *Hesperia* 48 (1979) 174–78. |
| ⁺*ArchEph* 1897 45 no. 14 | |
| EM 13235 | Unpublished. |

## Inscriptions in the style of

| | |
|---|---|
| *IG* II² 835 | Maier, *Gr.Mauerbauinschriften* 80–82; Peçirka, *Enktesis* 114–16. |
| *IG* II² 894 | Archon [Sym]machos (188/7). |

---

[1] I am indebted to Dr. Lazzarini for providing a photograph.

⁺Agora I 178       *Agora* XV no. 241.
Agora I 925       Published below.

## *Preliminary publication of fragments from the Athenian Agora*

**1** (pl. 9). Fragment of gray marble, face only preserved, found just below the floor of a Byzantine building east of the Stoa of Zeus (J 6) on February 12, 1934.

H. 0.075 m.; W. 0.10 m.; Th. 0.042 m.; LH. 0.005 m.

Inv. No. I 1330

        ca. a. 205 a.         NON-STOICH.

          *in corona*
          *two? lines lost*
          [ --- ]ν Ξέ-
2 [νων]α Σφῆτ-
          τιον

Line 1. The bottom stroke of dotted xi is clearly preserved; zeta is the only other possible reading.

Line 2. The two serifs at the bottom of alpha alone are visible.

This man is not attested elsewhere.

The type of decree from which this citation comes is unclear. The extant ephebic and prytany decrees by this cutter do not have incised crowns.

**2** (pl. 10). Fragment of gray marble, right side preserved, found in late Roman road fill west of the southern part of the Stoa of Attalos (P 11) on March 10, 1937.

H. 0.089 m.; W. 0.09 m.; Th. 0.06 m.; LH. 0.005 m.

Inv. No. I 4615

      ca. a. 205 a.       NON-STOICH.

    1 [ ---------- ]ΑΔ[ --- ]
      [ --------- ]ου καὶ ΛΕ[ . .]
      [ ------- ]ΣΥΩΝ καὶ ΙΔΙ
    4 [ ------- ] βιαζομένων
      [ ------- ] ἐν τοῖ[ς] νόμοις

[------]τοὺς νόμους ᵛ
[----]ως καὶ ἀκολού ᵛᵛ-
8 [θως -----] ΘΛΠΙΛΜ[..]

Line 1. Only the right slanting stroke of dotted alpha survives.
Line 3. The tip of a slanting stroke which appears at the edge of the break is the basis for reading dotted sigma.
Line 8. Only the tops of the dotted letters are visible above the break.

Despite the intriguing references to lawbreakers (?) and laws in lines 4-6, I can neither suggest any probable restorations nor offer enlightening parallels.

**3** (pl. 11). Fragment of gray marble, left side (smooth) preserved, found in the tower of the late Roman fortification at the southwest corner of the library of Pantainos (R 15) on June 1, 1933.

H. 0.175 m.; W. 0.11 m.; Th. 0.085 m.; LH. 0.006 m.

Inv. No. I 925

*ca. a.* 205 a. STOICH.

1 τοῖς Σι[--- γραμ]-
ματέα τ[ῆς ----]
ΘΑΡΑΠ[------]
4 σεν ε[------]
ἐφα[------]
[.]Ω[------]

Line 1. Just the right tip of the horizontal of tau and the serif at the bottom of dotted iota are preserved.
Line 2. Only the left end of the horizontal of tau is visible.
Line 3. Of dotted pi, the horizontal alone remains.
Line 5. There appears to be a slanting stroke at the edge of the break; this is the basis for dotted alpha.

The nature of this text is unclear. The sequence of letters in line three puzzles. The adjective καθαρά comes to mind but has no parallel in Attic inscriptions. These letters perhaps form part of a name. Lines 4-6 may be in part restored *exempli gratia* on the basis of IG II² 663 lines 30-31 as follows:

[----- ὅπως]
ἐφά[μιλλον ἦι πᾶσι χρείας παρέχεσθαι]
[τ]ῶ[ι δήμωι ----]

## Adnotatiunculae

### IG II² 994

Now that it can be established that this inscription most probably dates to the last quarter of the third century, it becomes one of a number of texts which reflect increased religious activity in the years after 229. The promotion of this activity appears to have been a deliberate policy of Mikion and Eurykleides (above, p. 53f.). Though the details are unclear, the present text makes reference to a *stephanites* competition of a musical character sacred to Apollo (lines 4 and 5) and to a sacred embassy to announce the festival (line 10). Similar activity is recorded on *IG* II² 993 which is likewise to be dated about this same time.[2] II² 993 records the reception of ambassadors from Megalopolis and the Athenian acceptance of the reestablishment of the Lykaian games.

### IG II² 1024

The date in *IG*, "*fin. s. II*," must be moved back approximately a century. For the reading of the name in line 25, see *SEG* II (1925) no. 12. The Ptolemy mentioned in lines 8–9 is either Ptolemy IV (221–205) or Ptolemy V (205–180).

### IG XII.v 647

These interesting regulations for a festival at Koresia, the port of Iulis on the island of Kea, can now be dated to the last quarter of the third century. Hiller von Gaertringen in *SIG*³ no. 958 dated this text to the beginning of the third century. This cutter is not the only Attic letterer whose work is known on Kea; see the I 6006 Cutter below.

### Agora I 1013 and 1518

These four fragments, if they all belong to the same stele, do seem to form part of an ephebic text, at least the reference in line 3 of fragment *a* to the *paidotribes* appears all but certain. However, the reading of παιδ[οτρίβην __] in the fourth line of fragment *c* (Reinmuth's line 15) cannot be maintained. There are remains of two slanting strokes to the right of the break which require the reading (dotted) kappa. This line reads [____] καὶ δ[____].

I list here corrections to Reinmuth's text of these *frustulae* and use his line numbers for convenience of reference:

---

[2] S. Dow, *HSCP* 48 (1937) 120–26 and above, p. 47.

Line 1. καὶ Σ

A slanting stroke, most probably (to judge from its angle and the fact that it has no serif) the lowest back angle of sigma, occurs just to the right of iota.

Line 9. The final sigma should be printed in square brackets (see Reinmuth's plate 3).

Line 10. Iota is visible at the break after phi.

Line 21. The second letter is upsilon—with this cutter's characteristically shallow v-shaped top—and not tau.

In general, the letters on these pieces fall short of being diagnostic and hardly justify the restorations offered. These pieces date to about 205 B.C. and not to the last quarter of the second century as the initial editor implies in his commentary.

## Agora I 1331

This fragment takes its place alongside Agora I 7181 + *IG* II² 944b, Agora I 7484, and I 1013a as the fourth known ephebic inscription by this cutter. It must be dated to about 205 B.C. and not to *ca.* 158 as in the *editio princeps*. Ephebic inscriptions were apparently a notable part of this man's output.

## Agora I 6530

This decree should be dated to about 205 B.C. and not to 250 B.C. as the editors of *Agora* XV. Note that Agora I 6258 (*Agora* XV no. 98), which records the same Priest of the Eponymous, likewise belongs to about 215 B.C. and was inscribed by the Cutter of *IG* II² 1706, *q.v.*

## ArchEph 1897 45 no. 14

Line 3. The last letter is omikron not beta.

Line 4. The first letter is omikron; it is preceded by a kappa.

This piece is very probably part of *IG* II² 1307, for the vertical spacing is the same, whereas it differs markedly from that of *IG* II² 1220 and 1303, the two other known Eleusinian inscriptions by this cutter. The present piece should be placed somewhat below *IG* II² 1307; it continues the praise of the phylarch for his good services to the garrison.

## Agora I 178

Dow (*Prytaneis* 155) thought this inscription was cut by the workman who inscribed *IG* II² 971 and dated it to about 140/39. The lettering on this fragment has serifs; the lettering of II² 971 is unadorned. There is little or no similarity between them; the writing is certainly not identical.

# The Cutter of *IG* II² 1318

## Date: 212/1

### General characteristics of the lettering (fig. 5)

This man cut letters which are plain and placed rather close together on the horizontal. He tends to use a rather large space between the lines. The letters vary in size giving the hand a slightly erratic feel.

### Peculiarities of individual letters

| | |
|---|---|
| *Alpha* | This is a wide and short letter, the apex of which is occasionally left open. The crossbar is straight, usually horizontal, and comes below the mid-point of the letter. |
| *Epsilon* | The central horizontal is often quite short. |
| *Nu* | The initial vertical almost always has a decided lean to the right. The cutter begins the letter as if it were to be a mu. |
| *Omikron* | This letter is very small most of the time. |
| *Sigma* | This letter is taller than the others. |
| *Phi* | The central part is composed of a rather wide, but very compressed, oval. |

### List of Inscriptions

| | |
|---|---|
| *IG* II² 848 | Archon Archelaos (212/1).[1] *Agora* XV no. 129. |
| *IG* II² 1318 | |
| Agora I 6827 | *Hesperia* 32 (1963) 14. |

---

[1] On the date, see Habicht, *Studien* 159–62.

*Figure 5. IG II² 1318.*

## Inscriptions in the style of

*IG* II² 2947
Agora I 4221     *Agora* XV no. 140.

# The Cutter of *IG* II² 913

## Dates: 210/09–171/0

### General characteristics of the lettering (fig. 6)

This cutter[1] inscribed texts which have a very neat, clean appearance. The individual letter-strokes appear as thin, sharply cut lines which are very clear despite having a minimum of depth. The letters themselves are spaced out, with a uniform amount of space left between them. Although this cutter does not cut his texts in *stoichedon* style, the spacing of the letters suggests that he cut them with a unit of space in mind for each letter. That is to say, he seems to be under the influence of the *stoichedon* style, which had been very much in use down to a short time before he began inscribing.[2] The general impression of his lettering is such that editors, when they have no evidence other than the style of the letters, tend to date inscriptions cut by him to the first half of the third century B.C. The dates of the following inscriptions need to be adjusted accordingly: *IG* II² 702, 789, 1243, 1296, 3211, Agora I 999, 3142, and 3675. Except for a definite tendency to leave an opening at the apex of alpha, delta, and lambda, the II² 913 Cutter places his letter-strokes carefully so that they meet quite neatly, one with another. Another sign of his careful craftsmanship is that his "round" letters are usually round.

### Peculiarities of individual letters

| | |
|---|---|
| *Alpha* | These three letters are all made in approximately the same way. The slanting vertical strokes are placed rather close together so that the space between them at the bottom is wide enough to accommodate only a short stroke; thus, these letters have a tall, slender |
| *Delta* | |
| *Lambda* | |

---

[1] Originally published in *Hesperia* 47 (1978) 255–61. Additions to the list of inscriptions there published are marked with an asterisk.

[2] See R. P. Austin, *The Stoichedon Style in Greek Inscriptions* (Oxford 1938) 101–12. Stoichedon did not go out of style completely until about 225 B.C.

*Figure 6. IG* II² 913 lines 61–68.

|||
|---|---|
| | appearance. In addition there is usually an opening at the apex and the left vertical stroke is significantly shorter than the right. |
| *Beta* | Beta tends to be a rho (see below) with the lower loop added by extending a short straight stroke down from rho (similar to capital R in the Roman alphabet) and by placing a curving stroke at the bottom. |
| *Kappa* | This is a wide letter; the lower slanting stroke tends not to approach the bottom of the letter-space. Rather it extends forward verging on being horizontal. |
| *Xi* | This letter is always made with a central vertical stroke. |
| *Pi* | This cutter usually begins the crossbar at the first vertical and extends it past the second. |
| *Rho* | The loop makes a nice round sweep back to the vertical, curving perceptibly in towards it. |
| *Phi* | This letter is made about the same height as the other letters. The central part is a single ellipse, which is |

|   |   |
|---|---|
| Omega | placed over the vertical at the mid-point or a little nearer to the bottom than to the top.<br>Omega is a nicely rounded letter with an opening left at the bottom. Small horizontal strokes are always attached to both sides; the one on the right tends to be larger than the one on the left. |

## List of Inscriptions

| | |
|---|---|
| IG II 398 | Osborne, *Naturalization* no. D120. Not (*pace* Kirchner) part of *IG* II² 978.³ |
| IG II² 702 =<br>Agora I 1125 | *Agora* XV no. 87. For discussion of the date, see *Hesperia* 47 (1978) 257–58, Habicht, *Studien* 172, 174–75, and, for an opposing view, *Hesperia* 50 (1981) 90. |
| IG II² 785 | Archon Charikles (184/3).⁴ Kirchner-Klaffenbach, *Imagines* no. 98. |
| *IG II² 789 | |
| IG II² 844 | Archon Phanarchides (193/2). |
| IG II² 851 | Osborne, *Naturalization* no. D91. |
| IG II² 854 | *Ibid.* no. D93. |
| IG II² 855 | *Ibid.* no. D103. |
| IG II² 864 | Archon Phanarchides (193/2). *Agora* XV no. 186. |
| IG II² 893a | Archon [Symmachos] (188/7). To be separated from fragments *b* and *c* (see *Hesperia* 47, 1978, 259). |
| IG II² 896 | Archon Zopyros (186/5). |
| *IG II² 899 | Archon Eupolemos (185/4). *Agora* XV no. 179. |
| IG II² 913 | *Agora* XV no. 137. |
| IG II² 914 | *Agora* XV no. 193. |
| IG II² 978 | Archon [Euthykritos] (189/8). |
| IG II² 1243 | |
| IG II² 1293 | *Hesperia* 28 (1959) 178–79. See also J. Labarbe, *Thorikos: les Testimonia* (Gent 1977) 75–76. |
| *IG II² 1296 | This text is wrongly described as *stoichedon*. |

---

[3] See *Hesperia* 47 (1978) 259.
[4] On this date, see below, p. 142 n. 5.

| | |
|---|---|
| +*IG* II² 1327,<br>    lines 1–29 | Archon Philon (180/79).⁵ |
| +*IG* II² 2314,<br>    col. I | |
| *IG* II² 2323, lines<br>    113–143 | Archon [Diodotos] 205/4. Ruck, *Victors* 12–13, lines 128–235. |
| \**IG* II² 2331 | Archon Sosigenes (172/1). Maier, *Gr.Mauerbauinschriften* no. 17. |
| \**IG* II² 2362 | Traill, *Demos and Trittys* (Toronto 1986) 52–74. |
| +*IG* II² 3211 | |
| *IG* II² 4441,<br>    lines 1–7<br>    (side A) | Archon Euandros (202/1–197/6).⁶ |
| \*Agora I 166 | Archon Antigenes (171/0). *Hesperia* 15 (1946) 198–201. |
| \*Agora I 999 | *Agora* XV no. 94. |
| \*Agora I 1422 | Unpublished. |
| Agora I 1553 | *Hesperia* 16 (1947) 161. |
| Agora I 1966 | *Hesperia* 10 (1941) 58–59. |
| Agora I 2334 | Archon [An]kylos (197/6 or, more probably, 202/1).⁷ *Hesperia* 11 (1942) 292–93. |
| Agora I 2527 | *Hesperia* 10 (1941) 59–60. |
| \*Agora I 2665 | Unpublished. |
| Agora I 3142 | *Hesperia* 37 (1968) 270. |
| Agora I 3675 | *Hesperia* 30 (1961) 10–11. This text is wrongly described as *stoichedon*. |
| \*Agora I 3782 | Unpublished. |
| \*Agora I 3954 | Published below. |
| \*Agora I 4427 | Unpublished. |
| Agora I 5224 | Unpublished; to be published in *Agora* XVI. |
| +*Agora I 5302 | *Hesperia* 30 (1961) 225. |
| Agora I 5722 | Pritchett-Meritt, *Chronology* 110–11. On the date, |

---

⁵ As Habicht points out in *Studien* 168–70, the archon Philon must be distinguished from the archon Philon after Menedemos. On his date see *ibid.* 173–74.

⁶ On the date see Habicht, *Studien* 159–63, 177.

⁷ Concerning the date of the archon Ankylos, see the discussion of Agora I 2498 above under the Cutter of *IG* II² 1706.

| | |
|---|---|
| | see *Hesperia* 47 (1978) 257–58 and Habicht, *Studien* 174–75. |
| *Agora I 5798 | Published below. |
| +Agora I 6057 | *Agora* XV no. 169. Agora I 6676 was inscribed by the Cutter of *IG* II² 886 and is not part of this inscription (*Hesperia* 47 [1978] 260–61). |
| Agora I 6329 | *Agora* XV no. 162. |
| *Agora I 6341 | *Hesperia* 30 (1961) 226. |
| Agora I 6420 | *Hesperia* 46 (1977) 268–76. |
| Agora I 6589 | Archon [Alexandros] (174/3). *Hesperia* 32 (1963) 20. |
| Agora I 6982 | Archon Sostratos (210/09 *vel* 209/8).[8] *Hesperia* 34 (1965) 90–92. Agora I 2499 is part of this inscription (*Hesperia* 47 [1978] 259–60). |
| *EM 12873 | Unpublished. |

## Inscriptions in the style of

| | |
|---|---|
| *IG* II² 822 | |
| +*IG* II² 2443 lines 1–12, 16, 18 | |
| Agora I 171 = *IG* II² 4931a | Archon Antigenes (171/0). |
| +Agora I 1033 | *Hesperia* 16 (1947) 161–62. |
| Agora I 4003 | Archon Eupo[lemos] (185/4). *Hesperia* 23 (1954) 239. |
| Agora I 4537 | Published below. |
| Agora I 6592 | *Agora* XV no. 144. |
| EM 2388 | Unpublished. |

## Preliminary publication of fragments from the Athenian Agora

**1** (pl. 12). Fragment of gray marble, face only preserved, found in a Turkish context west of the northern part of the Stoa of Attalos (P 8) on April 2, 1936.

H. 0.068 m.; W. 0.133 m.; Th. 0.081 m.; LH. 0.006–0.007 m.

Inv. No. I 3954

---

[8] Concerning the date, see *Hesperia* 41 (1972) 44–45.

*ca. a.* 190 *a.* NON-STOICH.

[ _ _ _ _ _ _ _ _ _ _ _ _ _ ] τοῖς φιλο[τιμουμένοις _ _ _ ]
2 [ _ _ εἰς δὲ τὴν ἀν]αγραφὴν τῆς σ[τήλης _ _ _ _ ]
[ _ _ _ _ _ _ _ _ _ _ ἐκ] τῶν εἰς τὰ κατ[ὰ ψηφίσματα]
*vacat to bottom* 0.023 m.

Line 3. Just the right tip of dotted tau appears at the break.

The language of these three lines bears a general similarity to that of honorary decrees, particularly citizenship decrees, of the third century B.C. I can adduce however no exact parallel. For the sentiment in line 1, see *IG* II² 808 lines 21–22 (Osborne, *Naturalization* no. D87) and 891 line 9. We may restore *exempli gratia* lines 2 and 3 as follows, using *IG* II² 809 and 707 (Osborne, *Naturalization* no. D88), both dated 250–230 B.C., as parallels:

[ _ _ _ _ εἰς]
[δὲ τὴν ἀν]αγραφὴν τῆς σ[τήλης μερίσαι τὸν ταμίαν τῶν στρα]-
[τιωτικῶν ἐκ] τῶν εἰς τὰ κατ[ὰ ψηφίσματα ἀναλισκομένων τὸ]
[ἀνάλωμα.]

The present text becomes the latest known example of this type of payment formula. But see the "Salaminian decrees," II² 1008 line 88 and 1011 line 63.

**2** (pl. 13). Fragment of white marble, face only preserved, found in a late Roman wall outside the market square south of the church of the Holy Apostles (N 17) on April 20, 1939.

H. 0.135 m.; W. 0.085 m.; Th. 0.11 m.; LH. 0.007 m.

Inv. No. I 5798

*ca. a.* 180 *a.* NON-STOICH.

[. .]ΟΑ[ _ _ _ _ _ ]
[κ]αὶ φι[ _ _ _ _ _ ]
3 ⟦ἐπὶ Φί[λωνος?]⟧ _ _ ]
ἀγωνο[θέτης _ _ _ ]
Ἀλέξα[νδρος _ _ _ ]
6 φιάλη [ _ _ _ _ ]
ἐ[π]ὶ Κα[ _ _ _ _ ]
[²¹⁄₂]ΠΑ[ _ _ _ _ ]
9 [ἀγ]ωνο[θέτης _ _ ]

The stone is preserved (blank) to the left of lines 3–6 for two or three letter-spaces.

The lower right part of an arc in line 1, the bottom tip of a slanting stroke in line 2, and the left slanting stroke in line 5 form the basis for reading the dotted letters.

This text remains a puzzle. The mention of the phiale in line 6 points perhaps to an inventory; line 6 might then be restored φιάλη [ἣν ἀνέθηκε].

**3** (pl. 14). Fragment of white marble, face alone preserved, recovered from loose stones in a Turkish (?) wall west of the northern part of the Odeion (K 9–10) on February 27, 1937.

H. 0.185 m.; W. 0.121 m.; Th. 0.104 m.; LH. 0.010 m.

Inv. No. I 4537

```
         ca. a. 190 a.           NON-STOICH.
        1 [____]ΛΗΕ[____]
         [_____]ου Κηφισ[ιεύς __]
         [_____]έμων Θε[___]
        4 [_____]χοῦντ[ες ___]
         [_____]ΤΑΙΟΝ[___]
```

This is perhaps a dedication. The most probable restoration of line 4 would appear to be φυλαρχοῦντες. Artemon and Polemon are two of the common names which might be restored in line 3.

## *Adnotatiunculae*

### IG II² 1327

Lines 30–33 are by a different hand and were clearly added after the initial inscribing in order to list by name the overseers referred to in line 27. The letters of these lines are larger, have serifs, and are awkwardly made. The horizontal of tau, for example, is overstruck. The strokes curve in an uncertain manner and the letters themselves vary quite a bit in height. Though these lines give the appearance of being much later, they probably are not. Rather they are likely to be the handiwork of a local, less expert, cutter from Piraeus.

### IG II² 2314

Lines 98–103 are not by either of the cutters who inscribed this text and do not belong to this inscription. Raubitschek (*Klio* 52 [1970] 379–81) plausibly associates them with a grave epigram, *IG* II² 13121, a work of the I 6006 Cutter, *q.v.*

## IG II² 3211

Just to the left of the initial tau and 0.037 m. above it are the bottoms of two slanting strokes with serifs. The angle of these strokes makes chi an almost certain reading. The remains suggest that the letters in this line were a centimeter or more in height.

## Agora I 5302

Just to the right of the sigma in line 1, in the line above (line a) there is preserved a clear alpha followed by the lower part of a vertical stroke, probably iota.

## Agora I 6057

It should be noted that the stone is blank above line 1 for *ca.* 0.05 m.

## IG II² 2443

The letters of the first column are not represented accurately in *IG*. There follows a new text:

```
 1  [-----------]ης
    [----------]ς
    [---------]ειδης
 4  [-----Ξυπε]ταιων
    [------Ἐλε]υσίνιος
    [---------]αῖος
 6a [---- ἐξ Οἴο]υ
    [----------]ς
 7a             vacat
    [----------]ιεύς
    [---------]σιεύς
    [---------]κίδης
10a [---------]ς
    [---------]αδης
    [----- Τρικ]ορύσιος
    [----------]αδης
```

```
14  [----------]ευς
              vacat
    [----------]ος
    [----------]ιευς
18  [----------]υς                    Φιλ[----]
```

Line 6. An unclear triangular shape is the basis for reading dotted alpha. Kirchner read sigma in this space.

Line 6a. The tips of two slanting strokes are all that remain of dotted upsilon.

Lines 13, 14, and 17 are inscribed by one or more different hands. They encroach on the space of the second column.

Kirchner misread the last preserved line. It contains the end of a demotic in the first column and the beginning of a name in the second.

The possible demotics in line 3 are Turmeides or Cholleides; in line 6 Aphidnaios, Eiteaios, or Oinaios; and in line 10 Berenikides, Epieikides, or Kothokides.

Lines 22–25 are by the Cutter of Agora I 247. The other lines are by a number of hands, none familiar. Except for most of the first column, the names were entered two or three at a time; the writing for the most part is not very neat. Most of these lines are probably the work of local cutters.

**Agora I 1033**

Part of the name survives in line 1. Read following sigma Ạ[.]Ọ. The apex of dotted alpha and the upper left part of dotted omikron are clear. The name began Apoll-.

\*

This man was one of the major cutters working in Athens around 190 B.C. The sixty-five or so extant examples of his work rank him among the most active cutters of the entire period covered by this study. He inscribed a wide variety of documents for the state—nine prytany decrees, three ephebic, four citizenship; he also worked for private organizations, such as the *orgeones* (*IG* II² 1327) and the *technitai* (II² 3211), as well as the Marathonian Tetrapolis (II² 1243). There is no observable pattern; rather it seems clear that any group needing a long inscription was likely to turn first to him or to his slightly younger (and equally prolific) colleague, the Cutter of Agora I 247. They collaborated (?)—at least their work appears together—on the panathenaic victor list, *IG* II² 2314 (see below, page 101) and they both, it would appear, inscribed sections of II² 2443.

# The Cutter of *IG* II² 1309

## Date: 208/7 ?

### General characteristics of the lettering (fig. 7)

This cutter inscribed neat regular lettering adorned with serifs. The letter-strokes tend to widen slightly at the ends. The serifs are small and v-shaped. The strokes of a number of his letters curve slightly, revealing that he inscribed with a furrowing technique. See, for example, the diagonals of alpha, delta, kappa, lambda, sigma, and upsilon; the horizontals of delta, epsilon, pi, and tau; and the verticals of epsilon, mu, and nu. These strokes do not curve all the time, but quite frequently.

### Peculiarities of individual letters

Alpha — The slanting strokes of this letter (and likewise its counterparts, delta and lambda) curve upwards, meet, and then proceed joined a short distance to the top of the letter.

Nu — The first vertical extends to the height of the letter-space; the second begins at the top of the space and comes down slightly more than halfway. The diagonal neatly connects them.

Omikron — This letter, quite nicely rounded, is smaller than the others and sits at or near the bottom of the letter-space, as do all of this cutter's round letters the majority of the time.

### List of Inscriptions

*IG* II² 939

*IG* II² 1309 — Archon Kal[ _ _ _ ]. This is probably Kallistratos, the archon of 208/7[1]; it could also be the archon Kalli[ _ _ _ ] of 218/7.

---

[1] On his date, see Habicht, *Studien* 164. This inscription has also been thought to refer, I think incorrectly, to a time around 260 (*ibid.* 53 and note 51).

*Figure 7. IG* II² 1309b.

∗

It is surprising that more examples of this man's work have not survived. It may be that he was a local cutter and, consequently, that the single decree from Athens (II² 939) was an experiment.

# The Cutter of
# Agora I 656 + 6355

*Dates: 203/2–164/3*

## *General characteristics of the lettering* (fig. 8)

The general impression is of evenly spaced letters with regular interlines. On the whole, the letters are uniform in height, including both theta and omikron which are, consequently, quite large. Theta, in fact, tends to be somewhat larger than omikron. Sigma alone tends to be taller than the surrounding letters. This cutter does not employ serifs, though there is a tendency to thicken the ends of some horizontals and verticals. I suspect this simply involves the initial position of the chisel in cutting rather than a deliberate decorative device.

With the exception of alpha and sigma, this cutter's lettering is very similar in shape to that of the Cutter of Agora I 6006, so much so that I suppose a direct relationship of master and apprentice—this cutter, obviously, the master and the I 6006 Cutter his apprentice (below, p. 232).

## *Peculiarities of individual letters*

| | |
|---|---|
| *Alpha* | This letter is relatively wide; the crossbar is placed at the mid-point or below and usually curves markedly. Very occasionally the bar is straight or virtually straight. |
| *Epsilon* | The three horizontals tend to differ in length slightly. It is normal for one or more not to meet the vertical with exactitude. |
| *Kappa* | Relatively narrow most of the time with short slanting strokes. |
| *Nu* | About half of the time this letter is made so that the first vertical begins below the base line and the second rises above the top line. |
| *Omikron* | Round in an awkward freehand way, this letter tends to be large and to stand out; it appears to be incised just a hair deeper than the other letters. |

*Figure 8.* Agora I 656 + 6355.

Pi    This letter varies quite remarkably: in relation to the horizontal, the verticals—the right is usually shorter than the left—can be placed neatly at the ends. Alternatively one, or both, can be positioned slightly in from the end. Consequently the space left between the verticals varies greatly.

Rho    One or more segments of the loop tends to be a straight line; the loop varies in shape and size.

Upsilon    This letter is made with three separate strokes. The vertical tends to be at least half the height of the letter. This is a relatively tall and wide letter.

Omega    A relatively small letter shaped, if made to its fullest extent, like a horseshoe. Most frequently the left side of the letter starts at the base and the curve is continued only part way down the right side stopping at the mid-point or even before. It does not usually have finials.

## List of Inscriptions

| | |
|---|---|
| ⁺*IG* II² 901 | To be dated *ca. a.* 185 *a.* (see *Hesperia* 51 [1982] 60). |
| *IG* II² 915 | Archon Proxenides (203/2). *Agora* XV no. 147. Kirchner-Klaffenbach, *Imagines* no. 97. |
| *IG* II² 938 | |
| *IG* II² 947 | Archon [Achaios] (ca. 190). |
| *IG* II² 948 | Archon [Achaios] (ca. 190). |
| Agora I 605 and 834 | Archon Charikles (184/3).[1] *Hesperia* 5 (1936) 419–28. |
| ⁺Agora I 656 + 6355 | Archon Sonikos (175/4). *Agora* XV no. 199. |
| Agora I 1025 | Archon [Ph]ilon after Menedemos (178/7). *Agora* XV no. 194. |
| ⁺Agora I 1029 | *Agora* XV no. 175. |
| Agora I 1886 | Archon [__ippos] (199/8). *Hesperia* 26 (1957) 62–63. |
| Agora I 2539 | Archon [Euergetes] (164/3). *Agora* XV no. 220. |
| ⁺Agora I 2861 | *Hesperia* 26 (1957) 219. |
| Agora I 3028 | *Hesperia* 29 (1960) 54. |
| Agora I 3785 | *Agora* XV no. 229. |
| Agora I 4144 | Archon Symmachos (188/7). *Hesperia* 15 (1946) 144–46. |

## Inscriptions in the style of

| | |
|---|---|
| ⁺*IG* II² 1708 | |
| Agora I 1318 | *Hesperia* 5 (1936) 428. |
| Agora I 3360 | *Hesperia* 37 (1968) 286. |
| Agora I 3365 | *Hesperia* 26 (1957) 61. |
| ⁺Agora I 6668 | *Agora* XV no. 190. |
| Agora I 7138 | *Hesperia* 51 (1982) 58–60. |

### *IG* II² 901 and Agora I 2861

Meritt noted in his *editio princeps* of the Agora fragment that it possibly belonged to II² 901. There can be no doubt that the pieces go together and give us parts of the first two columns of an ephebic register arranged in three columns of approximately equal length. The combined text is as follows:

---

[1] On the date, see below, p. 142 n. 5.

ca. a. 185 a.
(Column 1)

ca. 8 lines missing with the entries of
Erechtheis and Aigeis

[Πανδιονίδος]
[--- ca. 9 ---]μοτέλου [--- ca. 5 ---]εύς
Κλέαρ[χο]ς Σ[ωσι]στρά[του] Κ[ν]θήρρ
            Λεων[τί]δος
Σωσθένης [Σω]σθένου Κ[ρω]πίδης
5 Διονύσιος ['Ερ]μίου(?) Λευκ[ον]οεύς

18 Ἡ [β]ουλὴ
   ὁ δῆμος
   Ἑρμόδωρο[ν]
21 Ἀχαρνέα         26 Ἡ βουλὴ
                      ὁ δ[ῆμος]
                   - - -
                   - - -

(Column 2)

[Πτολεμαΐδος]
[---------]
6 [--- ca. 9 ---]ς Διοκλέου[ς -----]
        [Ἀκαμαν]τίδος
[Τιμοκλῆς Π]ολυκλέους Θορίκιο[ς]
[--- ca. 8 ---]ράτου Πόριος
10  [Οἰνεΐδ]ος
[--- ca. 9 ---]ς Δωροθέου Φυλάσ(ιος)
[--- ca. 10 ---] Κλεοδώρου Ἀχαρνεύ[ς]
     [Κεκροπίδ]ος
Δι[--- ca. 11 ---]νος Αἰξωνεύς
15 Διον[υσ---------]
    Σιμάρ[ιστος ------]
17 Ξένω[ν ----------]

22 Ἡ βουλὴ              - - -
   ὁ δῆμο[ς]            - - -
   Περσαῖο[ν]           - - -
25 Κικυνν[έα]
                        - - -
                        - - -
                        - - -

NON-STOICH.
(Column 3)

Column 3 missing
with the entries of
Hippothontis Aiantis
Antiochis and Attalis

- - -
- - -
- - -

- - -
- - -
- - -

Line 1. Δημοτέλης and Θυμοτέλης both of the deme Paiania are known, the first from the late fifth century in *IG* II² 1138 line 22, the second in an as yet unpublished inscription from the Athenian Agora. The restoration [_ca. 7_Θυ]μοτέλου [Παιανι]εύς is all but certain. The *nomen* Timoteles is also attested in Attica. The demotics Στειριεύς and Πρασιεύς are also possible.

Line 2. This man is probably the councillor of 155/4 attested in *Agora* XV no. 225 line 89.

Line 4. He is known as a contributor in 164/3 (*Hesperia* 36 [1967] 89 line 14).

Line 8. Meritt's restoration of the sculptor to be, Timokles (*PA* 13734; stemma published by Ch. Habicht in *AthMitt* 97 [1982] 179), suits the space and seems most probable. A. Stewart (*Attika*: *Studies in Athenian Sculpture of the Hellenistic Age* [London 1979] 42–46) discusses these artists and offers a slightly different stemma.

Line 16. Dotted rho is read on the basis of a clear vertical stroke just after alpha. I have restored the only *nomen* attested in Attica which suits the remains. Simaristos of Trinemeia, councillor about the year 200 (*Agora* XV no. 151 line 24), is doubtless a relative.

The enrollment in the ephebeia in the year of this text may be estimated at between thirty and thirty-six students, assuming that the central column is missing only one or two names and that all three columns had approximately the same number of names. This number conforms to the pattern of enrollment known to us in the first half of the second century B.C. when the norm seems to have been between thirty and fifty students enrolled in any given year. See *Hesperia* Suppl. 19 (1982) 159 for a list of the relevant texts and enrollments.

### Agora I 656 + 6355 and Agora I 1029

While there is no join between these two pieces, the lettering, marble, and textual considerations make it certain that they come from the same inscription. Agora I 1029 provides the ends of lines 8–20 and becomes fragment *c* in the combined text.

NON-STOICH. ca. 53

a. 175/4 a.

[ἐπὶ] Σωνίκου ἄρχοντος ἐπὶ τῆς Κεκροπίδος δευτέρα[ς πρυτανείας ἧι Παυσα]-
[νία]ς Βιοτέλου Περιθοίδης ἐγραμμάτευεν· Μεταγειτ[νιῶνος δεκάτει ὑστέραι]
[ὀγδ]όει καὶ δεκάτει τῆς πρυτανείας· ἐκκλησία ἐμ Πειρα[ιεῖ· τῶν προέδρων ἐπε]-
[ψή]φιζεν ᵛ Ἀντιχάρης Ἐπιζήλου Ἀγγελῆθεν Ἀγγελῆθεν καὶ συμπρό[εδροι· ᵛᵛ ἔδοξεν τῶι]
5 [δ]ήμωι· ᵛ Ὀρήσανδρος Οὐήτορος Κυδαθηναιεὺς εἶπεν· ὑπὲρ [ὧν ἀπαγγέλλουσιν]
οἱ πρυτάνεις τῆς Κεκροπίδος ὑπὲρ τῶν θυσιῶν ὧν ἔθυον τ[ὰ πρὸ τῶν ἐκκλησι]-
ῶν τῶι τε Ἀπόλλωνι τῶι Προστ[α]τηρίωι καὶ τεῖ Ἀρτέμιδι τεῖ Βουλαίαι καὶ τεῖ
[Φ]ωσφόρωι καὶ τοῖς ἄλλους θε[οῖ]ς οἷς πάτριον ἦν· ἀγαθεῖ τύχ[ει δεδόχθαι] τῶ[ι]
[δή]μωι τὰ μὲν ἀγαθὰ δέχε[σθ]αι τὰ γεγονότα ἐν τοῖς ἱε[ροῖς οἷς] ἔθυον ἐ[φ᾽]
10 [ὑγιεία]ι καὶ σωτηρίαι τῆ[ς β]ουλῆς καὶ τοῦ δήμου κ[αὶ τῶν σ]υμμάχων ᵛᵛ
[ἐπειδὴ] δὲ οἱ πρυτάνει[ς τ]άς τε θυσίας ἔθυσαν ἁ[πάσας ὅ]σαι καθῆκον ἐν
[τεῖ πρυτ]ανείαι καλῶ[ς καὶ] φιλοτίμως, ἐπεμελήθη[σαν δ]ὲ καὶ τῆς συλλο-
[γῆς τῆς τε βο]υλ[ῆς καὶ τοῦ] δήμου καὶ τῶν ἄλλω[ν ἁπάντων ὧ]ν αὐτοῖς προσέτατ-
[τον οἵ τε νόμοι καὶ τὰ ψηφίσμ]ατα τοῦ δήμου· [ἐπαινέ]σαι τοὺς πρυτάνε[ις]
15 [τῆς Κεκροπίδος καὶ στεφανῶ]σαι αὐτοὺς [χρυσῶι σ]τεφάνωι κατὰ τὸ[ν]
[νόμον εὐσεβείας ἕνεκεν τῆς] πρὸς τοὺ[ς θεοὺς καὶ φ]ιλοτιμίας τῆς εἰς
[τὴν βουλὴν καὶ τὸν δῆμον τὸν Ἀθ]ηναίων· [ἀναγράψαι δ]ὲ τόδε τὸ ψήφισμα
[τὸν γραμματέα τὸν κατὰ πρυτ]α[ν]ε[ίαν ἐν στήλ]ει λιθίν[ει καὶ στῆσαι ᵛᵛ
[ἐν τῶι πρυτανικῶι· εἰς δὲ τὴν ἀναγραφὴν τῆς στήλης] κ[αὶ] τὴν ἀνάθε-
20 [σιν μερίσαι τὸν ἐπὶ τεῖ διοικήσει τὸ γενόμενον ἀνάλωμα] vacat

## Adnotatiunculae

### IG II² 1708

Line 1 should read: [ταμίαν τῶν σ]τρατιωτικῶν. Only the bottoms of the dotted letters are visible along the break.

### Agora I 6668

The first preserved letter in line 2 is pi not gamma. The right vertical is short but clearly present. The name is spaced out indicating that it was quite a short one, having two or three more letters only. Π[ά]τ[ρων] seems to be the most probable restoration.

# The Cutter of *IG* II² 1131

## *Date: ca. 200*

### *General characteristics of the lettering* (fig. 9)

This lettering has small serifs on nearly every terminal stroke; it is somewhat squat in appearance and untidy, primarily because the vertical strokes of many of the letters lean or curve slightly to the right in an uncertain fashion. In addition, the crossbar of tau, which is large and therefore prominent, is placed rather precariously off-center to the left and often slopes downwards to the left. This cutter leaves a large interline, slightly exceeding the letters in height. This mannerism suggests a date near 200 or even a bit earlier.

*N.B.*: All five of his inscriptions have been dated from the letter-shapes, particularly the appearance of the serifs, to the mid-second century or later.

### *Peculiarities of individual letters*

| | |
|---|---|
| *Alpha* | This letter is quite wide. The crossbar comes at about the mid-point; it usually curves, but sometimes it is straight. |
| *Iota* | Serifs occur, quite unusually, at both ends of this letter. |
| *Nu* | This is a relatively wide letter; the diagonal tends to curve slightly. |
| *Pi* | The horizontal begins at the left vertical and continues past the right; the right vertical is short and curves or slants out away from the letter. |
| *Sigma* | The top and bottom strokes sometimes slant and sometimes they are parallel. |
| *Tau* | The vertical tends to be short; the crossbar is very wide and off-center to the left. |
| *Phi* | This letter is usually the same height as the others; an |

*Figure 9. IG II² 1131.*

|  | irregularly shaped oval, somewhat wider than omikron, is placed at approximately the middle. |
|---|---|
| Omega | This is a wide letter. Finials with attached serifs appear on both sides. |

## *List of Inscriptions*

*IG* II² 1131

| Agora I 2497 | *Agora* XV no. 242. |
| Agora I 4597 | *Hesperia* 37 (1968) 271. |
| Agora I 6097 and 6099 | *Agora* XV no. 247. |
| ⁺Agora I 6234 | *Hesperia* 30 (1961) 222–23. |

## Adnotatiunculae

### Agora I 6234

The reading of the initial letters in line 3 is ΑΣΣΩΝ. The second sigma, which Meritt read as dotted epsilon, does look like an epsilon in the published photograph. A good squeeze reveals that it is without doubt sigma; the lower half of the letter is clearly preserved. Dotted alpha is badly worn; only the right diagonal seems certain.

Robert (*Bull.épigr.* 1962 no. 107) points out that this text records a pact of friendship, perhaps an arbitration settlement, between two cities. He compares *IG* II² 1135 and suggests Crete. Unfortunately the improved reading does not support his conjecture of [Μυλ]ασέων.

This text should be compared to another fragment by this cutter, *IG* II² 1131, which also has Doric forms and may refer to Rhodes. The two pieces cannot apparently come from the same inscription (they reveal the same size lettering and vertical spacing), for the one (Agora I 6234) is of white marble and the other, according to *IG*, dark gray. It is a pity we cannot date these pieces more precisely, because they provide tantalizing evidence of Athens' active role in interstate relations.

# The Cutter of *IG* II² 1326

## Dates: 199/8–176/5

### *General characteristics of the lettering* (fig. 10)

This cutter made plain letters, a number of which tend to be tall and thin, *viz.* alpha, beta, gamma, delta, eta, lambda, rho, and omega. Letter-strokes are placed imprecisely with respect to one another and each letter reveals a surprising amount of variety. The lettering has a tall, narrow, somewhat sloppy look. Although this cutter can with care be distinguished from the Cutter of *IG* II² 897, his lettering shares many of the same general characteristics. I think it is likely that they worked in the same shop or trained under the same master (below, p. 231f.).

### *Peculiarities of individual letters*

| | |
|---|---|
| *Alpha* | The crossbar is placed in the middle to upper part of the letter. It either curves or is straight and reasonably horizontal. The apex of this letter, as well as of delta and lambda, is sometimes left open. |
| *Epsilon* | The vertical extends above the topmost horizontal most of the time. The horizontals are often nearly the same length, with the middle one being slightly shorter; all three tend to slant downward at times. |
| *Theta* | This letter is usually quite large, distinctly larger than omikron, and has no perceptible dot or mark in the center. |
| *Omikron* | This letter varies a great deal in size; it is often quite small and this seems to be his natural tendency. |
| *Rho* | The loop is small and frequently slightly squared. |
| *Sigma* | This letter is made asymmetrically; the two halves differ markedly in size, now one, now the other being larger. Quite often the lower part extends back be- |

*Figure 10. IG II² 1326 lines 4–17.*

|  | |
|---|---|
| | yond the end of the letter as established by the upper part. It varies also in height, being sometimes taller than the other letters but more frequently the same size or distinctly smaller. |
| Upsilon | This is a rather tall letter made with three distinct strokes. |
| Omega | This letter is roughly the shape of a horseshoe and is usually suspended from the top of the letter-space; it does not extend down to the bottom. The left side tends to be longer than the right. The letter is often awkwardly made and small. |

## List of Inscriptions

IG II² 1236
IG II² 1325          Archon Eupolemos (185/4).

| | |
|---|---|
| IG II² 1326 | Archon Hippakos (176/5). |
| ⁺IG II² 2858 | Archon E[ _ _ _ ]. |
| ⁺Agora I 432 and 2965 | Agora XV no. 170. |
| Agora I 3988 | Hesperia 29 (1960) 56. |
| Agora I 4966 | Archon Charikles (184/3).¹ Agora XV no. 166. |
| Agora I 6100 | Archon [ _³_ i]ppos (199/8). Hesperia 26 (1957) 61–63. |
| Agora I 7191 | Agora XV no. 158. |
| BCH 90 (1966) 727, 731 and fig. 14 | Archon Charikles (184/3). Concerning lines 10–12, see SEG 23 (1968) no. 98. |

## Inscriptions in the style of

| | |
|---|---|
| Agora I 1003 | Hesperia 36 (1967) 63. |
| Agora I 5651 | Osborne, Naturalization no. D110. |
| Agora I 7486 | Unpublished. |

## Adnotatiunculae

### IG II² 2858

The initial epsilon of the archon's name is clearly preserved. The possible archons between the years 210/09 and 166/5 in the Athenian archon list as currently established (primarily by Meritt in *Historia* 26 [1977] 161–91; for the late third and early second century archons, see also Habicht, *Studien* 176–77) are Euthykritos (189/8), Eupolemos (185/4), and Eunikos (169/8).

### Agora I 432 and 2965

Line 87. The name preserved is Olympiodoros not Olympios.

This man's career, so far as we can reconstruct it from his extant work, appears to have fallen into two phases. His early *oeuvre*, which all seems to date between 200 and 190, consists of official documents of the city, *viz.* three prytany decrees (*Agora* XV nos. 158, 166, 170), an ephebic (?) text (Agora I 1003), a citizenship decree (Osborne, *Naturalization* no.

---

¹ On this date, see below, p. 142 n. 5.

D110), a decree of uncertain nature (Agora I 6100), and a dedication of a board of *epimeletai* (*BCH* 90 [1966] 727). The later inscriptions, say 185 B.C. and after, all seem to be of a private nature: a decree of a genos (II² 1236), two decrees for the Dionysiasts (II² 1325, 1326—on them see below under the Cutter of *IG* II² 1324), and a dedication or two (II² 2858 and perhaps Agora I 3988).

# The Cutter of *IG* II² 886

## Dates: 194/3–178/7

### General characteristics of the lettering (fig. 11)

This cutter's lettering is rather ordinary and plain. He uses a serif once in a while at the bottom of vertical strokes. Pi has one quite often on one of its verticals; upsilon, tau, and eta occasionally. Although his lettering is not careless, there is enough inconsistency and inexactitude in the placement of letter-strokes that one would not characterize it as neat. The letters vary in height perceptibly. Sigma tends to be taller than the others, delta shorter. Omikron, usually quite round, varies; sometimes it is almost as large as the surrounding letters and sometimes it is much smaller.

### Peculiarities of individual letters

*Alpha*  This letter varies in width, being at times of normal width and height or, at other times, rather wide and consequently shorter in comparison to the other letters. The crossbar comes at the mid-point of the letter or higher and is usually a straight line. The apex is occasionally left open.

*Beta*  This letter has a very idiosyncratic shape. The upper loop is small and round; the lower is made by extending at the base of the upper loop a slanting stroke from the vertical to the bottom of the letter. This lower "loop" is then joined to the vertical with a straight or moderately slanting stroke.

*Epsilon*  The central horizontal is shorter than the others and, most often, does not quite touch the vertical. The upper horizontal slants upwards about half of the time.

*Rho*  The loop is usually quite large in height and width; it

Figure 11. IG II² 886.

|  | is rarely round. One or more segments consist of straight lines. |
|---|---|
| *Sigma* | The topmost slanting stroke tends to extend up into the interline. |
| *Tau* | The crossbar is short and often decidedly off-center to the right or left. |
| *Omega* | This is a large letter, the upper part of which has the shape of a brimless Homburg. It is always open at the bottom. Small serifs usually appear at both sides (the one on the right is sometimes omitted) with that on the left often being more prominent. |

## *List of Inscriptions*

| | |
|---|---|
| IG II² 850 | Archon Dionysios (194/3).[1] Osborne, *Naturalization* no. D96. |
| IG II² 886 | Archon [Phanarchides] (193/2). |
| IG II² 936 | |
| Agora I 4933, lines 5–8 | Archon Philon after [Menedemos] (178/7). *Hesperia* 26 (1957) 210. |
| Agora I 6676 | *Agora* XV no. 169, lines 8–13. This piece is to be separated from Agora I 6057 (= *Agora* XV no. 169, lines 1–7); I 6057 was inscribed by the II² 913 Cutter; see *Hesperia* 47 (1978) 260–61. |
| Agora I 6771 | Archon Hermo[genes] (183/2). *Hesperia* 32 (1963) 17. |

---

[1] On this archon and his date, see Habicht, *Studien* 165–68.

# The Cutter of Agora I 247

## Dates: 194/3–148/7

### *General characteristics of the lettering* (fig. 12)

This cutter[1] made unadorned letters and reduced to a minimum the number of strokes necessary to inscribe the alphabet. Rarely did he incise the crossbar of alpha or the central horizontal of epsilon. In addition, he rendered curving strokes in a most perfunctory manner, very often, in fact, substituting straight lines for curves. The result is especially noticeable in the case of omikron, for it often has the appearance of an "equals" sign. In general, the lower part of vertical strokes and the right side of horizontals is perceptibly deeper and wider than the opposite part. The strokes themselves rarely meet precisely. The overall impression is one of lettering produced rapidly in a type of shorthand which is, at first, rather difficult to decipher. Alpha, beta, epsilon, theta, kappa, omikron, rho, tau, phi, and omega are some of this cutter's most distinctive letters.

### *Peculiarities of individual letters*

| | |
|---|---|
| *Alpha* | This letter is usually indistinguishable from lambda. Occasionally a lightly inscribed horizontal bar appears. |
| *Beta* | This letter is often made with four straight strokes, namely a vertical and three horizontals. In isolation, it can easily be mistaken for epsilon. |
| *Epsilon* | A middle horizontal almost never appears. The upper and lower horizontals are rarely connected to the vertical. In addition the cutter had a tendency to place the upper horizontal noticeably below the top of the vertical. |
| *Theta* | In contrast to his treatment of omikron and omega, |

---

[1] Previously published as Cutter 5 in *GRBS* 14 (1973) 192–95 and plate 5. Inscriptions added to that dossier are here asterisked.

*Figure 12.* Agora I 247 lines 50–56.

|   |   |
|---|---|
|   | which he carved with one or more straight strokes, the cutter employed two curving semi-circles to render this letter; he made it rather large and round. No dot appears. |
| *Kappa* | The horizontally slanting strokes do not touch the vertical; rather, the cutter tends to place them at a significant distance from it, thus producing a rather wide letter. |
| *Omikron* | This letter tends to be rather small and to occur in the upper part of the letter-space. It is usually composed of two strokes which do not meet, but either curve slightly or are nearly straight. |
| *Rho* | The round upper segment is made like omikron; occasionally the straight strokes nearly meet at a point giving a distinctly pennant-shaped rho. |
| *Tau* | The horizontal and vertical rarely touch; the horizontal is usually not centered on the vertical and often slants perceptibly. |
| *Phi* | The central part of this letter is very compressed and unsymmetrical; at times it is roughly diamond- |

|  |  |
|---|---|
|  | shaped. Sometimes it even consists of a single curving stroke, which gives the letter a shape similar to that of the frame of a crossbow. |
| *Omega* | This letter is made with two strokes which do not touch each other. The left side is composed of a relatively long stroke beginning at the bottom of the letter-space and curving upwards and to the right; the right side consists of a single short slanting or vertical stroke. |

## List of Inscriptions

| | |
|---|---|
| ⁺*IG* II² 888 | Archon Dionysios (194/3). |
| ⁺*IG* II² 902 | Archon Timesianax (182/1). *Agora* XV no. 183. |
| *IG* II² 908 | The underlined letters appear on fragments numbered EM 2374 and 2375, which have been rejoined to the principal fragment (*Deltion* 29 [1973–74] B17). |
| *IG* II² 910 | Archon Eunikos (169/8). *Agora* XV no. 212. |
| *IG* II² 918 | *Agora* XV no. 214. |
| *IG* II² 946, lines 4–6 | Archon Achaios (ca. 190). These lines are inscribed *in rasura*. Kirchner-Klaffenbach, *Imagines* no. 102. |
| *IG* II² 954 | Osborne, *Naturalization* no. D100. |
| ⁺*IG* II² 972 | *Agora* XV no. 221. |
| *\*IG* II² 979 | Archon [Mnesitheos] (155/4). Osborne, *Naturalization* no. D101. |
| *IG* II² 990 | |
| *IG* II² 992 | |
| *\*IG* II² 997 | |
| *\*IG* II² 1938 | Archon Lysiades (148/7 or 149/8).[2] |
| *\*IG* II² 2314, column II | See above under the II² 913 Cutter. |
| *IG* II² 2332 | Archon Hermogenes (183/2). R. A. Padgug, "Polybios and the Population of Greece in the Third and Second Centuries B.C." (unpubl. diss. Harvard 1970), provides a new text and descriptive commentary. |
| ⁺*IG* II² 2357 | |

---

[2] On the alternate date, see Ch. Habicht, "The Eponymous Archons of Athens from 159/8 to 141/0 B.C.," *Hesperia* 57 (1988) 237–47.

| | |
|---|---|
| †*IG* II² 2443, lines 22–25 | See above under the II² 913 Cutter. |
| Agora I 77 | *Agora* XV no. 217. |
| Agora I 247, lines 1–65 | Archon Mn[es]itheos (155/4). *Agora* XV no. 225. For the list of names, see the Cutter of the Register of Agora I 247. |
| Agora I 896 | Published below. |
| *Agora I 968 | Published below. |
| †Agora I 983, lines 1–29 | Archon Eue[rgetes] (164/3). *Hesperia* 36 (1967) 88–91. For the other hands on this text, see the discussion under the Cutter of *IG* II² 1135. |
| Agora I 1325 | *Agora* XV no. 213. |
| *Agora I 1419 | *Hesperia* 16 (1947) 163–64. |
| Agora I 1572 | *Hesperia* 37 (1968) 287–88. |
| Agora I 1582 | *Agora* XV no. 185. |
| Agora I 2115 | Archon Alexandros (174/3). *Hesperia* 10 (1941) 279–80. |
| Agora I 2768 | Published below. |
| Agora I 2913 | *Agora* XV no. 204. |
| Agora I 3717 | *Agora* XV no. 189. |
| *Agora I 3777 | *Hesperia* 29 (1960) 18–19. |
| Agora I 3783 | *Agora* XV no. 210. |
| †*Agora I 4241 | Archon Achaios (*ca.* 190). *Hesperia* 23 (1954) 240. |
| *Agora I 4250 | Archon Hippakos (176/5). Pritchett-Meritt, *Chronology* 120–21. |
| Agora I 4253 | Archon Sonikos (175/4). *Agora* XV no. 200. |
| Agora I 4462 | Archon [Pleistainos].³ *Agora* XV no. 181. |
| Agora I 4503 | Published below. |
| *Agora I 4886 | Published below. |
| Agora I 4900 | Archon [_____] (177/6). *Hesperia* 16 (1947) 188–91. |
| Agora I 4915 | *Agora* XV no. 205. |
| Agora I 4917 | Archon Demetrios (ca. 170).⁴ *Agora* XV no. 171. |

---

³For a discussion of the date of Pleistainos, see below under the Cutter of *IG* II² 3479.

⁴Demetrios must be moved from 190/89; see Tracy, "The Date of the Athenian Archon Achaios," *AJAH* 9 (1984) [1988] 43–47, especially note 15. Two of the inscriptions dated to his year were inscribed by the Cutter of *IG* II² 903 (*q.v.*) whose dates are 179 to 160.

| | |
|---|---|
| Agora I 4933, lines 1–4 | Archon Philon after [Menedemos] (178/7). *Hesperia* 26 (1957) 210. |
| Agora I 5348 | *Agora* XV no. 224. |
| Agora I 5761 | Archon [Ale]xis (173/2). *Hesperia* 16 (1947) 163. See also *Hesperia* 26 (1957) 39 and 29 (1960) 417. |
| ⁺Agora I 5982 | *Agora* XV no. 211. |
| Agora I 6162 | Archon Alexandros (174/3). *Agora* XV no. 202. |
| Agora I 6165 | Archon Timou[chos?] (191/0). *Agora* XV no. 163. |
| Agora I 6190 | *Agora* XV no. 153. |
| Agora I 6671 | Archon Alexis (173/2). *Agora* XV no. 206. |
| Agora I 6750 | *Agora* XV no. 201. |
| Agora I 6843 | *Hesperia* 32 (1963) 15–16. |
| Agora I 7188 | Archon Pleistainos.[5] *Agora* XV no. 180. |
| *Agora I 7235 | *Hesperia* 51 (1982) 62. |
| *Agora I 7286 | *Hesperia* 45 (1976) 285–86. |
| *Agora I 7401 | Unpublished. |
| *Agora I 7529 | Unpublished. |
| **ArchEph* 1896 35 no. 18 | |
| ⁺*Corinth no. 5 | B. D. Meritt, *Corinth* VIII.1: *Greek Inscriptions 1896–1927* (Cambridge, Mass. 1931). |
| *EM 2282 | Unpublished. |
| EM 12379 | Unpublished. |
| EM 12727 + 13408 | Osborne, *Naturalization* no. D105. |
| EM 12763 | *Hesperia* 4 (1935) 172–73. |

## Inscriptions in the style of

⁺*IG* II² 867
   = *IG* II² 998

*IG* II² 946
   lines 1–3, 7–14

---

[5] See note 3 above.

Agora I 4267   Archon Ti[mesianax] (182/1). *Hesperia* 29 (1960) 15–16.
Agora I 4683   Archon T[i]mes[i]a[na]x (182/1). *Agora* XV no. 184.
Agora I 6257   *Agora* XV no. 231.
EM 454   Archon [Hippakos] (176/5). *Hesperia* 16 (1947) 187 and 26 (1957) 71.

## Preliminary publication of fragments from the Athenian Agora

**1** (pl. 15). Fragment of dark gray marble, face alone preserved, recovered from a marble dump east of the Metroon on June 2, 1933.

H. 0.09 m.; W. 0.065 m.; Th. 0.035 m.; LH. 0.006 m.

Inv. No. I 896

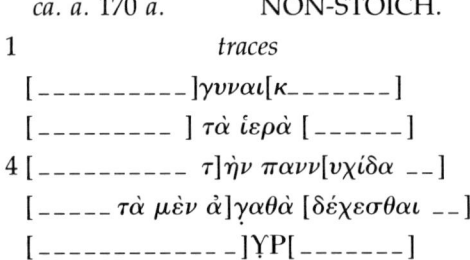

ca. a. 170 a.     NON-STOICH.

```
1                    traces
   [_____]γυναι[κ_____]
   [_____ ] τὰ ἱερὰ [_____]
4 [_____ τ]ὴν παννυ[χίδα __]
   [_____ τὰ μὲν ἀ]γαθὰ [δέχεσθαι __]
   [_____ -]ΥΡ[_____]
```

Line 5. The horizontal of dotted gamma appears above the break.

Line 6. The right slanting stroke of upsilon alone is visible; chi and sigma are also possible.

This fragment is apparently part of a decree praising a priest and his wife. For other inscriptions which mention a *pannuchis* see *IG* II² 334, 704, 775, 974–76, 1199. It was common in the cult of Asklepios.

**2** (pl. 16). Fragment of white marble, face alone preserved, found in a late wall east of the Propylon to the New Bouleuterion on June 15, 1933.

H. 0.10 m.; W. 0.045 m.; Th. 0.078 m.; LH. 0.006–0.007 m.

Inv. No. I 968

ca. a. 170 a.     NON-STOICH.

```
1  ΝΤ
   ΕΥΤΗ
   ΠΑΡΕ
4 ΝΩΝ
   Ν
```

Incised guidelines are readily visible on this fragment. Among this cutter's numerous other inscriptions, only three others, *IG* II² 2357, Agora I 1572, and I 4503 (no. **4** below) have incised guidelines. This fragment cannot apparently belong to either of the first two, since they are both of gray marble. Significant differences in letter size and vertical alignment make it impossible for this fragment and I 4503 to have belonged to the same inscription.

**3** (pl. 17). Fragment of white marble, left side preserved, found in a late wall south of the Tholos (G 12) on April 16, 1935.

H. 0.18 m.; W. 0.065 m.; Th. 0.052 m.; LH. 0.006 m.

Inv. No. I 2768

<pre>
        ca. a. 170 a.         NON-STOICH.
      1 [ca. 5]ΣI[ _____ ]
        [ca. 3]ενον [ _____ ]
        [ca. 3]ιον τ[ _____ ]
      4 [ca. 3]ΟΝΤΩ[Ν _____ ]
        [ca. 2 τ]ῆι βουλ[ῆι _____ ]
        [ca. 3]ειν εἰ[ _____ ]
        [τ]ῶν καὶ μι[σθοῦν? _____ ]
      8 ΝΟΝΤΩΝ Π[ _____ ]
        δὲ μηθεν[ _____ μετε]-
        νεγκεῖν τ[ὰ _____ ]
        καὶ ὁ ἐπιψ[ηφίσας _____ γραμ]-
     12 ματεὺς ὁ [ _____ ὀφειλόν]-
        των χιλία[ς δραχμὰς _____ ]
        τεῖ Φωσφό[ρωι _____ ]
        μενοι ὑπὸ [ _____ ]
     16 πράξωσι I[ _____ ]
        κεχωρισμ[ένα _____ ]
        μηδὲ στ[ _____ ]
        [μ]ήτε ὑπ[ὸ _____ ]
     20 [. . .]ΝΑΓΙ[ _____ ]
</pre>

Line 5. The beta is all but obliterated by a scratch.

Line 17. Only the left half of mu is preserved; it could also be lambda.

This is a most tantalizing fragment of what appears to be a sacred text prohibiting certain behavior (line 9) and specifying several categories of persons, including anyone who propounds a counterdecree (line 11) and, it seems, the secretary (line 12), as subject to pay a fine of one thousand drachmas to Artemis Phosphoros if the prohibition is not heeded.

Though I can offer no convincing restorations which result in consistent line lengths, the following reconstruction, purely *exempli gratia*, may suggest the general sense of lines 8–14.

[\_\_\_\_ μὴ ἐξεῖναι]
9 δὲ μηθεν[ὶ αὐτῶν εἰς ἄλλο τι μετε]-
νεγκεῖν τ[ὰ χρήματα. εἰ δὲ μή, ὅ τε εἴπας]
καὶ ὁ ἐπιψ[ηφίσας καὶ ὁ γραμ]-
12 ματεὺς ὁ [ἀεὶ λαχὼν ὀφειλόν]-
των χιλία[ς δραχμὰς ἱερὰς τεῖ Ἀρτέμιδι]
τεῖ Φωσφό[ρωι \_\_\_\_]

Lines 5–9 of *IG* II² 1243, a decree of the Marathonian Tetrapolis, provide the closest parallel. Similar sentiments also appear in lines 36–41 of *REG* 91 (1978) 290–91, a decree from Eleusis. One might also cite a number of texts from outside Athens; see, for example, the well-known law of Samos concerning grain which ends with a similar prohibition and fine aimed against persons who might propose a change (lines 85–90 of Wiegand and Wilamowitz-Moellendorff, *SB Berlin* 1904 917–31 = *SIG*³ no. 976 = Thür and Koch, *AAWW* 111 [1981] 61–88).

**4** (pl. 18). Fragment of white marble, face alone preserved, recovered from a marble pile in the area west of the Odeion (J–M 9–11) on February 9, 1937.

H. 0.076 m.; W. 0.041 m.; Th. 0.051 m.; LH. 0.007–0.008 m.
Inv. No. I 4503

*ca. a.* 170 a.        NON-STOICH.

1    Λ
     ΤΟ
    ΤΟΥ
4   ΠΛῚ
     ΓΡ
     – v

Line 4. There is a vertical stroke at the edge of the break.
Guidelines are visible on this fragment (see above on Agora I 968).

**5** (pl. 19). Fragment of white marble, molding above and part of inscribed face alone preserved, found in a late Roman disturbance in the classical floor of the Tholos (G 12) on May 22, 1937.

H. 0.10 m.; W. 0.13 m.; Th. 0.065 m.; LH. 0.006 m.

Inv. No. I 4886

ca. a. 170 a.     NON-STOICH.

1 [ _ _ _ _ _ ἐπὶ τῆς _ _ ἰδο]ς δεκά[της πρυτανείας]
 [ _ _ _ _ _ _ _ _ _ _ _ _ Μο]υνι[χιῶνος _ _ _ _ ]

Only the tips of the dotted letters survive.

Enough of the molding, i.e. its shape and the spacing of the letters in relation to it, is preserved to allow comparison with the other moldings on inscriptions by this cutter. This cannot, alas, be associated with any of the other known examples.

## *Adnotatiunculae*

### *IG* II² 888

There is a blank space above the first line of 0.097 m. Kirchner's restoration of [τοῦ μετὰ _ _ ] was probably incorrect as Habicht has shown in *Studien* 165–68. Line 11 should read [ .²½. ]ΑΓ[. .]ΝΤΟ[ _ _ _ ]. Dotted gamma could be tau.

### *IG* II² 902

The eta read by Meritt and Traill at the beginning of line 5 should at least be dotted. I can discern no sure traces of it and, in fact, the inscribed surface appears to be worn away at the point where it should occur. The area of wear slants as though along a stroke. Dotted alpha would appear to be a better reading.

### *IG* II² 972

The letters in the register of names are larger but are not (*pace* Meritt and Traill) in a different hand. The rho in line 25 is completely characteristic of this cutter.

### *IG* II² 2357

Except for the last letter, line 12 has been erased. The letters, awkwardly reinscribed, are much disfigured by the erasure. [[Εὐε]λπι]ς seems to be the correct reading and restoration. A clear apex forms the basis for reading dotted lambda. Pi, though unusually wide, is clear. The name, if correctly restored, is new to Attic prosopography.

Line 29. The name Ἀρχώ is quite clearly preserved on the stone; it is well attested in Attica. See, for example, *IG* II² 7321.

## *IG* II² 2443

The cutter inscribed K = ZΛ[.]KIΔI as the demotic in line 24. Kothokides, following Kirchner, does seem the most probable interpretation of what he meant to inscribe.

## Agora I 983

Line 2 reads Μηνογέ[νης].

## Agora I 4241

The cutter committed an haplography, omitting the second nu in line 2. Read Ἡρακλέων <Ν>αννάκου. It is at least amusing to note that the Cutter of *IG* II² 912 also had problems with the succession of nu's in this man's name; he omitted one of the central nu's from the patronymic (*Agora* XV no. 216, line 2).

## Agora I 5982

Line 7. Meritt and Traill's reading Ἀθμ[ονεῖς] cannot stand. The third letter is clearly a nu—the tops of the two verticals (and both are vertical) and part of the diagonal appear. Mu is impossible, for this cutter makes mu with slanting strokes. In the space before the first letter appears the top of a vertical stroke. The reading is probably [Φ]ίλων. Only the tops of dotted lambda and omega appear.

## Corinth no. 5

The lettering of this text (see the photograph published in *Corinth* VIII.1) is unmistakably the work of this cutter. Among the Greek inscriptions found in the excavations at Corinth there are only eleven known decrees which predate the resettlement in 44 B.C. It is quite surprising to find that one of them was inscribed by this prolific Athenian cutter. What brought him to Corinth one can only speculate. There was certainly not enough inscribing being done in Corinth to keep him employed for very long. No other of these eleven Corinthian decrees was inscribed, so far as I can determine, by an Attic cutter.

Neither the original editor (K. K. Smith, *AJA* 23 [1919] 333) nor Meritt offered a date for this decree. It belongs to the first half of the second century B.C., perhaps to a date not too long before Mummius' troops destroyed the city in 146.

Once the cutter is recognized as Attic, the Attic/Ionic form in line 5 is no longer surprising.

## *IG* II² 867 = *IG* II² 998

For a new text, see A. S. Henry, *ZPE* 38 (1980) 91–92. The last letter of line 3 (Henry's text) is not epsilon but eta.

Practically all of this cutter's very considerable output consists of decrees or other texts of an official character. He appears in fact to have done an extraordinary number of inscriptions honoring prytaneis. Twenty-five of his sixty-seven extant fragments belong to that class, i.e. just about thirty-seven percent.

# The Cutter of *IG* II² 1324

*Date: ca. 190*

## General characteristics of the lettering (fig. 13)

The lettering of this cutter is rather plain. The interlines are liberal and, though erratic, the spacing between letters is also quite generous. Despite these qualities, this lettering has an amateurish look about it, partly because the individual strokes of letters are not placed with precision and the letters themselves vary both in size and in placement in the letter-space. This cutter fails to align his letters either along the line (probably drawn on by most cutters) marking the top of his letters or along that at the bottom. His letters and lines in consequence wobble.

## Peculiarities of individual letters

| | |
|---|---|
| *Alpha* | The crossbar is usually straight and often slants upwards from left to right. It occurs quite low in the letter, at times so low that the letter could be taken for delta in isolation. |
| *Delta* | This letter is often asymmetrical; if placed on a vertical axis, the left half is larger. Or, to put it another way, the letter is elongated to the left. |
| *Rho* | The loop tends to be relatively small; the top is often formed by a straight stroke, down from which a slightly curving diagonal extends back to the vertical, giving to the letter an awkward pennant-like shape. |
| *Sigma* | This letter reveals a lot of variety, particularly in the top and bottom strokes: one, sometimes both, are horizontal, or nearly so; occasionally both clearly slant. The strokes which form the center of the letter meet with precision but, by contrast, they regularly overlap, or are overlapped by, the top and bottom strokes. |

*Figure 13. IG II² 1324 lines 6–13.*

Tau　　　　　The crossbar tends to be wider than the vertical and at times was clearly made with two horizontal strokes placed end to end.

Phi　　　　　This letter is taller than the others. A very short straight stroke, sometimes slanting upwards from left to right, crosses the vertical below the mid-point to finish off the letter. Another stroke is sometimes added below this to make a very perfunctory loop.

## List of Inscriptions

⁺*IG* II² 1324
*IG* II² 2948
*IG* II² 4454
*IG* II² 4459

## Adnotatiunculae

### IG II² 1324

This stone has been broken at the top with the consequence that there is now no trace of the letters in lines 1–2. In fact, the surface on which they were inscribed has been broken away.

### General comment

The four inscriptions by this cutter, a decree of the Orgeones of Bendis in Piraeus (II² 1324), the dedicatory poem for the temple of the Dionysiasts in Piraeus (II² 2948), and two dedications to Asklepios (?) from the south slope of the Acropolis (II² 4454 and 4459), suggest that he was a local workman from Piraeus who had some special association with religious organizations.

By contrast, Dionysios son of Agathokles of Marathon (*PA* 4213), the donor for the temple of the Dionysiasts (see II² 1325, lines 21–22), was an influential man; he was crowned for his beneficence by the Dionysiasts in 185/4 (II² 1325) and honored by the same group on his death in 176/5 (II² 1326). He was apparently quite wealthy; at least he appears with his sons Agathokles and Dionysios in the *epidoseis* inscriptions of 183/2 (II² 2332 lines 306–8) and of *ca.* 180 (II² 2333 lines 16–17). His grandson is known from II² 2452 line 99 and a female descendant was priestess at Eleusis in the first century B.C. (Clinton, *Sacred Officials* 73).

# The Cutter of *IG* II² 897

## *Dates: 189/8–178/7*

### *General characteristics of the lettering* (fig. 14)

This cutter inscribed a rather plain ordinary style of letters. The lettering reveals just enough inconsistency from letter to letter that it borders on being sloppy. When one studies the letters in detail, each seems to be made slightly differently each time. Occasionally strokes are simply omitted, specifically the central horizontal of epsilon and the crossbar of alpha. On the similarity of this hand to that of the Cutter of *IG* II² 1326, see below pp. 231–32.

### *Peculiarities of individual letters*

| | |
|---|---|
| *Alpha* | This letter and its counterparts delta and lambda all tend to be relatively wide. The crossbar, usually straight, is placed in the middle to upper part of the letter. Sometimes it is horizontal and sometimes it slants in one direction or the other. Occasionally it is slightly curved. |
| *Epsilon* | The horizontals thicken slightly at the ends. Usually the middle one is shorter and is quite often placed closer to the top. The other two tend to be quite long, i.e. as long as or longer than the vertical, and not quite parallel to each other. The vertical often extends a bit beyond the horizontals; this occurs more frequently at the top. One, or more, of the horizontal strokes does not quite touch the vertical. |
| *Theta* | In relation to omikron this letter is distinctly larger and has no dot. |
| *Kappa* | This letter is very wide; the slanting strokes often do not touch the vertical or one another. |
| *Omikron* | This letter is quite small and occurs in the middle or |

*Figure 14. IG II² 897.*

|  |  |
|---|---|
| | upper part of the letter-space. It was made in one or more segments and is sometimes slightly oblong; occasionally there is a small space left open along its circumference. |
| *Pi* | Usually the initial vertical extends slightly up beyond the horizontal; the horizontal begins at the vertical and extends consistently beyond the second vertical. The second vertical is only slightly shorter than the first and at times slants perceptibly outwards. |
| *Rho* | The loop is usually of ordinary size but it can be very small. It is often roughly oblong or pennant-shaped, though no two seem to be quite the same shape and size. |
| *Omega* | This letter has the shape of a horseshoe; it tends to be small and thin. |

## List of Inscriptions

| | |
|---|---|
| *IG* II² 856 | Osborne, *Naturalization* no. D97. |
| *IG* II² 897 | Archon Eupolemos (185/4). Kirchner-Klaffenbach, *Imagines* no. 100. |
| ⁺*IG* II² 898 | Archon [Eupol]emos (185/4). Ch. Habicht, *Hesperia* 56 (1987) 64–66, has demonstrated that Agora I 7197 +7199 belong. |
| ⁺*IG* II² 900 | Archon Eupolem[os] (185/4). |
| *IG* II² 909 | The lettering of this text is large (0.008–0.01 m.) and very neat. The cutter has added finials to most of the omegas; otherwise this lettering is the same as that on his other inscriptions. Note that Osborne, *Naturalization* III p. 105, dates this inscription to 160–150; this is probably a trifle late. |
| *IG* II² 929 | |
| *IG* II² 940 | |
| Agora I 979, 1015, 1017 | Archon Zo[pyros] (186/5). *Hesperia* 15 (1946) 193–97. |
| Agora I 1871, 6115 | Archon Euthykritos (189/8). *Agora* XV no. 173. |
| Agora I 5143 | *Deltion* 18A (1963) 106–7. |
| Agora I 5424 +3087 | I 5424 *a* and *b* are published in *Hesperia* 29 (1960) 17–18 and 3087 in the same volume, page 54. I 5424*a* and 3087 have been joined on the shelves. |
| ⁺Agora I 5800 | *Agora* XV no. 178. |
| Agora I 7226 | *Hesperia* 51 (1982) 56. The date should be *ca.* 185 rather than *fin. saec.* III *a*. |
| Agora I 7453 | Archon Philon [after Menedemos] (178/7). *Hesperia* 51 (1982) 61–62. On the restorations in lines 6–9, see *Bull.épigr.* 1982 no. 139. This decree honors Antiochos, later Antiochos IV Epiphanes; for more on him, see the references under *IG* II² 937 below. |

## Inscription in the style of

| | |
|---|---|
| Agora I 6546 | *Hesperia* 32 (1963) 47. |

## Adnotatiunculae

### *IG* II² 898

Koehler and Kirchner both thought that this decree might have been passed on the same day as II² 897, i.e. on the eleventh day of Mounichion, the tenth month of the year. If so, it would have been rather surprising, for it would have meant that the same cutter was commissioned to inscribe two decrees from the same meeting. The new fragments published by Habicht establish that this was not the case and it instead seems highly probable that II² 898 was passed in the first half of the year (*Hesperia* 56 [1987] 66).

### *IG* II² 900

0.046 m. below line 25 appear the faint remains of two citations. This area has been worn nearly smooth.
          [κοσμητή]ν                       ἐφήβ[ους]
The nu falls under the omikron of τό and the epsilon under the epsilon of εἰς in line 25.

Meritt, *Charisterion eis Anastasion K. Orlandon* I (1965) 194 n. 8, dissociates fragment *c*. This may well be correct. If so, it cannot be associated certainly with any of the known fragments.

### Agora I 5800

There are the remains of an incised olive crown below line 5. Eta is inscribed within the crown and, just below eta, a slanting stroke appears, probably alpha.

Notable in this cutter's work is the fact that he inscribed the annual ephebic record for two consecutive years, namely Agora I 979 of 185/4 and *IG* II² 900 of 184/3.

# The Cutter of *IG* II² 892

## Dates: 188/7–187/6

### General characteristics of the lettering (fig. 15)

This cutter inscribed neat, plain lettering and left liberal interlines. His spacing between letters tends to be somewhat uneven, most noticeably in the case of omikron. Note that the third omikron in line 3, that in line 7, and the second in line 9 follow very closely on the letter which precedes.

### Peculiarities of individual letters

| | |
|---|---|
| *Alpha* | The crossbar is placed at about the mid-point and varies between a straight line and a curve, with the frequency being about equal. |
| *Epsilon* | On each given example the horizontals tend to be roughly the same length but the length varies from example to example, some epsilons being in consequence quite thin and others quite wide. The horizontals were made so that they taper at the ends to needle points, as it were. |
| *Rho* | The loop is quite nicely rounded and relatively small. |
| *Sigma* | This letter tends to be slightly taller than the others. The upper and lower slanting strokes tend to curve slightly or to give that impression by being positioned slightly in from the ends of the central strokes of the letter. |
| *Upsilon* | This letter is composed of three strokes. The vertical tends to be about half the height of the letter. The slanting strokes are relatively long, thus making this letter quite wide and large relative to the others. |
| *Omega* | This letter is always open at the bottom with no finials of any sort. It tends to be roughly symmetrical and |

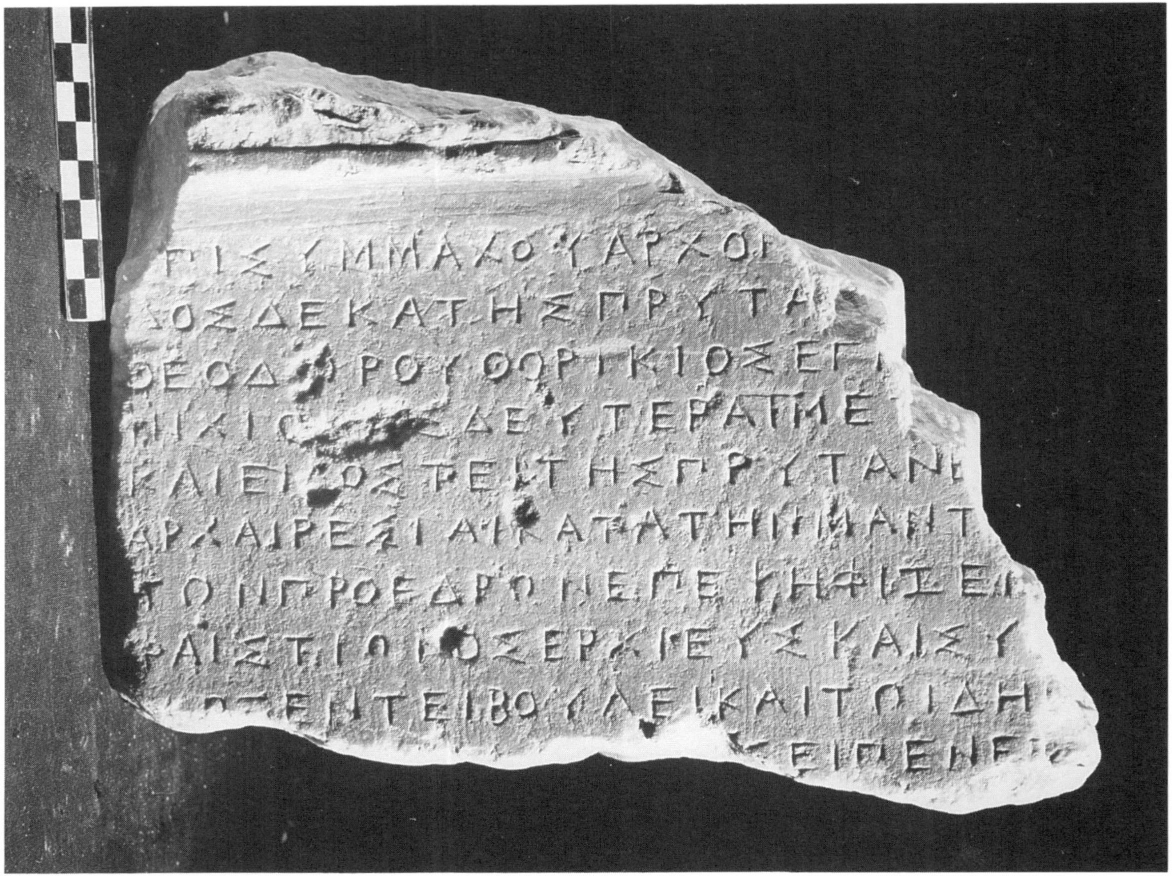

*Figure 15.* IG II² 892a.

varies in size quite dramatically. See the examples in lines 7–9.

## List of Inscriptions

| | |
|---|---|
| ⁺*IG* II² 892 | Archon Symmachos (188/7). Kirchner-Klaffenbach, *Imagines* no. 99. |
| ⁺*IG* II² 925 | Osborne, *Naturalization* no. D104. |
| ⁺Agora I 2155 | Archon [Theoxenos] (187/6). Pritchett-Meritt, *Chronology* 117–18. |

## Inscription in the style of

| | |
|---|---|
| Agora I 6244 lines 1–8 | *Hesperia* 33 (1964) 225–26. Lines 9 and 10 are inscribed by another hand (unfamiliar) and appear to be much later in date. The serifs and broken crossbar of alpha suggest a date 125 or after. |

## Adnotatiunculae

### *IG* II² 892

Wilhelm associated fragments *a* and *b*—an association which at first glance appears unlikely since the number of letters per line differs markedly on the two fragments. But, as Kirchner noted in *IG*, the letters on fragment *b* are rather crowded. In fact, measurement reveals that the lines on both fragments as restored would require the same horizontal space, just about 0.34 m.

### *IG* II² 925

Osborne has incorrectly recorded the vertical space; five full lines occupy not *ca.* 0.044 to 0.045 m. but 0.07 to 0.073 m.[1]

### Agora I 2155

*IG* II² 925 almost certainly belongs with this fragment from the Athenian Agora, for the spacing of the letters, the interlines, and the marble are

---

[1] At an early stage of this study I had tentatively placed this fragment in the dossier of another cutter and shared this information with Osborne who incorporated it into his work (*Naturalization* II p. 191 and n. 896).

identical. Moreover both pieces preserve the back rough-picked; the recorded thicknesses, 0.11 m. for II² 925 and 0.115 for I 2155, support the association, for the first is a small piece from the left edge whereas the second preserves more than half the original width. Since stelai tend to be slightly thicker in the middle, the difference in the recorded measurements is exactly what one would expect and well within accepted tolerances.

The combined text reveals that the Athenians conferred citizenship on someone close to King Seleukos IV. This decree was passed before the year 187/6 was out, around the middle of the tenth month. Not coincidentally Seleukos had come to power following the death of his father, Antiochos the Great, near the beginning of this very year.[2] The man honored had probably been sent to Athens as a goodwill ambassador. The Athenians responded favorably to this overture from the new king, who was doubtless concerned to reassert Seleucid influence in Greece in the aftermath of his father's decisive defeat by the Romans.[3]

---

[2] His father had died on the third or fourth of July 187 (*Bull.épigr.* 1955 no. 38).
[3] See E. S. Gruen, *The Hellenistic World and the Coming of Rome* (Berkeley 1984) 639–45.

# The Cutter of Agora I 6765

*Dates: 188/7–181/0*

## *General characteristics of the lettering* (fig. 16)

This lettering has a crowded and busy look about it. The letters are placed close together, occasionally actually touching. The letter-height varies, with sigma and upsilon tending to extend up above the line of the letters. This cutter did not employ serifs. His round letters tend to be quite round.

## *Peculiarities of individual letters*

| | |
|---|---|
| *Alpha* | This letter varies in width but it tends to be thin. The crossbar is straight and can be placed quite high in the letter to well below the middle. It also slants quite often. |
| *Epsilon* | The top and bottom horizontals tend to be as long as the vertical and at times longer, making this a wide letter; the central horizontal is short. |
| *Omikron* | This letter tends to be small and to hang down from the top of the letter-space. |
| *Sigma* | This letter varies in shape and size. It habitually appears to lean back because the top slanting stroke does not project as far forward as the point formed by the central part of the letter. The bottom stroke, though short, is placed so that it frequently projects beyond the central part. This treatment of sigma with the short bottom stroke placed quite far up the lower central diagonal is highly idiosyncratic. This bottom stroke often thickens perceptibly at the end. |
| *Upsilon* | This letter is made with three strokes; the vertical is often short. The letter tends to be tall and rather thin. |
| *Phi* | The vertical extends up into the interline. The central |

*Figure 16.* Agora I 6765.

part is usually round, in essence an omikron or just a shade smaller. This letter is very distinctive.

## List of Inscriptions

| | |
|---|---|
| ⁺*IG* II² 891 | Archon [Symmachos] (188/7). |
| *IG* II² 920 + Agora I 1462 | Archon [Hippias] (181/0). *Agora* XV no. 168. |
| Agora I 5344 | Archon Hippias (181/0). *Hesperia* Suppl. 4 144–47. |
| Agora I 6765 | Archon Hippias (181/0). *Agora* XV no. 167. |
| Agora I 7496 and *IG* II² 1707 | Archon [Hip]pias (181/0). *Hesperia* 53 (1984) 370–74. Gauthier, *REG* 100 (1987) 256, suggests some restorations and expresses doubt about the association. |

## Inscriptions in the style of

+ Agora I 3642     *Agora* XV no. 159.
+ Agora I 4673     *Hesperia* 26 (1957) 218.

## Adnotatiunculae

### IG II² 891

The chairman in this inscription of the year 188/7, Lakrates son of Mentor from Perithoidai, is also attested as a speaker four times during the year of Hippias (181/0). In that year he proposed a citizenship decree (*IG* II² 889 + 904 = Osborne, *Naturalization* no. D99), two prytany decrees (*Agora* XV nos. 167 and 168), and a decree praising a board refurbishing the Skias (*Hesperia* Suppl. 4 145). These last two were moved in meetings of the boule, revealing that he served twice as a councillor (see P. J. Rhodes, *ZPE* 57 [1984] 201–2).

Whether coincidence or not, it seems appropriate to note two strange facts about this cutter's work: four of his five inscriptions belong to the archonship of Hippias; also Lakrates from Perithoidai appears in four of the five either as chairman or as speaker. He is not the speaker of Agora I 7496 and *IG* II² 1707.

### Agora I 3642

Seven centimeters above the crown to the right appears the end of a column of names, as Meritt noted, though he made no reading. One name can be deciphered, [Δ]ιονυσόδω[ρος]. The basis for dotted omega is the lower left side of a round letter at the break. There are traces of another name above but I can discern no certain letter-stroke.

### Agora I 4673

Line 3. The first letter is omikron, not epsilon.

The date of this text is probably about 185 B.C. and, contrary to what Meritt thought, it does not provide any evidence for the composition of the phyle Demetrias.

\*

The four decrees from the archonship of Hippias were passed in the second half of the year in the sixth, eighth, eleventh, and twelfth prytanies. They provide the opportunity to pose questions of timing, i.e. how soon after passage was a text given to the cutter for inscribing and how quickly was he expected to produce the finished product? I have always assumed that inscriptions were ordinarily done on a piecework basis and that the secretary was both likely to act promptly and to seek out a cutter who could begin work at once. To put it another way, I think it unlikely that the secretary would hand over a text for inscribing to a cutter who was already engaged in a major job and could not work on it for some time. We cannot perhaps know. But it is notable that the present group of four inscriptions is sufficiently spaced out that they could have been inscribed according to these assumptions.

The interval between the passage of *Agora* XV no. 167 on the twenty-ninth day of the sixth prytany and the passage of Agora I 5344 on the eighth or ninth day of the eighth prytany is about thirty-seven days. A complete prytany inscription will have had about three thousand letters to be inscribed. Assuming a rate of work of three hundred letters per day, incised, corrected, and painted, a prytany inscription will have required ten days of work, not including the time required for fairly detailed layout and incising (or painting) of the crowns. The entire job will have required about twenty working days.[1] There is time to spare between jobs. The same was also probably true for *Agora* XV no. 168, passed in the eleventh month, and Agora I 7496 and *IG* II² 1707, passed in the third week of the twelfth month. In summary, the work we have evidence of would have kept this cutter quite busy during the last six months of Hippias' year as archon, but would probably not have consumed all of his time.

---

[1] The rate of work here assumed may be low. For more on this subject, see Tracy, *Lettering* 119 and note 70.

# The Cutter of *IG* II² 1329

## Dates: 183/2–175/4

### General characteristics of the lettering (fig. 17)

This man inscribed plain letters with only an occasional serif on a number of letters including epsilon and xi. The letters vary greatly in height and width, giving the lettering to my eye an erratic look. Alpha, gamma, delta, epsilon, lambda, mu, xi, sigma, tau, and omega are rather wide; beta, kappa, omikron, rho, and upsilon tend to be narrow. Epsilon, rho, sigma, upsilon, and phi are tall; delta, omikron, and tau tend to be short. Round letters are made with multiple short straight strokes so that, e.g., the omikrons often resemble hexagonal nuts for carriage bolts.

### Peculiarities of individual letters

| | |
|---|---|
| *Alpha* | The crossbar is sharply broken and extends down to the base of the letter. |
| *Delta* | This letter is very wide and compressed in height; it is this cutter's most idiosyncratic letter. |
| *Epsilon* | The central horizontal is usually shorter; the top and bottom strokes quite often curve perceptibly. |
| *Omikron* | This letter is small and occurs in the upper part of the letter-space. |

### List of Inscriptions

⁺*IG* II² 1328
    lines 4–20    Archon Her[mo]gen[es] (183/2)
*IG* II² 1329    Archon Sonikos (175/4). Kirchner-Klaffenbach, *Imagines* no. 101.

*Figure 17. IG II² 1329 lines 17–28.*

## Adnotatiunculae

### IG II² 1328

Above the preserved crown appears the bottom of another crown. This crown is not centered but is positioned to the left slightly. Perhaps it is part of a row of slightly smaller crowns which extended across the width of the stele at this point. In any case, one or more decrees are lost above. Note that this stone was apparently one of the major monuments of the association, for line 44 characterizes it as ἡ στήλη τῶν ὀργεώνων.

There are now parts of three decrees preserved on this stele. Each is by a different hand suggesting that each was inscribed at a different time, *scil.* soon after passage. There are not enough letters of the first (lines 1–3) to enable meaningful study; the third (lines 21–44) is so worn that positive study of the hand is scarcely possible. However, sigma has parallel top and bottom strokes, which is sufficient to show that the present cutter did not inscribe these lines. This third decree was passed in the archonship of Sonikos (175/4) in the month Mounichion at the major conclave. In fact, it was passed at the same meeting as *IG* II² 1329. Note that, as we would expect, two decrees passed at the same meeting were assigned to different cutters for inscribing.

The present cutter seems to be in essence a local workman from the Piraeus. He apparently had some special connection with the Orgeones of the Great Mother and her sanctuary in Piraeus.

# The Cutter of Agora I 6512

### Dates: ca. 180–162/1

## General characteristics of the lettering (fig. 18)

This cutter inscribed lettering which, though rather plain, is crowded together and makes a rather sloppy impression. The letters vary in height and width and often are so close together that they actually touch. The letter-strokes themselves are quite long and thin.

## Peculiarities of individual letters

| | |
|---|---|
| *Alpha* | This is a very wide letter with a sharply broken crossbar which reaches down to the base of the letter. The crossbar is clearly two separate strokes which sometimes vary markedly in size. |
| *Epsilon* | The middle horizontal tends to be shorter; all three taper at the end to points. |
| *Tau* | This letter is very wide and invariably has a serif at the bottom of the vertical. |

## List of Inscriptions

| | |
|---|---|
| Agora I 175 | Archon Poseidonios (162/1). *Hesperia* 2 (1933) 503–5. |
| +Agora I 6035 | *Hesperia* 17 (1948) 13–14. |
| +Agora I 6512 | *Hesperia* 30 (1961) 12. |
| +Agora I 6545 | *Hesperia* 51 (1982) 201–2. |

## Adnotatiunculae

### Agora I 6035

Meritt in the *editio princeps* dated this citation from an ephebic inscription to *ca.* 232 B.C. This is certainly part of Agora I 175. I now (June 1988)

Figure 18. Agora I 6512.

am informed, thanks to the kindness of J. McK. Camp II, that the two fragments join, with I 6035 going directly on top of I 175 (pl. 20). The join reveals that the second decree for the *kosmetes* had no preamble but began with the name of the speaker. This general citation for the ephebes was probably the central one flanked by one on each side for the *kosmetes*. A nearly contemporary text, *IG* II² 1027 of 160/59, offers a parallel in that it also had three crowns between the two decrees. The position of its one preserved crown for the *kosmetes* has been misrepresented in *IG*. Its center appears directly above the eta of the relative pronoun, revealing that it was the third of three crowns. The two to the left are lost. The order of praise in II² 1027 seems to have been the ephebes and *kosmetes* together, the ephebes alone, and the *kosmetes* alone. Agora I 175 apparently had a similar arrangement.

### Agora I 6512

On the date of this text, *ca. a.* 180 *a.*, and the reading of the demotic in line 10 as [Φλ]υεύς and not [ Ἀχαρ]νεύς, see *Hesperia* 51 (1982) 60. The marble of this text is predominantly white and different in character from the other three fragments by this cutter, which are all of the same gray marble.

### Agora I 6545

In the *editio princeps* J. S. Traill dated this fragmentary ephebic roster to the years 224/3 to 200. The hand, the vertical spacing, and the gray marble make it virtually certain that this fragment too is part of the same monument as Agora I 175, a decree praising the ephebes of 162/1. That text has line lengths, counting iota as half a letter, of about 72 letters; it was quite a wide monument. The roster was arranged in three columns with the present fragment coming from the top of the second column. As his *"vestigia coronae?"* and *"vacat"* attest, Traill was puzzled by the broken remains above his line 1. These are in fact the remains of two letter strokes from a heading in large letters: just above the right side of epsilon there is the lower part of a vertical stroke with a serif. This stroke terminates at about the mid-point of the letter-space. Directly above the center of mu appears the lower part of a vertical stroke with serif. These can only be the remains of pi iota in the title

[οἱ ἐφηβεύσαντες οἱ ἐ]πὶ [Ποσειδωνίου ἄρχοντος]

Line 5. The first letter is tau as the serif at the bottom reveals and not pi.

Line 7. The strokes read as mu cannot be part of mu, for this cutter makes mu with slanting strokes. The only clear letter-stroke is a vertical.

The very light mark, which does have the correct position for a stroke and which Traill interpreted as part of the central complex of mu, seems to be a scratch. Iota appears to be a preferable reading.

Line 8. Before the first letter, the bottom right angle of delta may be discerned below the break.

It seems an odd happenstance that from this man's work parts of only two texts survive. Both are ephebic inscriptions, i.e. major monuments, and, if our dates are correct, they are separated by about eighteen years. A major cutter active for almost twenty years—other examples of his writing ought to survive.

# The Cutter of *IG* II² 903

## Dates: 179/8–161/0

### General characteristics of the lettering (fig. 19)

This cutter tends to incise his letters lightly and does not employ serifs. His lettering is neat and often rather large. The round letters are quite round. His most distinctive idiosyncrasy is his tendency to thicken the ends of strokes cuneiform-like, particularly the horizontals of epsilon, the second vertical of pi, the vertical of tau, and all three strokes of upsilon.

### Peculiarities of individual letters

| | |
|---|---|
| *Alpha* | The cutter makes this letter reasonably wide. The crossbar is straight and tends to be nearly horizontal. The strokes at the apex often do not quite meet. |
| *Kappa* | The lower slanting stroke tends to be shorter than the upper and is placed so that it often touches neither of the other strokes. |
| *Omikron* | Though it is clearly incised freehand and reveals some unevenness, this letter is usually quite round. Its size varies markedly, though it tends to be slightly smaller in height than the other letters. |
| *Pi* | The second vertical is short, is placed just inside the end of the horizontal, and is thickened at the end. |
| *Sigma* | This letter is definitely taller than the other letters. |
| *Tau* | The horizontal is placed off-center to the left, occasionally so far that the letter resembles a backwards gamma. The vertical and the horizontal often do not quite touch. |
| *Omega* | This letter is relatively small, open at the bottom, and has small serifs of the inverted-v variety or sometimes straight lines. |

*Figure 19.* IG II² 903.

## List of Inscriptions

| | |
|---|---|
| IG II² 820 | *Hesperia* 28 (1959) 179–81. |
| IG II² 903 | Archon Hippakos (176/5). Gauthier presents a new text and full discussion in *REG* 95 (1982) 275–90. |
| IG II² 911 | Archon [Eunikos] (169/8). |
| IG II² 951 | Archon Nikosthenes (167/6). |
| IG II² 956 | Archon Aristolas (161/0). |
| IG II² 2404 | The date in the *Corpus, post med. s.* IV, needs adjustment. Dow in *Ancient World* 8 (1983) 95–106 noted that this text and *IG* II² 2392 are identical. |
| Agora I 94 + 189 + 647 | *Hesperia* 13 (1944) 254–57. |
| Agora I 684a, b | Archon Demetrios (ca. 170).¹ *Agora* XV no. 172. |
| Agora I 2184 | *Agora* XV no. 122. The date, *ca. a.* 225 *a.*, is at least fifty years too early. |
| Agora I 2967 | *Agora* XV no. 126. Note that a date *ca.* 220 is too early. |
| ⁺Agora I 5912 | *Agora* XV no. 150. |
| Agora I 6081 | Archon [D]emet[rios] (*ca.* 170). *Hesperia* 26 (1957) 30–31. |
| Agora I 6161 | *Agora* XV no. 230. |
| Agora I 6166 | Archon [___i]ppos (177/6). *Agora* XV no.197. |
| ⁺Agora I 6367 | *Hesperia* 26 (1957) 47–49; but see also Robert, *Hellenica* 11–12 (1960) 92–111, esp. 107–8. |
| Agora I 6459 | Joins I 5912, *q.v.* |
| Agora I 6675 | Archon Euergetes (164/3). *Agora* XV no. 219. |
| Agora I 6986 | Archon Menedemos (179/8). *Hesperia* 34 (1965) 89. |

## Inscriptions in the style of

| | |
|---|---|
| IG II² 814 | If this attribution is correct, the date *med. s.* III *a.* should be adjusted to *ca. a.* 170 *a.* |
| IG II² 1536 | For a new edition with commentary see S. B. Aleshire, *The Athenian Asklepieion: The People, Their Dedications and The Inventories* (Amsterdam 1989) 351–53. |

---

¹On Demetrios' date, see *AJAH* 9 (1984) [1988] 47 and note 15.

*IG* II² 3148
*IG* II² 3874
Agora I 6103   *Hesperia* 36 (1967) 64.

## *Adnotatiunculae*

### Agora I 5912 + I 6459

Agora I 6459, a small, previously unpublished fragment (pl. 21) from the excavations in the Athenian Agora, joins I 5912. It is a fragment of gray marble, with the inscribed face alone preserved; it was found in a Roman context west of the Odeion (J 10–11) on March 5, 1952.

H. 0.12 m.; W. 0.12 m.; Th. 0.046 m.; LH. 0.008 m.

The combined text is as follows (the new fragment provides the first two letters in line 1):

ἡ β[ου]λὴ
[τὸν τα]μίαν
3 [τῆς βο]υλῆς
[ ca. 5 ]ωνα
[ca. 3]έα

The calculations of letters lost in lines 4 and 5 are rough estimates which assume that the cutter preserved symmetry and spaced the letters evenly, as he seems to have done in the parts preserved. Therefore, the restoration of the paymaster of the boule of 168/7, viz. [ ᾽Αρτέμ]ωνα [Πειραι]έα, though tempting, is probably not correct.

### Agora I 6367

This inscription, which honors Arrhidaios, general of Antiochos IV Epiphanes, alone among this cutter's decrees[2] has carefully incised guidelines, as though it were especially commissioned. Stamires in his *editio princeps* drew a parallel with *IG* II² 945, an inscription which honors a certain Diodoros, a friend of King Eumenes. Although I cannot accept Stamires' prosopographical conclusions, II² 945 does have pronounced guidelines and was inscribed in very distinctive writing, otherwise unknown in Attica. It does in fact appear that, at least on some occasions, inscriptions honoring important foreigners were given special treatment.

---

[2] *IG* II² 3874, the base from Eleusis with its large letters (0.022 m.), also has guidelines.

Stamires pointed out (p. 49) and is followed in this by Henry (*Prescripts* 83–84) that the name of the secretary is absent in the four known prescripts of Alexis' archonship (173/2) just as it is in this decree and that Alexis suits the space. Robert, who calculates less space for the archon's name, thinks (p. 93 n. 5) that the chronological limits are wider than Stamires' 173/2 to 168/7.

✻

Like his contemporary, the I 247 Cutter, this workman inscribed quite a large number of prytany inscriptions. More than a third of his extant inscriptions, eight of twenty-three, are decrees honoring councillors.

# The Cutter of *IG* II² 3479

Dates: 175/4–ca. 135

*Caution:* The inscription chosen as the standard has ninety-two letters, barely enough to permit study. This Cutter's phi is, however, quite idiosyncratic. This is the only large hand that I feel I have had any success in isolating.

## General characteristics of the lettering (fig. 20)

This lettering is large and carefully made. The strokes are relatively thin with small serifs. The serifs occur quite regularly, but not invariably.

## Peculiarities of individual letters

| | |
|---|---|
| *Alpha* | This letter is relatively thin with a curved crossbar which occurs at the mid-point of the letter. |
| *Iota* | This letter very often has a serif at the top; sometimes it is distinctly larger than the one at the bottom. |
| *Kappa* | The slanting strokes are quite short and extend neither to the top nor bottom of the letter-space. The serif at the top is often a straight line which is quite long. |
| *Nu* | The second vertical tends not to extend down as far as the first. |
| *Omikron* | This letter is quite round and nearly as tall as the surrounding letters. |
| *Rho* | The loop comes down about one-third of the height of the letter; it curves in quite idiosyncratically as it meets the vertical, namely in such a way that the loop seems to sag. |
| *Sigma* | The top and bottom strokes slant; the diagonals which form the central part are the same length as the other two strokes. |

*Figure 20. IG II² 3479.*

| | |
|---|---|
| *Upsilon* | This letter is composed of three strokes; the vertical is half the height of the letter or a bit more. |
| *Phi* | The central part of this letter is made with two rather flattened ovals; the shape is very idiosyncratic. |
| *Omega* | This letter is quite large and round, open at the bottom, with short finials adorned with serifs. |

## List of Inscriptions

| | |
|---|---|
| *IG* II² 3469 | This text dates to soon after 150 B.C. Clinton, *Sacred Officials* 27, provides an improved text. For this man's brother and immediate predecessor as hierophant, see the discussion of II² 1934. |
| *IG* II² 3479 | Archon Pleistainos (?)—see below for a discussion of his date. |
| *IG* II² 3482 | |
| ⁺*IG* II² 3781 | This inscription was rediscovered during the course |

|   |   |
|---|---|
|   | of the American excavations in the Athenian Agora. It is presently on exhibit outside the museum in the lower colonnade of the Stoa of Attalos and sits at the base of the nineteenth (from the south) interior column. For a good photograph, see *Agora* XIV pl. 55c. |
| ⁺*IG* II² 3867 | |
| ⁺*IG* II² 3871 | |
| ⁺*IG* II² 4298 | |
| Agora I 388 + 719 | D. W. Bradeen, *The Athenian Agora XVII Inscriptions, the Funerary Monuments* (Princeton 1974) no. 207. The date *saec*. IV *a*. is much too early. |
| ⁺Agora I 3527 + 3601 | *Hesperia* 23 (1954) 252–53. |
| Agora I 4246 | *Hesperia* 15 (1946) 215–17. The date should be lowered from *ca*. 180 to *ca*. 155. |
| ⁺Agora I 6200 | *Hesperia* 30 (1961) 269. |
| Agora I 7186 | *Hesperia* 40 (1971) 257–58. |

## *Inscriptions in the style of*

|   |   |
|---|---|
| ⁺*IG* II² 3058 | *ABSA* 50 (1955) 24. |
| ⁺*IG* II² 3088 | Archon Sonikos (175/4). |
| ⁺*IG* II² 6398 | |
| ⁺Agora I 6135 | *Hesperia* 26 (1957) 83–88, 104–5. |

## *Adnotatiunculae*

### *IG* II² 3781

Kirchner's intuition (*IG ad loc.*) that the two dedicants of this statue honoring Karneades, Attalos and Ariarathes of Sypalettos, were respectively the future kings, though attractive, is impossible. Mattingly (*Historia* 20 [1971] 28–32) had correctly pointed out that Attalos surely must have belonged to the tribe Attalis—Sypalettos belongs to Kekropis. This is now borne out by an as yet unpublished inscription from Athens which lists Attalos' tribe as Attalis.[1]

---

[1] For more on this point, see now page 16 of Ch. Habicht's 1988 David Magie Lecture, "Hellenistic Athens and Her Philosophers," published by Princeton University, Program in History, Archaeology, and Religions of the Ancient World.

The Ariarathes of this text is probably identical with Ariarathes son of Polemaios of Sypalettos, the paymaster of Prytaneis in *ca.* 140.[2] Note also the Ariarathes son of King Ariobarzanes of Sypalettos who was an ephebe in the years after Sulla (*IG* II² 1039 *b'* + *c'* + *p* lines 3–5).

## *IG* II² 3867

This is a statue base for Miltiades son of Zoilos of Marathon. He is attested as *agonothetes* of the Theseia in Phaidrias' archonship (*IG* II² 958), as Archon Basileus (Agora I 7186), and was honored for his services to the city about 140 (*IG* II² 968).

This base was signed by Eucheir and Euboulides, a father and son team, who were working in Athens in the years 140 and after. Note in support of this date that three bases signed by them were inscribed by the Cutter of Agora I 286 (*q.v.*), whose dated work falls in the years 130–116, and one by the Cutter of *IG* II² 937, who dates *ca.* 135–123/2. Furthermore, Euboulides III's service as an *epimeletes* in Piraeus (*IG* II² 1939 line 64) is to be dated to *ca.* 140 or even a bit earlier and not to *ca.* 125.[3]

## *IG* II² 3871

This is a base for a statue of Apelles son of Pollis of Sounion set up by his sons Apelles and Pollis. The Apelles of Sounion known as a *hierope* about 150 (*IG* II² 1938 line 11) is probably, as Kirchner notes, identical with the man honored in this inscription.

## *IG* II² 4298

This base is signed by Euboulides alone and not with his father; it need not be much later, if at all, than II² 3867 which is signed by them both. This may well be the statue base to which Pausanias (1.2.5) refers. A. Stewart, *Attika: Studies in Athenian Sculpture of the Hellenistic Age* (London 1979) 52, discusses the remains of the sculpture group associated with this base.

## Agora I 3527 + 3601

This dedication by King Attalos and his queen in honor of the Athenian Theophilos, his *syntrophos*, must belong to the King's reign (158–138).

---

[2] Agora I 6053, line 46 (*Agora* XV no. 261). On the date, see the discussion of I 6053 under the Cutter of Agora I 6006.

[3] II² 1939 was inscribed by the Cutter of Agora I 6006, *q.v.*

## Agora I 6200

It appears certain that this fragmentary base, like the closely similar one at Eleusis which is also by this cutter (*IG* II² 3469), records a dedication by Amynomachos son of Eukles of Halai. He made the dedication in Eleusis and presumably also the matching one in Athens after he became hierophant.

## *IG* II² 3088

The lettering of this text reveals fewer serifs than normal and has alpha with a broken (as well as curved) crossbar. Otherwise, the shapes and mannerisms conform precisely to the lettering of this cutter. D. M. Lewis (*ABSA* 50 [1955] 24) rightly saw that *IG* II² 3058 was a companion piece to this inscription.

## *IG* II² 6398

This is the gravestone of Habryllis daughter of Mikion (IV) of Kephisia (*PA* 2, stemma under *PA* 5966). She served as priestess of Athena Polias sometime after 138/7 (*IG* II² 3477; see the discussion below under the Cutter of *IG* II² 937). Her grave monument, therefore, must be dated after 138/7.

## Agora I 6135

This is the dedicatory inscription on the epistyle of the Stoa of Attalos. It must date to the king's reign (158–138) and can hardly be earlier than 150. The letters are *ca.* 0.14 m. or four times larger than the next largest letters by this cutter, 0.035 m. on *IG* II² 6398. Considering their great size, they are very lightly inscribed and are essentially this cutter's lettering writ large. The characteristic shapes of alpha, kappa, nu, and rho all but guarantee the attribution. Rho appears on plate 20 no. 31 fragment 3 of *Hesperia* 26 (1957); for a loop of rho similar, if not quite as awkwardly executed, see line 3 of II² 3479. The very large omega has finials which are elaborated; but these can already be seen in nascent form in the omega of line 5 of Agora I 3527 + 3601 and in developed form on *IG* II² 6398.

The great majority of this man's work, *viz. IG* II² 3469, 3781, 3867, 3871, 6398, Agora I 3527 + 3601, I 6200, I 6135, and I 7186 all strongly pull towards 150 B.C. and well after, thus raising serious doubt about the date of Pleistainos in 184/3. In fact, the gravestone for Habryllis (*IG* II² 6398)

brings the lower date for this cutter to about 135. Upon examination, the date of Pleistainos rests on a questionable reading of the secretary's demotic in Agora I 4462 (*Agora* XV no. 181 line 26) as PA. Pritchett in his *editio princeps* (*Hesperia* 10 [1941] 277–79) read only dotted rho. On two separate and good squeezes, I can see no trace of alpha—the photograph and squeezes in fact suggest that the inscribed surface is gone at this point—and only a possible vertical at the edge of the worn area. I say possible because, though the surface seems to be preserved, this "stroke" does not extend up much beyond the middle of the letter-space. Rho should, at the least, be dotted. I think, in fact, that we have almost no real evidence for the demotic of this secretary.[4] In consequence, Pleistainos is by no means fixed to 184/3 but must be considered a "floating" archon.[5] His date is very likely, the evidence of this hand suggests, to be rather nearer to 150 than has previously been thought. Two of the four inscriptions other than II² 3479 which name him, *viz.* Agora I 4462 and 7188, were inscribed by the Cutter of Agora I 247 who dates 194/3 to *ca.* 150. A date of 150 or thereabouts would appear, then, to be the lower limit for Pleistainos.[6]

---

[4] The name of the secretary, Philoxenides, is attested not only in Rhamnous (II² 1939 line 56), but in Hagnous (see the stemma under II² 3510), Aigilia (II² 5380), Aixone (*AthMitt* 66 [1941] 218), Apollonieus (II² 1008 line 107 IV), and Semachidai (*Stud. D. Robinson* II [1953] 351 no. 9 = *SEG* 13 [1956] no. 130).

[5] In Autumn of 1988 I learned *per litteras* both from D. M. Lewis and Ch. Habicht that a soon to be published fragment of *IG* II² 2323 would reveal that the archon of 184/3 was [Charik]les. See now A.P. Matthaiou, *Horos* 6 (1988) 13–18.

[6] The two others are a horos near Brauron (*Deltion* 17A [1961/62] 215–16) and *IG* II² 1019. The horos fits comfortably around 150. The woman named on it is not attested elsewhere. II² 1019 offers no obstacle to this, though I do not think its date can be fixed with certainty. Dinsmoor (*The Athenian Archon List in the Light of Recent Discoveries* [New York 1939] 194–95) identified the priest mentioned in lines 13 and 42, Leonides of Phlya, with the priest of 138/7 from Phlya honored by *IG* II² 974. This identification is possible but far from assured. Whatever the case, the mention of Ple[istainos] in line 44 comes in a context of repairing offerings made some years earlier by the ephebes of Pleistainos' year. In an article forthcoming in *Horos* 7 (1989), I attempt to delimit more precisely the year of Pleistainos.

# The Cutter of *IG* II² 783

## Dates: 173/2–161/0

### General characteristics of the lettering (fig. 21)

This cutter inscribed plain rather ordinary letters. He places them close together but does not crowd them, i.e. each letter has its own space. His round letters tend to be round. His lettering is quite similar to that of the Cutter of *IG* II² 903 (below, p. 232).

### Peculiarities of individual letters

*Alpha*  This letter is quite wide and usually open at the top just a little. The crossbar is straight and normally comes at the mid-point of the letter or a little below.

*Epsilon*  The central horizontal usually thickens at the end. Sometimes it is quite short and sometimes it is almost as long as the others.

*Kappa*  The diagonals are short and incline sharply, making this a relatively thin letter.

*Rho*  The loop is large and some part of it, if not the whole, curves nicely.

*Sigma*  This letter tends to be taller than the others.

*Upsilon*  This letter is made with three strokes; it tends to be slightly taller than the other letters. The vertical is normally no more than half the height of the letter.

*Phi*  The central oval is neat and nicely rounded; the letter itself tends to be the same height as the others.

*Omega*  Small inverted-v serifs are placed at the bottom so that the letter seems almost to tiptoe on them.

### List of Inscriptions

*IG* II² 783  Archon [Erastos] (163/2). For the secretary's name, see *Hesperia* 3 (1934) 29–30. Photograph, *ibid.*

*Figure 21. IG II² 783.*

IG II² 952 — Archon [Aristo]las (161/0). *Agora* XV no. 222.
IG II² 996 — Archon [Alexis] (173/2).[1] *Hesperia* 28 (1959) 181–84 and plate 37.
Agora I 838 — *Agora* XV no. 209.

## Inscriptions in the style of

Agora I 1938, 1939, 1943, and 1948 — Archon [Sosigenes] (172/1). *Agora* XV no. 208.

---

[1] This decree, the name of the chairman reveals, was passed on the same day as Agora I 5761 (so Meritt in *Hesperia* 26 [1957] 39).

| | |
|---|---|
| Agora I 3755 | *Hesperia* 54 (1985) 324–25. |
| Agora I 3941, lines 3–6 | *Agora* XV no. 218. The first two lines of this text are in different and unfamiliar lettering. The first line, not to mention what appear to be abortive letters above it (see pl. 11 no. 19 in *Hesperia* 26 [1957]), is very crudely inscribed as though an inexperienced cutter began this text. |
| Agora I 5032 | Archon [Eu]ergetes (164/3). *Hesperia* 28 (1959) 273. |

# The Cutter of Agora I 6006

## Dates: 169/8–135/4

### General characteristics of the lettering (fig. 22)

This cutter[1] inscribed a neat, plain alphabet. The letter-strokes are usually quite thick and the letters are evenly spaced. A thickening or point at the ends of strokes suggestive of serifs appears frequently. See, for example, the lowest diagonal of sigma and kappa, the right vertical of pi, and the horizontals of epsilon. The end result is lettering which makes a strong, solid impression. This cutter also tends to leave the apex of alpha and lambda, and delta less frequently, slightly open; thus his lettering is often assigned to the so-called "disjointed style," i.e., to a period around 200 B.C. or earlier.

### Peculiarities of individual letters

*Alpha* — This is a relatively thin letter. There is normally a slight gap at the apex. The crossbar occurs at about the mid-point of the letter and varies, with about an even frequency, between a straight, horizontal bar and a curving stroke.

*Epsilon* — The three horizontal strokes are frequently the same size. About half of the time, the central stroke is somewhat shorter than the other two. In addition, this stroke is sometimes placed noticeably nearer one of the others. Occasionally all three strokes intersect the vertical giving the letter the appearance of a xi with a central vertical (note that this cutter normally makes xi *without* a central vertical).

*Omikron* — This letter is round and large.

---

[1] First published in *Hesperia* 47 (1978) 261–66. Inscriptions added to the list there published are asterisked.

*Figure 22.* Agora I 6006 lines 36–43.

| | |
|---|---|
| *Pi* | The initial vertical tends to extend up beyond the horizontal. |
| *Sigma* | This letter tends to be taller than the other letters. The upper and lower strokes always slant. The letter appears to be leaning backwards because the central and bottom strokes extend slightly further to the right than the upper stroke. In addition, there is a tendency for the angle of the gap to be wider in the lower half of the letter than in the upper. |
| *Tau* | The crossbar is very often markedly off-center to the left and slanting. |
| *Phi* | This letter is usually the same height as the other letters. The central part makes a rather awkward impression; it normally consists of a lower straight stroke (slanting upwards somewhat from left to right) surmounted by a curving stroke. This whole complex is more or less centered over the vertical. The total effect is awkward, striking, and exceedingly idiosyncratic. |

*Omega*       This letter is most often rendered by a rounded horseshoe shape. The right side very often extends somewhat lower than the left. Occasionally horizontal strokes are placed at the bottom on one or both sides.

## List of Inscriptions

*IG* II² 736
*IG* II² 853  Osborne, *Naturalization* no. D107.
*IG* II² 868
\**IG* II² 895  Part of Kerameikos I 1, *q.v.*
*IG* II² 907  Peçirka, *Enktesis* 118–20.
\**IG* II² 924  Osborne, *Naturalization* no. D118.
\**IG* II² 926
\**IG* II² 930
\**IG* II² 941
  = *IG* XII.v
  no. 596B, *q.v.*
\**IG* II² 953  Archon Tychandros (160/59). Kirchner-Klaffenbach, *Imagines* no. 103. For a new text and discussion, see R. E. Allen, *The Attalid Kingdom* (Oxford 1983) 117–18 and 223 no. 18.
\**IG* II² 955
*IG* II² 960
*IG* II² 961
*IG* II² 962
*IG* II² 966  *Hesperia* 47 (1978) 265.
*IG* II² 967  Archon Metrophanes (145/4). *Agora* XV no. 238.
*IG* II² 968  Archon Theaitetos (143/2 or 144/3).[2] Kirchner-Klaffenbach, *Imagines* no. 105. *Hesperia* 47 (1978) 265–66. D. Peppa-Delmouzou has joined EM 5182 (*Deltion* 1973–74 [1979] B 17 = *SEG* 29 [1979] no. 119) allowing us to read more letters in the crown.
*IG* II² 970  Archon [Hagnotheos] (140/39).
\**IG* II² 974  Archon Herakleitos (137/6). *Hesperia* 28 (1959) 188–94.

---

[2]This and all alternate dates offered in this list are those presented by Ch. Habicht in *Hesperia* 57 (1988) 237–47.

| | |
|---|---|
| *IG* II² 981 | Osborne, *Naturalization* no. D108; *Hesperia* 47 (1978) 266. |
| *IG* II² 983 | |
| *\*IG* II² 987 | Osborne, *Naturalization* no. D116. |
| *\*IG* II² 988*a* | *Ibid.* no. D114. |
| ⁺*\*IG* II² 988*b* | *Ibid.* no. D115. |
| *\*IG* II² 1027 | Archon [Aristaichmos] (159/8). On the date see Meritt, *Historia* 26 (1977) 183 and Pelekidis, *BCH* 81 (1957) 478–82. Concerning the crown, see above under the Cutter of Agora I 6512. |
| *\*IG* II² 1045 | Clinton, *Sacred Officials* 119–21. |
| ⁺*IG* II² 1224 | *Hesperia* 47 (1978) 266. |
| ⁺*\*IG* II² 1934 | Agora I 5708 belongs; see *Hesperia* 15 (1946) 158. |
| *\*IG* II² 1937 | Archon Kall[istra]tos (156/5). |
| *IG* II² 1939 | |
| *IG* II² 1940 | |
| *IG* II² 2323, lines 205–52 | Archon [Theaitetos] (143/2 or 144/3). Ruck, *Victors* 15–17, lines 386–576. |
| *IG* II² 2330 | |
| ⁺*IG* II² 2334 | |
| ⁺*IG* II² 2435 | |
| ⁺*\*IG* II² 2436 | The date given in *IG* II² should be moved down a century. |
| *\*IG* II² 2864a | Archon Poseidonios (162/1). Dow, *Prytaneis* 198–202. |
| ⁺*\*IG* II² 2944 | The archon Eunik[os] (169/8) is mentioned in one of the crowns. Clinton informs me that this inscription dates *ca.* 140. |
| *IG* II² 3215 = Agora I 453 | *Hesperia* 47 (1978) 262. |
| ⁺*\*IG* II² 3463 | Note that the date in the *Corpus* is too early. |
| *\*IG* II² 8494 | The date in *IG* is more than a century too early. |
| *\*IG* II² 13121 | *IG* II² 2314 lines 98–103 and *Hesperia* Suppl. 7 p. 6 no. 8 are part of this grave epigram; see *Klio* 52 (1970) 379–81; new edition by Peek, *Attische Versinschriften* (Berlin 1980) 60 no. 74. |
| ⁺*\*IG* XII.v 596B = *IG* II² 941 | |

| | |
|---|---|
| *IG XII.v 600 | |
| +*Agora I 884 lines 8, 11, 13, 15, 18, 23, 26–28 | Hesperia 36 (1967) 86–89. |
| *Agora I 907 | Agora XV no. 164. |
| *Agora I 984 + 7492 | Archon Aristolas (161/0). Hesperia 53 (1984) 374–77, 16 (1947) 164–68. Agora I 6700 also belongs; see Hesperia 32 (1963) 33–36. |
| +*Agora I 1005 + 1007 | Agora fragments I 2309 and 5916 also belong; see Hesperia 46 (1977) 259–67. |
| *Agora I 1659 | Hesperia 6 (1937) 457–58. |
| Agora I 1680 | Agora XV no. 161. |
| Agora I 1720 | Hesperia 47 (1978) 263. |
| Agora I 2010 | Agora XV no. 198. |
| *Agora I 2016 | Published below. |
| Agora I 2145 + 6295 | Archon Dionysios after Timarchides (135/4). Agora XV no. 243. |
| *Agora I 3054 | Archon Nikosthenes (167/6). Agora XV no. 215. |
| Agora I 3791 | Hesperia 47 (1978) 264. |
| Agora I 4234 | Ibid. 264–65. |
| Agora I 4389 + 5556 | Archon Lysiades (148/7 or 149/8). Clinton, Sacred Officials 24–27. |
| *Agora I 5427 | Agora XV no. 156. The date must be adjusted somewhat. |
| Agora I 6003 | Archon [Diony]sios [after Timarchides] (135/4). Hesperia 17 (1948) 22–23. |
| Agora I 6004 | Agora XV no. 143. |
| +*Agora I 6005 | |
| Agora I 6006 | Archon Hagnotheos (140/39). Agora XV no. 240. |
| +Agora I 6053 | Agora XV no. 261. On the date, see Hesperia 47 (1978) 263. |
| *Agora I 6140 | Archon Eunikos (169/8). Hesperia 26 (1957) 82–83. |
| *Agora I 6333, lines 1–3 | Archon Andreas (144/3 or ca. 150). Hesperia 30 (1961) 252. See the discussion of this text below under the Cutter of FD III 2 no. 5. |
| *Agora I 6977 | Archon Lysiades (148/7 or 149/8). Meritt published |

| | |
|---|---|
| + 6980 + 6978 | Agora I 6977 in *Hesperia* 34 (1965) 89–90; the other fragments are published below. |
| *Agora I 7421 | Osborne, *Naturalization* no. D109. |
| *Agora I 7510 | Unpublished. |
| *AthMitt 62 (1937) 3–5 | |
| *AthMitt 62 (1937) 5–6 | |
| AthMitt 66 (1941) 228 | Archon Timarchos (138/7). |
| *EM 4699 | Unpublished. |
| Hesperia 28 (1959) 186 | |
| +*Kerameikos I 1 | Archon Theoxenos (187/6). *AthMitt* 76 (1961) 127–41. |
| *Kerameikos I 10, lines 1–18 | Archon Andreas (144/3 or *ca.* 150). *AthMitt* 97 (1982) 171–84. |

## Inscriptions in the style of

| | |
|---|---|
| Agora I 1057 | Archon Speusi[ppos] (153/2 or 150/49). *Agora* XV no. 228. |
| Agora I 1312 | *Agora* XV no. 235. |
| Agora I 2264 | *Agora* XV no. 90. The date must be lowered about 100 years. |
| Agora I 2943 | *Agora* XV no. 195. |
| Agora I 5414 | *Agora* XV no. 123. The date needs to be lowered about 75 years. |
| +Agora I 5988 | *Hesperia* 17 (1948) 40 and 26 (1957) 62. |
| +Kerameikos I 10 lines 19–21 | *AthMitt* 97 (1982) 171–84. |

## Preliminary publication of fragments from the Athenian Agora

**1** (pl. 22). Fragment of white marble, inscribed face alone preserved, retrieved from a marble dump in the northwest corner of the Agora (E–H 10–12) in November 1934.

H. 0.08 m.; W. 0.034 m.; Th. 0.023 m.; LH. 0.006 m.
Inv. No. I 2016

  *ca. a.* 150 *a.*   NON-STOICH.

     ΙΚ
     ΑΙṬ
  3 ΤΗΣẸ
     ΕΚΑ
     ΤΟΔ
  6 ΑΝΕ
     ΕΙ

Line 2. Dotted tau could also be zeta; the letter is broken at the bottom.

Line 3. A worn vertical stroke at the break is the basis for reading epsilon.

This piece could be restored in a number of ways; one might restore lines 4–7 as follows for example.

  [καὶ στεφανῶσαι] ἕκα[στον αὐτῶν θαλλοῦ στεφάνωι·]
  [ἀναγράψαι δὲ] τόδ[ε τὸ ψήφισμα τὸν γραμματέα]
 6 [τὸν κατὰ πρυτ]ανε[ίαν εἰς στήλην λιθίνην καὶ στῆ]-
  [σαι ἐν ἀκροπόλ]ει· [τὸ δὲ γενόμενον etc. ___ ]

The fragment does not obviously belong with any of the other pieces by this cutter.

**2** (pl. 23). An Athenian Decree Concerning Allotment

This partially preserved stele is composed of three joining fragments of gray marble.[3] The top is flat and dressed to a pebbly smoothness; the left side is preserved (claw-chiselled). The original thickness is preserved only by the top fragment. The combined dimensions are:

H. 0.486 m.; W. (face) 0.135 m., (with molding) 0.16 m; Th. 0.145 m., (with molding) 0.17 m.; LH. 0.007 m.

The inventory numbers, find spots, and dates of discovery of the three fragments from top to bottom are:

Agora I 6977. Found in a late Roman wall over the southeast corner of the Middle Stoa (O 13) on January 28, 1964.

---

[3] I am indebted to Homer Thompson and B. D. Meritt for the opportunity to study and publish the joining fragments. S. Dow and A. L. Boegehold offered helpful suggestions.

Agora I 6980. Same find spot, May 12, 1964.

Agora I 6978. Same find spot, January 28, 1964.

B. D. Meritt published Agora I 6977 the year after it was found (*Hesperia* 34 [1965] 89-90) and before it had been joined to the other fragments.

a. 148/7 a.  NON-STOICH. ca. 49

1 ἐπὶ Λυσιά[δου ἄρχοντος ἐπὶ τῆς ___ca. 16___ πρυτανείας]
 ἧι Διόδω[ρος __ca. 23__ ἐγραμμάτευεν __ca. 5__]-
3 ὧνος ὀγ[δόει _____]
 ἐνάτ[ει _____ca. 26_____ τῆς πρυτανείας· ἐκκλη]-
 σία [_____ τῶν προέδρων ἐπεψήφιζεν _____]-
6 [1-2 ο]ν Ο[___ καὶ συμπρόεδροι·                    vacat ]
   vac. [vac. ἔδοξεν τῆι βουλεῖ καὶ τῶι δήμωι vac. ]
  [ Ἀφθ]όνητο[ς _____ εἶπεν· ἐπειδὴ _____]
9 [ . . . . ]ιας το[_____]
  [ . . . ]κληρω[_____]
  [3-4] ὑπαρχ[_____]
12 [τῶ]ν ἀναγε[γραμμένων _____]
 ὁλοσχερῶ[ς _____ τὰς γε]-
 γονείας ἀρχ[ὰς _____]
15 ὑπαρχοῦσα [_____]
 πολλοὺς το[ὺς _____]
 διὰ τὸ μετὰ [_____]
18 ἑτέρας καὶ [_____]
 κληρώσεω[ς _____]
 [.]εν τοιουτ[_____]
21 [.]η καὶ ἡ κλήρω[σις _____ τοὺς]
 λαχόντας π[ροέδρους εἰς τὴν ἐπιοῦσαν ἐκκλησίαν χρηματίσαι πε]-
 ρὶ τούτων, γνώ[μην δὲ ξυμβάλλεσθαι τῆς βουλῆς εἰς τὸν δῆμον ὅτι]
24 δοκεῖ τῆι βου[λεῖ _____]
 τόδε τὸ ψήφισ[μα _____]
 [.]Δ[.]Γ[ . . . ]Π[_____]
27 [___]Ο[_____]
 σονται τὴν ἀν[αγραφὴν _____]
 στήλας λιθίν[ας _____]

30 γεγραμμένα [_____]
   [.]υλει τὰς ἐπὶ [_____]
   Φίλωταν Θριάσ[ιον _____]
33 στήλας ΔΟΛ[_____]
   τῆς στοᾶς τῆ[ς _____]
   ται τὴν ἀναγρ[αφὴν _____ τῶν ἐν]-
   νε᾽ ἀρχόντων π[_____]
37 ἐξετάζειν· ᵛ τόδ[ε τὸ _____]
   τῶν στηλῶ[ν] Λ[_____]

*uncertain number of lines lost*

Line 3. Only the upper third of dotted gamma is discernible.

Line 26. There are the remains of three letters in this line. A single apex occurs directly under the initial omikron of line 25. Parts of two horizontal strokes appear, each in the top of the letter-space; one is under epsilon and the other under the eta of line 25.

Line 27. The lower half of a round letter under the psi in line 25 is the only legible trace in this line.

Line 33. A triangular shape, a round shape, and a triangular shape provide the basis for the dotted letters.

Line 36. The verticals of dotted pi alone are clearly legible.

This decree provides tantalizing evidence of actions pertaining to sortition about 150 B.C. Restoration does not seem possible. The practice of allotting offices, described by Aristotle (*Ath.Pol.* 55), was central to the Athenian political system and continued apparently almost to the time of Sulla with little change.[4] This text does not seem to relate to allotting the law courts, for it makes no mention of dikastai or dikasteria; nor is it apparently similar to the two tribal decrees, Agora I 3625 = *Hesperia* 7 (1938) 95 and *IG* II² 1163, which praise individuals for, among other things, allotting the law courts. The present decree is more elaborate than these tribal decrees and probably refers to the allotment of the board of archons (line 36). Dow in his discussion of allotment machines noted considerable activity in the mid-second century.[5] Perhaps this decree is connected in some way.

Line 8. The only attested Attic *nomen* is Aphthonetos; see *PA* 2771–74 and *sub nomine* in the index of *Agora* XV.

Line 32. A Philotas Thriasios (*PA* 14933) is attested on a gravestone of the third century B.C. (*IG* II² 6268).

---

[4] S.V. Tracy, "Athens in 100 B.C.," *HSCP* 83 (1979) 220–21.

[5] *Prytaneis* 209–10 and note 2.

## Adnotatiunculae

### IG II² 988b

The first five letters of the patronymic, editors have failed to note, are reoriented to the left a half letter-space and are inscribed over ΑΧΜΩ. Iota was initially omitted.

### IG II² 1224

Line 10 of fragments *a b c* begins [ . . . . . .]ς. A slanting stroke which can only be sigma occurs at the bottom of the letter-space before epsilon. Three demotics suit the space exactly, Ἀτηνεύς, Ἰκαριεύς and Πλωθεύς. Another eleven are either a half space too short or too long.

It is quite likely that this important man named Herakleitos son of Poseidippos, hoplite general for the second time, belongs to a well attested family from Ikarion. We may list Ἡράκλειτος Ποσειδίππου Ἰκαριεύς (IG II² 2445, line 4), a dedicant in about 140, Ἡράκλειτος Ἰκαριεύς, who contributed one hundred drachmas for the repair of the theater in Piraeus about mid-century (II² 2334, lines 6–9), Ἡράκλειτος Ἰκαρ[ιεύς], who was paymaster of the boule in 135/4 (*Agora* XV no. 243 line 53), Ἡράκλειτος Διονυσογένους Ἰκαριεύς, polemarch about 150 (*Hesperia* 35 [1966] 242–43), and Διονυσογένης Ἡρακλείτου Ἰκαριεύς, gymnasiarch on Delos in 115/4 (*ID* 2589 line 63).[6]

### IG II² 1934

This text has been wrongly dated to the fourth century B.C. The new date, now made possible, has some very happy consequences. Hieronymy, i.e. the replacement of the hierophant's name with Ἱεροφάντης, became regular practice by the late second century B.C. This text had been an anomaly by seeming to give evidence for it just once earlier, in the fourth century B.C.[7] Since this text is now seen to date between about 170 and 135, it provides evidence for the first hierophant to adopt hieronymy and, even more importantly, a fairly precise date for the introduction of the practice. The man named in it, [Ἱεροφάν]της Νουφράδου Περιθοίδης is identical with the hierophant Aristokles of Perithoidai who took office in 183/2 and served at least until the archonship of Lysiades in about 150 B.C. when he was honored by Agora I 4389 + 5556, a decree of the Eumolpidai.[8] His full name, Ἀριστοκλῆς Νουφράδου

---

[6] Ch. Habicht kindly drew my attention to these last three references.

[7] See Clinton, *Sacred Officials* 22.

[8] *Ibid.* 24–27 and the discussion there. I am greatly indebted to K. Clinton for his help on these matters.

Περιθοίδη[s], is attested by good fortune in an ephebic list from the year of Sostratos (210/9 or 209/8).[9] He was therefore born about 227 B.C., was about forty-four years old when he became hierophant, and nearly eighty years of age when he was honored by the Eumolpids. He apparently was very active and did much to restore the cult.[10] One of his innovations was to adopt the practice of hieronymy on at least some official occasions. *IG* II² 1934, then, will be dated sometime in the years 170–150 B.C. and constitutes our first evidence for hieronymy.

In addition to the prosopographical references cited *ad loc.* in *IG* II², one should note that Theoboulos son of Theophanes from Piraeus (line 11) is attested as general ἐπὶ τὴν παρασκευήν in the archonship of Dionysios around 200 B.C. (*IG* II² 2798). He also probably served as councillor in 178/7 (*Agora* XV no. 194 line 73).

Line 12. A relative, his grandfather or great uncle, was secretary in 267/6 (*IG* II² 661 lines 2–3).

Line 15. *PA* 175 is doubtless an ancestor.

## *IG* II² 2334

Line 68 reads Σωσικρατε[ίας].

## *IG* II² 2435

J. S. Traill republished II² 2435 in *Hesperia* 51 (1982) 204–206 and, by an oversight, entitled it "Prytaneis of Leontis"; it is a list of Akamantis. D. M. Lewis (*per litteras*) has suggested that this piece and Agora I 2010 (*Agora* XV no. 198) join. Though the suggestion is attractive, I do not think it possible because of the reported difference in the marble and the fact that the demotics are indented 2½ letter-spaces on I 2010 and only 1 to 1½ on II² 2435.

## *IG* II² 2436

The spacing reveals that the first three lines are not part of a list of names as Kirchner's text implies. The letters in these lines appear above the demotics, i.e. out of line with the list which follows. They are almost certainly the last three lines of the text which preceded the list of names and record a sacrifice to Apollo.

---

[9] *Hesperia* 34 (1965) 90–91, line 25.
[10] He is also honored in *IG* II² 1045 (Clinton, *Sacred Officials* 119–21). Two inscriptions honoring *epimeletai* of the Mysteries, also by this cutter, *IG* II² 3463 and Agora I 6140, belong to his time as Hierophant. *IG* II² 736 also may reflect his activity, for it seems to refer to repair of sacred buildings and makes mention of a hierophant.

IKA

[ --- τάς τ]ε θυσί[ας ____]
[____ τῶι] Ἀπόλλω[νι ___]

Line 15. Read ΑΙΟ. Dotted omikron is broken at the bottom and could also be omega. The first letter falls under the space between pi and epsilon in the line above. These letters, therefore, are part of the demotic; five letters at most can have followed (based on the longest demotics preserved in this list). The possible demes are: Ἀφιδναῖος (V), Εἰτεαῖος (VI or XI), Ἐλαιούσιος (IX), Ἑστιαιόθεν (II), Ξυπεταιών (VIII), Οἰναῖος (V or XII), and Παιονίδης (IV). The list is not arranged in tribal order and there seems no way to choose.

## *IG* II² 2944

More can be read in the lower wreath on the front as follows:

*in corona aurea*

17a [ _____ ]
17b [ _____ ]
17c μυστ[ηρίων]
18 [ἐ]πιμελ[ητὴν]
18a [γενόμενον ἐπὶ]
18b Εὐνίκ[ου ἄρχον]-
18c [τος]

Line 17c. Just the lower part of the right slanting hasta of dotted mu survives.

Line 18. The left slanting stroke of dotted lambda appears at the break.

## *IG* II² 3463

Line 7 is inscribed *in rasura*. Of the erased letters eta is visible between epsilon and lambda. The cutter at first apparently tried to squeeze the entire word ἐπιμελητήν into this line and then respaced when it became clear that the space would not allow it.

## *IG* XII.v 596B

Wilhelm (*SAWW* 224 [1947] 14) first recognized that *IG* II² 941 was identical with this text. It must be dissociated from 596A, which is inscribed by a very different hand: the lettering has serifs and differs in every way from that of the I 6006 Cutter.

Kirchner read the initial line as ΑΛΚΟΥ; Hiller von Gaertringen as ΛΕΙΕΥ. The last letter is upsilon and the third letter from the end is kappa. Alpha or lambda—the slanting strokes are clear—may safely be read as the fifth letter from the end. The next to last letter seems to be round. I can make out no certain traces of strokes in the fourth letter-space from the end. Read Λ[.]ΚΟΥ.

Line 7. The tau is not at all certain. Kirchner's iota may be correct; the top of the letter is damaged. The square brackets around alpha in this line and line 9 are unnecessary.

This text and no. 600, also by this cutter, were both found on Kea and later transported to the Epigraphical Museum in Athens. There can be no question that they are local texts as opposed to, let us say, Athenian copies set up in Athens. It seems inescapable that this very prolific Athenian artisan was hired to do some work on Kea. The trip is, and was, not a difficult one and the island not unpleasant. It may have been an attractive assignment. It is also not unlikely that artisans capable of inscribing long decrees in an efficient manner were not plentiful in local communities. Athens would have been the nearest place to find such craftsmen. Furthermore, this man is not the only Athenian cutter whose handiwork is known on Kea—the Agora I 7181 Cutter (*q.v.*) of the late third century also did some work on the island.

The hand provides us for the first time with a reasonably precise date for these inscriptions from Kea, i.e. *ca.* 150 B.C.

**Agora I 884**

This is a type of inscription which begins to occur not infrequently about 150, i.e. a list of names inscribed by a number of different hands. This appears to be one of the early examples. Why the phenomenon occurs we can only speculate. Perhaps, for example, each individual had to pay to have his name inscribed. Whatever the case, space has been left in this text for expected entries. Guidelines appear at intervals, as though to mark off sections. Perhaps these names were to be arranged by tribe. The I 6006 Cutter made several entries probably at several different times. There seems no way to be sure. His entry in line 11 is probably a late one, for he made larger letters here than his norm on this text; he was probably influenced to do it by predrawn guidelines.

Of the nineteen lines of text—the other lines are blank—he inscribed nine. There are six other hands: (1) lines 1–4, (2) lines 5–6, (3) line 7, (4) line 12, (5) line 24, (6) line 25. None of these is identical, so far as I can determine from the scant evidence, with any of the cutters of this study.

## Agora I 1005 + 1007

Line 60 should read ὑμητ[τία].

## Agora I 6005

This small fragment, recognized by the hand, joins Agora I 6006 of 140/39[11] (pl. 24) and gives the ends of lines 33-35 as follows:

γραμματέ[α]
Εὐκτίμενον
Εἰτεαῖον

Published by M. B. Walbank (*Hesperia* 54 [1985] 323-24) as the end of a decree and dated to *ante med. s.* III *a.*, this fragment illustrates the difficulties which these tiny edge breaks can offer. Walbank's reading, however, of omega (dotted)[12] in line 2 for a clear omikron is indefensible. Despite his claim *ad loc.*—"the feet of the omega have been omitted (or, rather, drawn in to form its base), as often occurs in documents of this date"—I know of no omega of this shape. Misshapen omikrons, however, are commonplace.

## Agora I 6053

The secretary's name in this text is partially preserved; it is [ _ _ ]ου Παιανιεύς (III). The places in the archon list for secretaries from tribe III during the span of this man's working career are known and, with the exception of one year in the 140s (probably 143/2), will not accommodate the secretary of this text:

179/8 Ἀγγ[ελῆθεν]
167/6 Μ[υ]ρ[ριν]ο[ύσι]ος
155/4 Φιλίσκος Κράτητος Παιανιεύς
143/2(?) open
131/0 Ἀ[γγελῆθεν]

It would appear that this text and whatever archon we assign to 143/2 go together. It must, however, be acknowledged that the name of the herald of the council and people listed in this text, Kleon of Kikynna (line 55), does not support this date. Eukles of Trinemeia held this office it seems until at least 140/39 (*Agora* XV no. 240 line 49). I note this conflict-

---

[11] I am indebted to K. Clinton for corroborating the join in Athens.
[12] But in his commentary he writes: "The third preserved letter is definitely an omega."

ing evidence, but can offer no happy solution. It is probable that the eventual explanation will involve a break in the secretary cycle and the adjustment of the dates of some archons.

**Kerameikos I 1**

The date of this text is troublesome. The decree definitely belongs to the year of Theoxenos (187/6) and honors a hipparch for his service in the preceding year, the year of Symmachos. Seleukos IV, who succeeded to the throne in June or July 187, was already in power when Theoxenos served as archon.[13] Theoxenos seems quite firmly dated. The hand, on the other hand, is certain. This cutter's career cannot be pushed back eighteen years. I am forced to conclude that the present text was part of an elaborate monument honoring a distinguished man at the height of his career by inscribing copies of earlier documents passed in his honor. Unfortunately his name is not preserved on either part of this text. As hipparch he received signal honors, including a bronze statue. He may be conjectured to have been an ambitious man on the rise and with the resources to support his ambition. A hipparch will have gone on to serve as general.[14] *IG* II² 844 offers not an exact parallel but at least an example of a stele with several earlier decrees quoted verbatim. Thus, although not totally satisfactory, this explanation seems at least theoretically possible.

Is there a likely candidate and a likely occasion for the extraordinary honors here conjectured? I believe the answer is a qualified yes to both. I must caution, however, that what follows is the purest speculation. At the time when Athens recovered Lemnos, Delos, and other islands by action of the Romans in 167 B.C., Herakleitos son of Poseidippos probably from the deme Ikarion was hoplite general for the second time (*IG* II² 1224 *b* 9). Soon after this, the Theseia, a festival of a military character commemorating one of the heroic founders of Athens, was reestablished in a grand fashion. The cavalry of each tribe took prominent part and events in armor were featured (*IG* II² 956–64). It would be strange indeed if a two-time hoplite general were not involved in the reorganization of this festival. If he were the moving force, say the principal sponsor, that would provide the occasion we are looking for.

There are other possible candidates. Miltiades son of Zoilos of Marathon, for example, served as *agonothetes* of the Theseia in 153/2, Phai-

---

[13] See Habicht, *AthMitt* 76 (1961) 130 and n. 6.
[14] See for example the careers of two generals who commanded at Eleusis. One was hipparch, the other phylarch on the way to becoming general (*IG* II² 1285 and 1299 lines 51ff.).

drias' archonship (*IG* II² 958), and was honored about 140 for his signal services to the state (*IG* II² 968). He also served as archon basileus (Agora I 7186) and was honored with a statue, the work of Eucheir and Euboulides (*IG* II² 3867). And then there is Leon son of Kichesias of Aixone, discussed fully by Habicht (*Studien* 194–97). Kichesias in fact proposed Kerameikos I 1 (line 13).

**Agora I 5988**

B. D. Meritt has used this text in an attempt to establish the demotic of the secretary in Agora I 6100; see *Hesperia* 26 (1957) 62. The downdating of this text from about 200 to about 150 B.C. makes that argument, never very convincing, even more unconvincing.

**Kerameikos I 10**

Habicht in his *editio princeps* accepted my discussion of the hands. I now am of the opinion, based on further study, particularly of this cutter's larger letters (*ca.* 0.01 m.), that lines 19–21 are also his work. These lines, the blank space of 0.14 m. before and the larger letter size reveal, were inscribed (as Habicht also reasoned) at a time later than the first eighteen lines. How many years we cannot say, perhaps not many. I am obliged to make one correction. Line 22 is not by the same hand as lines 19–21 as I first thought. The omega with serifed finials in line 22 sets it apart as a separate hand. None of the four hands in lines 22–28 is familiar. The last three lines are by the I 286 Cutter (130/29–117/6) and suggest that lines 22–31 form a series of subsequent additions. Habicht's rich prosopographical discussion underlines this conclusion.

This cutter, one of the most active of his time, was almost certainly associated with the Agora I 656 + 3655 Cutter, probably as his apprentice. He may have started working in the shop as a young boy. Their inscribing careers overlap for five years, more than enough time for the strong influence over the letter-shapes to have occurred. The I 6006 Cutter inscribed a wide range of documents on both Hymettian and Pentelic marble with no clear preference. The percentage of work done on each is about 50/50. The variety in his work is notable. He seems not to have specialized but rather been willing to take on any type of text. He is, for example, one of only two cutters of long decrees known to me whose work includes grave monuments (*IG* II² 8494 and 13121).[15] The first of

---

[15] The other is the Cutter of *IG* II² 1706.

these was not his best effort, for he apparently omitted some verses. Was his copy defective or did he simply knock the monument out too quickly? In any case such a short text must have seemed like nothing to him. He also moved around a fair amount doing significant inscribing in Eleusis, Piraeus, and Kea. Except for the last, he is not so exceptional, for most major cutters do some work in Piraeus and Eleusis. He began his career as a cutter just a year or two before Athens recovered Delos and the other islands in 167. The period of his working life thus coincided with a significant shift of building and inscribing activity away from Athens to the flourishing international trading community on Delos. The number of Athenian inscriptions cut by him suggests that he concentrated his efforts in Athens primarily. As records on stone in Athens came to be inscribed less frequently in the years 150 and after, he and the other cutters of his time who remained in the city had to take on a variety of jobs to make a living.

# The Cutter of the Register of Agora I 247

*Date: 155/4*

## General characteristics of the lettering (figs. 23–24)

This man cut very plain, lightly incised letters. The individual letters are quite large and spaced apart. In all, though neat his letters have an insubstantial quality.

## Peculiarities of individual letters

*Epsilon* — The horizontals all tend to be about the same length; they are as long as the vertical, making this a wide letter.

*Pi* — A wide letter, the horizontal begins at the first vertical and sometimes extends markedly beyond the second. It tends to curve some.

*Rho* — The loop is oblong or square in shape and extends down a bit less than half the height of the letter.

*Sigma* — Taller than the other letters, the top and bottom strokes curve at times. The upper stroke is the longest and tends to flare up above the line of letters in a most idiosyncratic fashion.

*Upsilon* — This letter is composed of three strokes: the vertical extends up about half the height of the letter and usually more. The v at the top is shallow and unusually wide.

*Phi* — This letter is just slightly taller than the surrounding letters. The central element is created by two horseshoe-shaped strokes placed roughly opposite one another at the midpoint of the letter.

*Figure 23.* Agora I 247 lines 97–103.

*Figure 24.* Agora I 247 lines 116–121.

## List of Inscriptions

<sup>+</sup>*IG* II² 2440      *Agora* XV no. 136.
<sup>+</sup>Agora I 247,      Archon Mn[es]itheos (155/4). *Agora* XV no. 225.
  lines 66–122

## Inscription in the style of

*IG* II² 3462      Pouilloux, *Rhamnonte* 155. This text should be down-dated from *fin. s.* III *a.* to *ca. a.* 155 *a.*

## Adnotatiunculae

### *IG* II² 2440

Line 2. This cutter makes both a horseshoe-shaped omega and one with finials. The first preserved word, therefore, is τῶν not τόν; restore [____ τὸν ταμίαν] | τῶν [στρατιωτικῶν ____].

Line 10. The third omikron is preserved only at the top and should be dotted. Omega is also possible. Apollodo[tos] (Meritt/Traill) is thus far from a certain reading.

The date of this fragment must be adjusted downwards about two generations to *ca.* 155.

### Agora I 247

The list of names contains a surprising number of incorrect letters which are very hard to explain. The cutter appears to have been very careless. Perhaps the copy from which he worked was also a mess. In any case the following inscribing errors have gone unnoticed through three editions (by Meritt in *Hesperia* 3 [1934] 31–35, by Dow in *Prytaneis* [1937] 148–53, and by Meritt and Traill in *Agora* XV [1974] no. 225):

Line 67. Sigma is inscribed instead of xi. The initial alpha should be dotted, for just the tip of the right slanting stroke is visible at the break.

Line 72. Gamma appears for pi and beta for rho.

Line 73. Omega was inscribed and not lambda.

Line 74. Instead of the second omikron, iota was inscribed.

Line 76. Lambda appears instead of mu and omikron instead of omega. Τί<μ><ω>ν does appear to be the most probable interpretation of the remains. The area at the edge is worn; I am not at all certain of the tau.

Line 84. Beta was inscribed, not iota.

Line 85. Eta appears on the stone, not pi.

Line 87. Eta appears instead of kappa.
Line 104. Gamma was inscribed for rho.
Line 117. The first letter on the stone is chi, not alpha. The initial gamma appears to be inscribed over an epsilon.

I add the following comments on readings:
Line 91. The letter read as rho is, I think, an omikron. The stone is worn but I can see no trace of the vertical of the putative rho.
Line 106. I can find no trace of the initial letter. The next to the last letter is quite clearly a nu. Eta should be printed in pointed brackets. I do not think the name restored in this line has much chance of being correct.
Line 122. Read [Δ]ιονυ[σ]ο[__]. Only the tops of the dotted letters are preserved.

# The Cutter of Agora I 5469

## Date: 151/0[1]

## General characteristics of the lettering (fig. 25)

This cutter inscribes plain letters with rather thin strokes. He employs very small serifs intermittently. Every third or fourth letter may have one. The letters are not made with precision but vary quite a lot.

## Peculiarities of individual letters

| | |
|---|---|
| Alpha | This letter tends to be quite wide; the diagonals sometimes curve slightly and the crossbar is broken. |
| Epsilon | The top and bottom horizontals are longer than the vertical; the central one is shorter. All three taper to points. Occasionally a serif occurs on the top and/or bottom stroke. |
| Kappa | The slanting strokes are quite short and lightly inscribed. |
| Nu | The vertical strokes usually lean to the right just a bit. |
| Omikron | This letter tends to be quite large and somewhat misshapen. |
| Pi | The verticals are virtually the same length; the horizontal crossbar does not extend beyond the verticals. |
| Sigma | About half the time the top and bottom strokes slant slightly and about half the time they are parallel to one another. The upper part of the letter is sometimes larger. |

---

[1] This is the date proposed by Ch. Habicht in *ZPE* 20 (1976) 193–99, especially 196–98; the secretary cycle and prosopographical arguments constitute the evidence. I am bound to observe that alpha with a sharply broken crossbar and sigma with parallel top and bottom strokes suggest, but do not absolutely demand, a date nearer to 100 B.C.

*Figure 25.* Agora I 5469.

Upsilon      This letter is quite large and usually composed of three strokes; the vertical is normally quite short.

## List of Inscriptions

⁺*IG* II² 933      Part of Agora I 5469; see *ZPE* 20 (1976) 193–99. For a stemma of Kleomachides Larisaios, see H. Kramolisch, *Die Strategen des Thessalischen Bundes vom Jahr 196 v. Chr. bis zum Ausgang der Römischen Republik, Demetrias II* (Bonn 1978) 29.[2] If the later date suggested in note 1 proves to be correct, Kramolisch's stemma can easily accommodate it, since the names Kratinos and Kleomachides appear to alternate in the branch of the family with which we are dealing.

---

[2] I owe this reference to the kindness of Ch. Habicht.

*IG* II² 1037

Agora I 5469    *Hesperia* 29 (1960) 76–77.

## *Adnotatiunculae*

### *IG* II² 933

The nu in the first line is smaller than the other letters preserved on this piece and is part of the last line of the decree, surely part of the payment formula. The letters KA recorded by Kirchner in line 2 are large—the same size as the letters in the crown—and clearly part of the heading for the crown. After alpha and directly above the center of the tie a vertical is preserved at the edge of a worn area. The restoration [ἡ βουλή] καὶ [ὁ δῆμος] is inevitable. The heading, as is customary, will have been inscribed by eye without exact measurement and thus is slightly off-center to the left.[3]

---

[3] On this lack of centering, see Tracy, *Lettering* 116, 122.

# The Cutter of *FD* III 2 no. 24

## Dates: 138/7–128/7

### General characteristics of the lettering (fig. 26)

This lettering has a solid appearance. Strokes are precisely placed in relation to one another and the letters each have their own space, though the spacing between letters is somewhat uneven. The letter-strokes thicken into prominent serifs which occur at the end of every terminal stroke. The letter-strokes vary in thickness from quite thin to rather thick. For a brief description of this hand, see *BCH* 99 (1975) 212–13.

### Peculiarities of individual letters

| | |
|---|---|
| *Alpha* | The crossbar is straight and occurs at about the midpoint of the letter. |
| *Omikron* | This letter varies in size but is usually quite large and round. |
| *Pi* | This is a relatively wide letter. |
| *Sigma* | The top and bottom strokes are usually just about parallel. The diagonals which form the central part of the letter overlap the horizontals. |
| *Tau* | The horizontal is normally as wide as or wider than the vertical. Occasionally the vertical is quite short, rendering this letter distinctly shorter than the surrounding letters. |
| *Upsilon* | This letter is composed of three strokes. The v-shaped top is quite wide and prominent. The vertical is usually about half the height of the letter, though sometimes it can be rather short. |
| *Omega* | The loop is large and round; horizontal strokes with prominent serifs extend to right and left making this a very wide letter. |

*Figure 26.* FD III 2 no. 138 (top), no. 24 lines 1–16 (bottom).

## List of Inscriptions

| | |
|---|---|
| EM 2857 | Unpublished. |
| Record of the Pythaïs, *FD* III 2 nos. 7, 11, 23, and 29. | Archon Timarchos (138/7). On these texts, see *BCH* 99 (1975) 185–88. |
| Record of the Pythaïs, *FD* III 2 nos. 3, 8, 24, 27, 33, 34–42, 46, 47, 50, 52, 56a, 137, and 138. | Archon Dionysios after Lykiskos (128/7). *BCH* 99 (1975) 188–95. |

*

The lone unpublished inscription from Athens reveals that this cutter, like the other workmen who did the major work of inscribing the texts of the Pythaïdes on the Athenian Treasury, was an Athenian. See the Cutters of *FD* III 2 no. 5, *FD* III 2 no. 26, and *IG* II² 1028.

# The Cutter of *IG* II² 937

## *Dates: ca. 135–123/2*

### *General characteristics of the lettering* (fig. 27)

This lettering adorned with serifs is unusually precise and elegant. The serifs, small v-shaped ones, occur regularly at the end of every terminal stroke. Round letters are indeed round with the exception of phi (for which, see below). This cutter was an exacting craftsman. Letter-strokes are placed with care and each letter is made the same way each time. There is little meaningful variation, certainly not the kind that one normally sees in the lettering of this period. The individual *hastae* are long and thin. In addition, the long diagonals of alpha and lambda curve ever so slightly. These mannerisms along with the precision give the lettering its elegance.

### *Peculiarities of individual letters*

| | |
|---|---|
| *Alpha* | This is a tall, thin letter with a sharply broken cross-bar. |
| *Beta* | This is quite a thin letter; the lower loop tends to be a bit larger than the upper. |
| *Gamma* | The horizontal usually extends back across the vertical a slight, but noticeable, amount. |
| *Xi* | This is a tall wide letter made with a central vertical; the central horizontal is very short. |
| *Pi* | The horizontal extends beyond the verticals about the same distance on each end most of the time. Occasionally it extends more to the left than to the right. The second vertical is shorter, half, or slightly more than half, the length of the first. |
| *Sigma* | The top and bottom strokes are either parallel to each other or slanting just a little. The top half of the letter tends to be larger. |

*Figure 27. IG II² 937 lines 34–46.*

Phi	This letter is about the same height as the others. The central part is not round but rather seems to have been made in two parts. It is asymmetrical with the left side being larger. In profile it has the appearance of an unshelled peanut.

## *List of Inscriptions*

| | |
|---|---|
| IG II² 937 | See the new edition and study in GRBS 29 (1988) 383–88. |
| ⁺IG II² 977 | Archon Epikles (131/0). Agora XV no. 246. D. M. Lewis (ZPE 20 [1976] 300) has attributed IG II² 921 to this text and J. S. Traill (Hesperia 47 [1978] 286) has noted some corrigenda. Kirchner-Klaffenbach, Imagines no. 107. |
| IG II² 1331 and addenda p. 673 | |
| IG II² 2949 | J. v. Freeden, ZPE 61 (1985) 215–18, discusses the various dates proposed for this altar and concludes that the date must be between 123 and 120 B.C. |
| ⁺IG II² 3477 | |
| Agora I 750 | Published below. |
| Agora I 1912 | Published below. |
| Agora I 3668 | Hesperia 23 (1954) 242. |
| Agora I 4811 | Hesperia 33 (1964) 195. |
| EM 5588 + 6062 | Part of IG II² 977, q.v. |

## *Inscriptions in the style of*

| | |
|---|---|
| IG II² 1132 | Archon Demostratos (130/29). |
| IG II² 3784 | |
| Agora I 25 | Archon Demetrios (123/2). Hesperia 3 (1934) 71. This text was republished by J. Kirchner as IG II² 2993a and incorrectly dated to 50/49. |
| ⁺Agora I 3699 | Hesperia 6 (1937) 463. |

Agora I 3804a    Osborne, *Naturalization* no. D121.
Agora I 4758    *Agora* XV no. 245.

## *Preliminary publication of fragments from the Athenian Agora*

**1** (pl. 25). Fragment of white marble, face only preserved, found in a late context east of the Civic Offices (J 12) on June 2, 1933.

H. 0.162 m.; W. 0.095 m.; Th. 0.047 m.; LH. 0.008 m.

Inv. No. I 750

```
        ca. a. 130 a.         NON-STOICH.
          [ _____ ]ΜΑ[ _____ ]
          [ _____ ]ΞΕΣ[ _____ ]
        3 [ _____ ]εμελή[θη? _____ ]
          [ _____ ]τὰ θύματα [ _____ ]
          [ _____ δι]ετέλεσεν [ _____ ]
        6 [ _____ ὑπ]ὸ τῶν ταμιῶ[ν __ ]
          [ _____ ]Ι ταῦρον ΥΠ[ ____ ]
          [ ____ ἐν τῶι] βουλευ[τηρίωι __ ]
        9 [ _____ ]ΜΕΝΤ[ _____ ]
          [ _____ ]τοῖς βου[λευταῖς? _ ]
          [ _____ προεν]οήθη δὲ [καὶ ___ ]
```

Line 1. There is a stroke which slants slightly just to the right of the break. Mu is an almost certain reading.

Line 2. The tips of the three horizontals of xi appear just to the left of epsilon.

Line 3. At the bottom of the letter-space before mu appears a serif. It is the basis for dotted epsilon. A number of other letters are also possible, such as sigma and omega.

Line 9. Just the indistinct outline of mu can be discerned.

Some official, probably a priest, is being praised for sacrifices (lines 4 and 7) which he undertook. The reference to the paymasters and to the bouleuterion (lines 6 and 8) is intriguing. Do we have here a record of sacrifices made by councillors?

**2** (pl. 26). Fragment of white marble, left side (smooth) preserved, found in late fill south of the Tholos (G 12) on May 4, 1934.

H. 0.13 m.; W. 0.064 m.; Th. 0.042 m.; LH. 0.008 m.

Inv. No. I 1912

*ca. a.* 130 *a.*     NON-STOICH.

ΘΕ[ _ _ _ _ _ _ _ ]
ΤΑΣ[ _ _ _ _ _ _ _ ]
3 ΘΗΚ[ _ _ _ _ _ Πει]-
ραιεῖ [ _ _ _ _ ὁ]
δῆμος [ _ _ _ _ _ ]
6 τοῦ δή[μου _ _ _ _ ]
ΜΑΔΙ[ _ _ _ _ _ _ ]
ΝΕΕ̣[ _ _ _ _ _ _ _ ]

Line 8. Only the vertical and upper horizontal of dotted epsilon appear clearly.

Restoration does not seem possible. This fragment has the same size lettering and has the same vertical spacing as the foregoing piece; they may well come from the same text.

## *Adnotatiunculae*

### *IG* II² 977

Two unpublished fragments from the Epigraphical Museum, now joined[1] and bearing inventory numbers 5588 and 6062 (pl. 27), belong to this stele. The text is as follows (note that the placement of the fragments so that the two partially preserved columns are the last two is somewhat arbitrary):

---

[1] The join was made by the Ephor of the Epigraphical Museum, Dr. D. Peppa-Delmouzou, who kindly turned it over to me to publish since I had discovered, as a result of my work on hands, the relationship to *IG* II² 977. It is a pleasure to record here my debt to Dr. Delmouzou and her fine staff at the Museum.

[See Agora XV no. 246 for the opening lines of this text.]

1 [— — — — — — — — — — —]ν ⟨ Ἁρμοξένο[ν — — — καὶ τὸν γραμματέα τὸν]
[κατὰ πρυτανείαν Γόργυλον Ἀγγελ]ῆθεν ⟨ καὶ τὸν [ἐπὶ τὸ ἀπόρρητον — — —]
[— — — — — — — καὶ στεφαν]ῶσαι ἕκαστον [αὐτῶν θαλλοῦ στεφάνου·]
4 [ἀναγράψαι δὲ τόδε τὸ ψήφισμα τὸν γραμματ]έα τὸν κατὰ [πρυτανείαν εἰς στήλην]
[λιθίνην καὶ στῆσαι οὗ ἂν εὔκαιρον ἦν· εἰς δὲ τὴν ἀ]ναγρα[φὴν τῆς στήλης καὶ τὴν]
6 [ἀνάθεσιν μερίσαι τὸν ταμίαν τῶν στρατιωτικῶν τὸ] γεν[όμενον ἀνάλωμα.]

columns I–III lost

7 [— — — —]     25 [— — — —]
[ *demotic?* ]     [— — — —]
[— — —]ιδης     Ἀτ[ηνεῖς?]
10 [— — —]ς     28 Δ[— — —]
[— — —]ης     Τ[— — —]
[— — —]ας     Α[— — —]
13 [— — —]λης     Ἀ[— — —]
[— — —]ας     32 Π[— — —]
15 [— — —]τέλης     [*four or five*
[ *demotic* ]εἰς     *names lost;*
[— — —]νος     *two or three*
18 [— — —]     *lines blank*]
[*three lines*
*blank*]
22 [ἡ βουλή]     40 [ἡ βουλή]
[— — —]ην     [— — —]
[— — —]     [— — —]

Line 2. Just the top of the right vertical of dotted eta is legible.

Line 3. Merely the top of dotted omega is preserved; just the bottom of the left vertical of dotted nu survives.

Line 4. Of dotted epsilon the right tip of the topmost horizontal is discernible at the break.

Line 5. The lower third of the left slanting stroke of dotted alpha is visible.

Line 6. Only the initial vertical of dotted nu is preserved.

Line 23. A vertical preserved along the edge is the basis for dotted eta.

Line 27. After alpha a serif appears. It is placed somewhat up from the bottom of the letter-space and is quite probably the serif at the bottom of a tau. It could also be part of gamma or pi, thus the demotics Ἀγρυλεῖς, Ἁγνούσιοι, and Ἀπολλωνιεῖς are also possible.

Line 31. The edge is damaged at this point. There appears to be part of a slanting stroke preserved, thus my reading of dotted lambda.

I have restored this text with five columns of names on the analogy of *Agora* XV no. 206.

The exact spatial relationship of the two new fragments to the other fragments must remain conjectural pending further examination of the stones in Athens. It appears certain, however, that the first line either aligns with the last line of fragment c (line 37) or comes one line lower (new line 38). The restoration in the second line of the secretary κατὰ πρυτανείαν seems certain, so the fragments cannot be placed higher. If they are aligned with line 37, there were thirteen officials praised as in *Agora* XV no. 243 of 135/4. If they are placed lower, there were fourteen officials as in *Agora* XV no. 261 of 143/2 (?).[2]

For the officials praised and their order of listing compare *Agora* XV nos. 243 and 261. The name Harmoxenos (line 1) is not common in Attica. He is perhaps related to the victor in the Theseia of 157/6 (*IG* II² 957 line 73). There is also an Harmoxenos known with Xenokles on several coin issues around 100 B.C. (*PA* 2237; M. Thompson, *The New Style Silver Coinage of Athens* 555).

## *IG* II² 3477

This text honors an unnamed girl as hearth initiate, as *kanephoros* in the Pythaïs, and as *kanephoros* at the Panathenaia; it is dated to the priestes-

---

[2] *Agora* XV no. 261 was inscribed by the Cutter of Agora I 6006 and must date to 135/4 or earlier. See above, p. 159, on the date.

ship of Habryllis. The Pythaïs mentioned in this text is surely a reference to the Pythaïs to Delphi of 138/7 (*FD* III 2 nos. 7, 11, 23, 29). The *kanephoroi* are listed in number 29. She will have been one of them; we cannot determine which one.

More importantly, Habryllis' tombstone, *IG* II² 6398, which was inscribed by the Cutter of *IG* II² 3479, *q.v.*, must then postdate 138/7.

**Agora I 3699**

This circular base is, I am of the opinion, by this cutter. Completely certain identification is impossible, however, because so few letters are preserved. The initial eta and sigma are inscribed with slightly larger and deeper letters and are a correction. Under the left half of eta an erased omikron can be made out clearly; an erased upsilon appears between eta and sigma. Initially the patronymic was inscribed. It appears then that the base was first signed as the work of Eucheir alone and then changed to the joint signature. More than one erasure will have been required to make the change.

# The Cutter of *IG* II² 1028

*Dates: 131/0–98/7*

## *General characteristics of the lettering* (fig. 28)

The letter-strokes of this cutter[1] are comparatively thin and carefully placed. Prominent serifs are the chief feature of his lettering. He made two types, an inverted v and a straight-line serif. The v serif appears only at the ends of terminal vertical and vertically slanting strokes, the straight-line only on horizontal and horizontally slanting strokes. He had the habit of beginning the straight-line serif at the horizontal and extending it upward, thus giving epsilon, sigma, and tau highly distinctive shapes.

## *Peculiarities of individual letters*

| | |
|---|---|
| *Alpha* | This letter is relatively narrow and normally has such large serifs that it seems to "walk" on them crab-like. The crossbar varies, being either a curve or a straight, but slanting, line. |
| *Omikron* | This letter is smaller than the surrounding letters and is usually composed of two semicircles; occasionally it approximates a diamond in shape. |
| *Sigma* | The top and bottom strokes always slant. Serifs are usual, though occasionally the upper stroke lacks the serif. Very rarely does no serif occur. |
| *Upsilon* | This letter consists of two principal strokes—the right begins at the bottom and slants or curves to the height |

---

[1] A full-length study of this cutter appeared in 1975; see *Lettering*. It was preceded by a description of his lettering and a list of inscriptions in *GRBS* 11 (1970) 331–33, with addenda published in *GRBS* 14 (1973) 189. I include an account of this cutter here so that the present volume will be complete and users will not be forced to go outside of it for the basic reference material.

*Figure 28. IG* II² 1028 lines 93–99.

|  | of the letter, the left (a shorter straight stroke) meets the right at the bottom of the letter or just slightly above it. Often it is the left stroke which is longer and is joined by the right. |
|---|---|
| *Phi* | This letter is taller than the surrounding letters; it consists of a long vertical to which two small, complete circles adhere at about mid-point. |
| *Omega* | The bottom of this letter is always open. Two horizontal strokes usually with serifs extend to the left and right making the letter substantially wider than the others. |

## *List of Inscriptions*

| IG II² 989 | Archon Herakleides (104/3). *Lettering* 23–26; *Agora* XV no. 254. |
|---|---|
| IG II² 1023 | *Lettering* 74–77. |

| | |
|---|---|
| IG II² 1028 | Archon Medeios (101/0). *Lettering* 32–48. |
| IG II² 1136 | Archon at Delphi Xenokrates (106/5). *Lettering* 20–22. |
| IG II² 1227 | Archon Epikles (131/0). *Lettering* 15–18. |
| IG II² 1228 | Archon Sarapion (116/5). *Lettering* 18–20. |
| IG II² 1341 | *Lettering* 77–78. |
| IG II² 1942 | *Lettering* 79–80. |
| ⁺*IG II² 2336* | Lines 48–90, 123–26, 147–49, 162–63, 178–79, 237–38, 243–44, 257, 262–63, 270–71 in the edition by Tracy (*IG II² 2336*). See also *Lettering* 26–32. |
| IG II² 4991 lines 1–3 | *Lettering* 80–82. |
| Agora I 1773*a* | *Lettering* 69; *Agora* XV no. 255. |
| Agora I 2945 | *Lettering* 69–70; *Agora* XV no. 256. |
| Agora I 3871*a* | *Lettering* 70. |
| Agora I 3871*b* | *Lettering* 71. |
| Agora I 5919 | *Lettering* 71–72; *Agora* XV no. 257. |
| EM 649 | *Lettering* 72–73. |
| EM 5228 | *Lettering* 73–74. |
| EM 5581 | *Lettering* 74. |
| Record of the Pythaïs, *FD* III 2 nos. 2, 6, 10, 16, 17, 26, 31, 45, 48. | Archon Argeios (98/7). *Lettering* 45–68 and *BCH* 93 (1969) 371–95. |
| *Kerameikos* III A5 | *Lettering* 82–84; *Agora* XV no. 260. |

## Inscriptions in the style of

| | |
|---|---|
| IG II² 959 | See the discussion of the lettering of this inscription on page 10 of *Lettering*. This text should probably be dated to 115 B.C. or later. I now discover that this text joins (pl. 28) to the bottom left of II² 1014.[2] |
| IG II² 1014 | Archon Jason after Polyklei[tos] (109/8). |

---

[2] K. Clinton (May 1988) kindly confirmed the join for me in Athens.

IG II² 1014 + 959

a. 109/8 a.

NON-STOICH. ca. 59

ἐπὶ Ἰάσονος ἄρχοντος τοῦ μετὰ Πολύκλει[τον ἐπὶ τῆς ca. 3 ἴδος τετάρτης πρυτανεί]-
ας, ἧι Ἐπιφάνης Ἐπιφάνου Λαμπτρεὺς ἐγρα[μμάτευεν περὶ Θησείων ca. 10 ]·
Καλλικράτου Στειριεὺς γράμματα τάδε π[αρέδωκεν εἰς τὴν βουλὴν καὶ τὸν δῆ]-
μον· ⋮ Πυανοψιῶνος ἕκτηι ἱσταμένου, πέ[μπτηι τῆς πρυτανείας· βουλὴ ἐν βουλευτη]-
5 ρίωι· τῶν προέδρων ἐπεψήφιζεν Δεξίχαρις Φι[ ca. 11 ⋮ ἀντιγραφεὺς Στρά?]-
τιος Φηγαιεύς·

ἔδο[ξεν τῆι βουλῆι καὶ τῶι δήμωι]·

[Θ]ε[μ]ιστοκλῆς Ὀλ[βίου Κηφισιεὺς εἶπεν· ἐπειδὴ _____ ca. 25 _____ ]
ος χειροτονηθεὶ[ς ὑπὸ τοῦ δήμου Θησείων ἀγωνοθέτης εἰς τὸν ἐπὶ Ἰάσονος ἄρχον]-
10 τος ἐνιαυτὸν τό[ν μετὰ Πολύκλειτον τὴν τε πομπὴν ἔπεμψεν εὐσχήμονα]
καὶ τὴν θυσίαν σ[υνετέλεσεν τῶι Θησεῖ κατὰ τοὺς νόμους καὶ τὰ ψηφίσματα]
τοῦ δήμου, προε[νοήθη δὲ _____ ]
καὶ ἐποιήσατο τή[ν ἐπιμέλειαν τῆς λαμπάδος καὶ τοῦ γυμνικοῦ ἀγῶνος, προνοηθεὶς τοῦ μηδὲν]
ἀδίκημα γενέσθ[αι τοῖς ἀγωνιζομένοις _____ ὁμοί]-
15 ως καὶ τῆς τῶν [ _____ ca. _____ ἔθηκεν δὲ καὶ ἆθλα καλὰ καὶ εὐσχήμο]-
να τοῖς ἀγωνιο[αμένοις κατὰ τὰ ἐψηφισμένα τῶι δήμου σπουδῆς οὐδὲν ἐλλείπον, παρεσ]-
κεύασεν δὲ κα[ὶ ταῖς φυλαῖς ταῖς νικώσαις ἆθλα τῶν ἱππέων καὶ τῶν ἐπιλέκτων],
ὁμοίως δὲ καὶ τοῖς ἐκ τῶν ἐθνῶν τάγμασιν, καὶ ταῦτα ἀνέθηκεν· ἔδωκεν δὲ καὶ τεῖ βουλεῖ
[καθέσιμο]ν δ[ραχμὰς _____ ]

Note that in estimating line lengths and letters lost, I count iota as half a letter.

Line 1. The tribe in prytany will have been either Aigeis or Oineis.

Line 6. Just the right tip of the horizontal of tau is now visible.

This now becomes the latest known decree honoring an *agonothetes* of the Theseia and the first with a preamble. The other decrees are *IG* II² 956, 957, and 958. This preamble contains in lines 2–3 and 5–6 some unusual, indeed unparalleled, additions.[3] A reference to the Theseia seems probable in line 2. The family of Kallikrates of Steiria is well attested (see *PA* 7981, 7988, 7989). Syndromos (*PA* 13038), father of Kallikratides and Theorikos, ephebes in 107/6 (*IG* II² 1011 lines 107–8 I), is probably to be restored at the end of line 2.

The chairman is not attested elsewhere.

The speaker, Themistokles son of Olbios of Kephisia, is known from *IG* II² 2452 line 54 and was himself a contestant and victor in the Theseia around 140 B.C. (II² 961 line 41).

The language of the decree in lines 11–15 seems to be somewhat fuller than the earlier decrees from which it has been restored by Kirchner. His restorations in lines 13, 16, and 18 convey the sense required but result in lines which may be a bit long. In any case, I have corrected the verb at the end of line 16; Kirchner's [κατεσ]|κεύασεν was a slip.

Line 4 reveals that these honors were conferred at a meeting on the sixth of Pyanopsion, surely after or at the conclusion of the contests. This provides us with a valuable new indication of the date for the festival, i.e. prior to the sixth. The eighth was the day appointed for the largest sacrifice to Theseus (Plutarch, *Thes.* 36) and it had generally been taken as the main day of the festival.[4] We now see that the elaborate games honoring Theseus, no doubt of several days duration, came during the week before the great sacrifice.

## *Adnotatiunculae*

### *IG* II² 2336

I have discussed fully elsewhere (*IG* II² 2336 25–31) the hands of this important stele. Several are identical with cutters who appear in this

---

[3] See Henry, *Prescripts*, 92–93.

[4] A. Mommsen, *Feste der Stadt Athen im Altertum* (Leipzig 1898) 288–89; L. Deubner, *Attische Feste* (Berlin 1932) 224. J. Mikalson, *The Sacred and Civil Calendar of the Athenian Year* (Princeton 1975) 70–71, had seen that the Theseia was not necessarily to be dated to the eighth.

study, *q.v.* The following will provide a summary (line numbers are those of the new edition).

| *Lines* | | *Lines* | |
|---|---|---|---|
| 48–90 | II² 1028 Cutter | 178–79 | II² 1028 Cutter |
| 123–26 | II² 1028 Cutter | 180–81 | *FD* III 2 no. 5 Cutter |
| 131–32 | *FD* III 2 no. 5 Cutter | 182–89 | II² 1135 Cutter |
| 138–39 | *FD* III 2 no. 5 Cutter | 190–200 | II² 2983 Cutter |
| 142–43 | II² 2983 Cutter | 203–16 | *FD* III 2 no. 5 Cutter |
| 146 | *FD* III 2 no. 5 Cutter | 226–27 | II² 2983 Cutter |
| 147–49 | II² 1028 Cutter | 237–38 | II² 1028 Cutter |
| 150–60 | II² 2983 Cutter | 243–44 | II² 1028 Cutter |
| 162–63 | II² 1028 Cutter | 257 | II² 1028 Cutter |
| 164–65 | II² 1135 Cutter | 262–63 | II² 1028 Cutter |
| 167–75 | II² 2983 Cutter | 270–71 | II² 1028 Cutter |
| 176–77 | *FD* III 2 no. 5 Cutter | | |

None of the other hands distinguished on this inscription can be identified certainly with any of the cutters or writing on the fragments included in this study. Hands A (lines 1–46), C (lines 92–122), F (lines 245–56), and G (lines 228–36) are quite idiosyncratic and appear to be unique.

# The Cutter of Agora I 286

### Dates: 130/29–117/6

## General characteristics of the lettering (fig. 29)

This workman[1] tends to crowd his letters so closely together that they seem to bump against one another. The letter-strokes are thick and give an impression of haste since often strokes do not meet exactly or overlap noticeably. This cutter employs serifs frequently but irregularly, most often at the bottom of vertical strokes. The serif is usually of the inverted-v type; occasionally it is merely suggested by a thickening at the end of the letter-stroke. The overall impression is one of crowding and lack of precision.

## Peculiarities of individual letters

| | |
|---|---|
| *Alpha* | The crossbar is usually curved; occasionally it is sharply broken. The letter itself is quite wide. |
| *Delta* | This letter tends to be elongated to the right; it is rather wide and squat in appearance. |
| *Epsilon* | This letter tends to be thin with short, stubby horizontals which are often thickened perceptibly at the ends. Although there is no regularity of practice, the horizontals are usually about the same length; occasionally the middle or lowest is definitely shorter than the other two. They tend to curve slightly, sometimes fail to meet the vertical, and have a serif fairly frequently. When a serif appears, it is usually on the bottom stroke. |
| *Zeta* | The cutter makes this letter in the shape of Z. |

---

[1] First published in *GRBS* 11 (1970) 330–31 and figs. 4–7 and with an addendum in *GRBS* 14 (1973) 189; additions to the list of inscriptions previously published are here asterisked.

*Figure 29.* Agora I 286 lines 8–15.

| | |
|---|---|
| *Mu* | This letter is rather wide; the strokes which form the central v seldom extend down to the base of the letter and often intersect one another. |
| *Sigma* | This letter consists of four slanting strokes of approximately the same length. The strokes often curve |

|  |  |
|---|---|
|  | slightly, especially the top one, and tend to overlap; this is especially noticeable where they meet at the vertical mid-point of the letter. Serifs usually appear on the top and bottom strokes, although the one at the top is frequently omitted. Only rarely are there no serifs. |
| *Tau* | The crossbar tends to curve. |
| *Phi* | This letter is usually the same height as the other letters. The oval which forms the center is somewhat flattened in appearance and off-center to the right. |
| *Omega* | This letter is never a complete circle. The cutter has a tendency to place a relatively large horizontal line on the left and a small line or v serif on the right. |

## List of Inscriptions

| | |
|---|---|
| *IG* II² 1133 | Archon at Delphi [Aristion] son of Anaxand[rides] (130/29). Agora I 5679 belongs; see *Hesperia* 39 (1970) 309–11. This decree reproduces in part *FD* III 2 no. 68. |
| *IG* II² 1134 | Archon at Delphi E[ukleides] (*ca.* 125).[2] Lines 1–60 are identical with *FD* III 2 no. 69. Kirchner-Klaffenbach, *Imagines* no. 108. |
| *IG* II² 1171<br>= *IG* II² 1124 | *ZPE* 38 (1980) 92–93. |
| *IG* II² 1332 | Archon Jason (125/4). |
| *IG* II² 1333 | |
| *IG* II² 3147 | *Hesperia* 4 (1935) 81–90 and *Hesperia* 29 (1960) 56. |
| *\*IG* II² 3474 | On the priestess honored and her father, see Osborne, *Naturalization* II 187–88. |
| Agora I 138<br>and *I 7478 | *Agora* XV no. 248 and *Hesperia* 51 (1982) 63 and 206. |
| Agora I 286 | Archon Theodorides (127/6). *Hesperia* 24 (1955) 220–39 and *Hesperia* 34 (1965) 22. |

---

[2] On the date see G. Daux, *Chronologie Delphique, Fouilles de Delphes* III fasc. hors série (Paris 1943) 59 and the recent discussion by D. Mulliez, *BCH* 107 (1983) 429–34.

Agora I 3939      *Hesperia* 26 (1957) 77–78.
Agora I 4547      *Hesperia* 39 (1970) 311.
Agora I 5782      Published below.
*Agora I 6231     *Hesperia* 30 (1961) 256–57.
Agora I 6422      Archon Lenaios (118/7). *Agora* XV no. 253.
*Agora I 7156     Archon [Menoites] (117/6). *Hesperia* 45 (1976) 287–88.
*Kerameikos I 10  *AthMitt* 97 (1982) 171–84. See the discussion above
  lines 29–31      under the Cutter of Agora I 6006.
*Kerameikos* III A6

## Inscriptions in the style of

*IG* II² 4295
Agora I 5238      *Hesperia* 30 (1961) 260.

## Preliminary publication of a fragment from the Athenian Agora

Fragment of white marble (pl. 29), face only preserved, found in packing under the paving which covered the Library of Pantainos (R 14) on April 17, 1939.

H. 0.059 m.; W. 0.041 m.; Th. 0.036 m.; LH. 0.01 m.

Inv. No. I 5782

ca. a. 125 a.          NON-STOICH.

Μ̣

Χ̣ΙΣ

3 ΗΤΡ

ΑΛΛ

Line 1. The remains in this line are very difficult to be sure of. There appears to be a left slanting stroke with serif and part of a central slanting stroke; thus my reading of dotted mu.

Line 2. The bottom of a slanting stroke with serif appears at the break. This is the basis for dotted chi; kappa is also possible.

✶

There are two notable aspects of this cutter's surviving *oeuvre*. His hand appears on three bases signed by the sculptors Eucheir and Euboulides of Kropidai (*IG* II² 3474, 4295, Agora I 6231). All three should probably be dated to about 130 B.C., that is, toward the end of Eucheir II's career (see the stemma under *PA* 5330 and the commentary at *IG* II² 4291). In addition, inscriptions recording the activities of the Dionysiac Artists, *viz. IG* II² 1133, 1134, 1332, Agora I 7156, and *Kerameikos* III A6, comprise a significant portion of his work.

# The Cutter of Agora I 1594

### Date: 122/1

*Caution*: Only scraps of this man's work survive. I am forced therefore to characterize the hand based on a very small sample of the lettering. This sample under ordinary circumstances would be too small for one to speak about the hand. However, this cutter's peculiarities are so marked, I feel, that one can begin to characterize it from a very small sample.

## General characteristics of the lettering (fig. 30)

The width of the strokes varies and straight strokes tend to curve somewhat. The cutter employs small serifs regularly. Occasionally the small serif becomes quite a long line—note the serif on the horizontal of gamma in line 2.

## Peculiarities of individual letters

*Alpha*
: The single example is quite wide with a straight crossbar at about mid-point. There is a slight extension of the apex; see also delta.

*Delta*
: This letter is very wide, in fact elongated to the right, and flat. The strokes which meet at the apex extend up in a short straight line.

*Omikron*
: This letter is somewhat smaller than the surrounding letters and hangs from the top of the letter-space. It is quite round.

*Sigma*
: The single example is very idiosyncratic. The top and bottom strokes are parallel. The top bends a bit. The letter is out of proportion—the top is much wider than the bottom.

*Upsilon*
: This letter is quite large and composed of two strokes. The left curves up to the top of the letter. The right, a straight stroke, joins it at about the mid-point of the letter.

*Figure 30.* Agora I 1594.

## List of Inscriptions

Agora I 1594      Archon [Nik]odemos (122/1). *Hesperia* 10 (1941) 61.

Agora I 6086      *Agora* XV no. 262.

It is tempting to try to bring these two pieces together and make them parts of the same inscription. The line lengths, however, prevent it. In any case, *Agora* XV no. 262 should be dated about thirty years earlier than Meritt and Traill have it.

## Inscription in the style of

Agora I 4908      *Hesperia* 26 (1957) 218–19. If this attribution is correct, the date in *Hesperia* is about 75 years too early.

# The Cutter of *IG* II² 1008

## Dates: 118/7–97/6

### *General characteristics of the lettering* (fig. 31)

This workman places small serifs on his letters and crowds them together. Letters encroach on each other so much that it is difficult at times to tell letters apart. Gamma followed by iota, for instance, will be indistinguishable from pi. Letter-strokes are thin; long diagonal strokes tend to curve. This cutter leaves definite interlines which are in size about half to three-quarters the height of the letters.

### *Peculiarities of individual letters*

| | |
|---|---|
| *Alpha* | This letter is quite wide and often has a sharply broken crossbar. The crossbar can also be straight or curved. |
| *Epsilon* | The horizontals vary in size, curve, and are usually seriless. The middle horizontal is often slightly shorter. |
| *Mu* | This letter is of medium width. The outer strokes tend to be vertical or slant only a little. The central v extends down less than half the height of the letter and sometimes curves. |
| *Nu* | The second vertical tends not to extend down to the base of the letter. |
| *Omikron* | This letter tends to be small and to occur in the middle to upper part of the letter-space. It is made rather awkwardly and is rarely very round. |
| *Sigma* | The top and bottom strokes are parallel; occasionally they even slant downwards a little. The strokes which meet at the mid-point often overlap. Sometimes the cutter even adds a short horizontal stroke as if to extend the central part. |
| *Upsilon* | This cutter makes three varieties: the most frequent is composed of two strokes—the left curves to the height |

*Figure 31.* IG II² 1008 lines 79–106.

| | of the letter, the right joins above the mid-point; the next most frequent is the three-stroke variety with the vertical being at least half the height of the letter; a v-shaped upsilon also appears on occasion. |
|---|---|
| *Omega* | This letter tends to be rather small and to hang from the top of the letter-space. It is open at the bottom and has small horizontal lines attached to both sides; the one on the left sometimes extends into the letter instead of away from it. These strokes do not have serifs. |

## *List of Inscriptions*

| | |
|---|---|
| IG II² 840 | F. Sokolowski, *Lois sacrées des cités grecques* (1969) 78–79. |
| IG II² 932 = IG II² 1008, lines 132–33 (I). | See D. Peppa-Delmouzou, *Deltion* 29 (1973–74) B 16. |
| IG II² 1008 | Archon Lenaios (118/7). Agora I 6319 *a-g* and 6695 belong (*Hesperia* 33 [1964] 213–15). |
| IG II² 1036 | Archon Demochares (108/7). New edition by C. A. Hutton in *ABSA* 21 (1914–16) 155–62. The listing of Akamantis (VI) ahead of Ptolemais (V) is notable. B. Nagy, *GRBS* 19 (1978) 311–13, associates *IG* II² 1060. |

## *Inscriptions in the style of*

IG II² 1054
IG II² 2990       Archon Herakleitos (97/6).

# The Cutter of *IG* II² 1009

## Dates: 116/5–94/3

## *General characteristics of the lettering* (fig. 32)

This cutter inscribes letters which have thin strokes and small serifs. These serifs tend to be straight lines or thickenings, rather than of the inverted-v variety. They occur regularly on all terminal strokes; in addition, the points of alpha, delta, lambda, nu, and the central point of sigma are often thickened or actually have a small serif. The letter-strokes proper often curve slightly. The cutter tends to place the letters as close together as possible, so that, although his lettering is quite neatly executed, it has a crowded or busy look.

## *Peculiarities of individual letters*

*Alpha*      This letter varies in width from thin to normal and, in this regard, it contrasts with delta and lambda which are often quite wide. The crossbar tends to be sharply broken, though a straight crossbar does occur occasionally when the letters approach 0.005 m. in height.

*Beta*      The upper loop is quite round and occupies a little more than half the height of the letter; the lower is somewhat compressed and elongated.

*Delta*      This letter is often very wide and slightly shorter than the surrounding letters.

*Zeta*      This letter has the shape of Z; serifs appear on all four corners.

*Mu*      This is a very wide letter, essentially two lambdas placed side-by-side.

*Sigma*      The top and bottom strokes definitely slant. The upper half of the letter is about half the time slightly larger. The letter often leans forward a bit.

*Upsilon*      This letter tends to be made from three strokes, with

*Figure 32.* Agora I 5952 lines 8–14 (part of *IG* II² 1009).

|  | the vertical being half the height of the letter or less. Occasionally the vertical curves to the height of the letter in a single stroke. |
| --- | --- |
| Phi | This letter routinely extends up into the interspace. The round part, slightly ovoid, is placed just above the mid-point of the letter. |

## List of Inscriptions

| | |
|---|---|
| *IG* II² 1009 | Archon Sarapion (116/5). Agora I 582 (*Hesperia* 15 [1946] 213–14), Agora I 5952 (*Hesperia* 16 [1947] 170–72), and *IG* II² 2456 and 2457 (*ArchEph* 1950–51 41–42 no. 19) join. EM 4722 preserves the initial letters underlined in lines 71–79 (III) of *IG*. |
| *IG* II² 1030 | |
| ⁺*IG* II² 2459 | |
| ⁺Agora I 7203 | *Hesperia* 47 (1978) 283–84. |

## Inscription in the style of

*IG* II² 1033      Archon Kal[lias] (94/3). *Hesperia* 28 (1959) 200–201.

## Adnotatiunculae

### *IG* II² 2459

Line 4. Following the iota and just to the left of a gouge in the surface appears the lower third of a slanting hasta with attached serif. The reading must be alpha and the reference is to the festival known as the Apollonia, most probably the Delian festival of that name, for the Apollonia are not otherwise attested in Athens.

We are concerned here with the record made by a gymnasiarch of games celebrated under his aegis. Delian inscriptions provide the closest parallels; see *ID* 2590, 2591, 2593, and 2598. The reference to the Eumeneia, presumably a one-day fête honoring the king celebrated as part of the Apollonia, was placed to the right. On the left, and balancing it, was a reference to another festival, perhaps the Attaleia. The Attaleia are attested on Delos[1]; the Eumeneia are not.

Line 6. There is a blank space left between the first two letters; it falls precisely under the omega in line 4, the first tau of line 3, the first alpha of line 2, and the right side of pi in line 1. This space marks the approximate center of the text if it was arranged in two columns. In any case the width required for Medeios' name in line 6 provides an approximate indication for how far the text will have extended to the left. Kirchner's suggested restorations do not fit the space. The lines, we must keep in mind, may have been considerably longer than restorations have suggested. There will have been, for example, some such word as ἱεροποιήσαντας or ἀγωνοθετήσαντας to govern the accusative τὰ ᾿Απολλώνια in line 4.

Medeios in line 6 is surely the famous Medeios of the Piraeus (*PA* 10098). He is listed here either as a victor or, more probably, as one in charge of the festival. He grew up on Delos[2] and, in fact, his prominence in this text, the reference to the Apollonia, plus the parallels of language with Delian texts combine to suggest that this is a Delian text set up in Athens.

---

[1] Ph. Bruneau, *Recherches sur les cultes de Délos* (Paris 1970) 572–73.
[2] See Tracy, *IG* II² 2336 160–64, 210.

**Agora I 7203**

Traill dated this text *init. saec.* II *a.*; it should be dated to about 110 B.C. The unusual features in the language and organization of this text are, by the way, better suited to the later date.

Ammonios son of Ammonios of Anaphlystos will either be identical with the *epimeletes* of Delos of 128/7 (*PA* 712; P. Roussel, *Délos colonie Athénienne* [Paris 1916] 104) or, more probably, his son. The son should then be added to Roussel's stemma (*loc. cit.*).

The final word of line 6 should be ἔθυον.

# The Cutter of Agora I 6108

### Dates: 112/1–111/0

## General characteristics of the lettering (fig. 33)

This cutter makes serifed letters which have a reasonably neat, orderly appearance. This effect is created by his careful use of blank space. He leaves a distinct space between each letter and the next. The interlinear space is also clearly defined and respected; letters do not intrude into it, with the exception of phi, which is slightly taller than the other letters. He achieves this while placing his letters very close together and allowing only a very small interline.

## Peculiarities of individual letters

| | |
|---|---|
| *Alpha* | This is a relatively wide letter; the crossbar usually curves though occasionally it is straight. |
| *Epsilon* | The central horizontal is usually shorter, comes to a point, and rarely has a serif. |
| *Lambda* | The two strokes often curve slightly; the left stroke sometimes extends at the top of the letter beyond the apex. These remarks apply also to alpha and delta. |
| *Sigma* | The top and bottom strokes are more often than not horizontal or virtually horizontal; occasionally they slant. The top stroke tends to bend downward in a most idiosyncratic fashion. |
| *Omega* | This letter is quite round, open at the bottom, and has finials with small serifs. These finials tend to slant downwards perceptibly. |

## List of Inscriptions

| | |
|---|---|
| IG II² 975, 1061, and EM 4697 | *Hesperia* 28 (1959) 195–98. |
| Agora I 6108 | Archon Sosikrates (111/0). *Hesperia* 30 (1961) 229–30. |

*Figure 33.* Agora I 6108.

Agora I 6282    Archon Dionysio[s after Par]amonos (112/1). *Hesperia* 30 (1961) 229.

## Lines in the style of

Agora I 983,    *Hesperia* 36 (1967) 88–91. For a discussion of the hands
lines 38–40    on this inscription, see below under the Cutter of *IG* II² 1135.

*

Whether it is chance or not, it seems appropriate to note that this cutter's three independent inscriptions all relate to cults. Two (Agora I 6108, 6282) are decrees of a religious organization which worshipped the Great Gods; the third is a decree of the city praising a priest of Asklepios.

# The Cutter of *IG* II² 1135

*Dates: 111/0–98/7*

## *General characteristics of the lettering* (fig. 34)

This cutter makes his letters with precision and spaces them regularly. He tends to add small serifs, particularly to horizontal strokes. He employs them quite regularly for ten or more lines and then for another group of lines uses them hardly at all. But for this mannerism, his lettering is very neat and regular.

## *Peculiarities of individual letters*

| | |
|---|---|
| *Alpha* | This letter usually has a sharply broken crossbar. |
| *Theta* | The cutter uses a short horizontal line to articulate the center of this letter. |
| *Omikron* | This letter is often almost as large as the surrounding letters. |
| *Pi* | The crossbar is long and extends beyond the verticals an equal amount to the right and left. |
| *Sigma* | The top and bottom strokes always slant and sometimes curve. All four diagonals are approximately the same length. |
| *Upsilon* | This letter is usually made with three strokes; the vertical tends to be quite short. Once in a while the letter is v-shaped. |
| *Phi* | The central part is composed of two small circles attached at the mid-point of the vertical or a little below. This letter is only slightly taller than the surrounding letters. |
| *Omega* | This letter is almost a full circle; that is, it curves in at the bottom so that only a small opening is left. Two finials of about the same size usually with serifs always appear; sometimes they slant downwards a bit. |

*Figure 34. IG II² 1135a.*

## List of Inscriptions

*IG* II² 1135
Archon Sosikrates (111/0). *ICreticae* I 187 no. 9. Kirchner-Klaffenbach, *Imagines* no. 109. For a new edition of fragment *c*, see V. Kontorini, *Inscriptions inédites relatives à l'histoire et aux cultes de Rhodes au II$^e$ et au I$^{er}$ s. av. J.-C., Rhodiaka* I (Louvain-La Neuve 1983) 36–37 = *SEG* 33 (1983) no. 134.

*IG* II² 2336
This cutter is Hand M in the edition by Tracy, *IG II² 2336*; see page 30 and figure 18 for the hand. He inscribed lines 164–65 and 182–89, entries which belong almost certainly to 98/7 (*ibid*. 97–98).

+Agora I 983,  Hesperia 36 (1967) 88–91.
   lines 51–58

## Inscription in the style of
IG II² 4034

## Adnotatiunculae

**Agora I 983**

Line 57. The demotic is Φιλαίδης not Αἰθαλίδης. This man is not attested elsewhere.

Lines 1–29 (face A) of this fragmentary list of contributors were inscribed in 164/3 by the Cutter of Agora I 247. The rest of the names were inscribed in the last quarter of the second century by a number of hands which are unfamiliar except for lines 38–40 (style of I 6108 Cutter) and 51–58 (by the present cutter). Note that lines 30–32 are inscribed out of line (three spaces to the left) and in different lettering from the rest of face A. This lettering has serifs and alpha with a sharply broken crossbar, indicating that they belong to the later additions to this monument.

# The Cutter of *IG* II² 2983

*Dates: 111/0–98/7*

## General characteristics of the lettering (fig. 35)

This cutter incised his letters lightly and employed small serifs intermittently. His round letters stand out because they are unusually large and are more deeply incised.

## Peculiarities of individual letters

| | |
|---|---|
| *Alpha* | This letter is wide and usually has a sharply broken crossbar; one of the serifs is often omitted. |
| *Omikron* | This letter is usually as tall as the other letters. |
| *Rho* | The loop is often quite large. |
| *Sigma* | The top and bottom strokes usually slant and sometimes curve slightly. If there is a serif, it is more often on the top stroke. |
| *Upsilon* | This letter is quite tall and wide; it is composed of three strokes. The vertical is often quite short. |
| *Omega* | This letter has a large opening at the bottom; finials with serifs are attached to right and left making this a very wide letter. These finials sometimes slant upwards noticeably. The serifs are usually the crow's-foot variety, but straight-line ones also occur. |

## List of Inscriptions

| | |
|---|---|
| *IG* II² 1335, lines 1–24 | Archon Theokles (103/2). This lettering is very sloppy as though done in great haste. |
| *IG* II² 2336 | Archons [The]odos[io]s, [Prokles], and Argeios (100/99–98/7). This cutter is Hand D and N in the edition by Tracy (*IG* II² 2336).[1] See page 28 and figure 13 for a |

---

[1] The lettering of Hand N in lines 190–200 is rather sloppy, but the shapes are the same as those of Hand D. I am now of the opinion that these are one hand and not two. For what-

*Figure 35. IG II² 2983.*

|  |  |
|---|---|
| IG II² 2983 | brief characterization and illustration of Hand D and pages 30–31 and figure 19 for Hand N. He inscribed lines 142–43, 150–60, 167–75, 190–200, and 226–27. Archon Sosikrates (111/0). Lines 6 and 8 are inscribed with letters which are deeper. Though very similar in style, they are probably by another hand. |

## Inscription in the style of

IG II² 2448

---

ever reason, the workman inscribed lines 190–200 with less than his usual precision; the same is true of lines 1–24 of *IG* II² 1335. He was capable on occasion of very slipshod work.

# The Cutter of *IG* II² 1011

### Date: 106/5

## General characteristics of the lettering (fig. 36)

Although the letters are crowded and vary in height from example to example, this lettering has a solid, neat appearance. The cutter achieves this by maintaining a definite interline, by making the letter-strokes thick and deep, and by placing the strokes with precision. He decorates the ends of strokes with very small serifs.

## Peculiarities of individual letters

| | |
|---|---|
| *Alpha* | This letter tends to be thin and slightly taller than the other letters. The right slanting stroke often extends slightly beyond the top of the letter—delta and lambda show this same tendency. The crossbar is either sharply broken or has a definite curve. |
| *Mu* | The first and last strokes tend to be vertical; the central v normally does not come down to the base of the letter. |
| *Nu* | This is a relatively thin letter; there is occasionally a definite serif at the bottom of the second vertical. |
| *Omikron* | This letter is quite small and round and is placed in the center to upper part of the letter-space. |
| *Pi* | The verticals tend to be the same length. |
| *Sigma* | The top and bottom strokes tend to be horizontal. The central v is made with shorter strokes. |
| *Upsilon* | This letter is usually composed of three strokes; the vertical is at least half the height of the letter. |
| *Omega* | This letter is often shorter than the others and open at the bottom; it has two finials with small serifs. These strokes tend to be approximately the same size. |

*Figure 36. IG II² 1011 lines 35–87.*

## List of Inscriptions

IG II² 1011        Archon Agathokles (106/5). Kirchner-Klaffenbach, *Imagines* no. 110.

IG II² 3485

IG II² 4305

## Inscription in the style of

IG II² 3217        *Agora* XV no. 274. If this attribution is correct, the date should be adjusted to *ca. a.* 100 *a.*

# The Cutter of *FD* III 2 no. 5

*Dates: 106/5–96/5*

## General characteristics of the lettering (fig. 37)

This cutter makes letters which are plain and quite neat in appearance. He exhibits a tendency to thicken slightly the bottom of upsilon and the second vertical of pi. By contrast, most of his contemporaries were using serifs regularly. For brief treatments of his lettering, see the present writer's accounts in *BCH* 99 (1975) 212 and *IG II²* 2336 28–29.

## Peculiarities of individual letters

| | |
|---|---|
| *Alpha* | The crossbar is placed slightly above the mid-point of the letter. It can vary from straight to sharply broken. |
| *Epsilon* | The horizontal strokes tend to be quite short and are often all approximately the same length. They usually curve slightly and taper at the ends to points. |
| *Kappa* | The upper slanting stroke often curves. |
| *Mu* | This letter consists of two lambdas placed side-by-side. |
| *Pi* | The horizontal is quite long and extends beyond both verticals. In consequence, this letter is quite wide. |
| *Sigma* | The top and bottom strokes always slant; they often curve as well. |
| *Tau* | The crossbar is often off-center to the right. |
| *Upsilon* | The vertical is usually quite short and sometimes non-existent. |
| *Phi* | This letter is taller than the others. The central part is made with two loops roughly round and sometimes differing in size attached at the mid-point or slightly above. |

*Figure 37. FD* III 2 no. 13 lines 2–20 (continuation of *FD* III 2 no. 5).

## List of Inscriptions

| | |
|---|---|
| *IG* II² 1029 | Archon [___krates] (96/5). |
| *IG* II² 1552a | |
| *IG* II² 2336 | Archons Medeios–Argeios (101/0–98/7). This cutter is labelled Hand E in the edition by S. Tracy (*IG* II² 2336). He inscribed lines 131–32, 138–39, 146, 176–77, 180–81, 203–16. |
| ⁺*IG* II² 2452, line 42 | |
| *IG* II² 3488 | |
| ⁺Agora I 6333, lines 5–8 | *Hesperia* 30 (1961) 252. |
| Agora I 6885 | Archon Pr[okles] (99/8). *Hesperia* 32 (1963) 23–24. |

| | |
|---|---|
| Record of the Pythaïs, *FD* III 2 nos. 4, 5, 9, 13, 14, 15, 25, 28, 30, 43, 44, 49 | Archon Agathokles (106/5). On these texts, see *BCH* 99 (1975) 195–210. |
| EM 3191 | Unpublished. |

*Line in the style of*

⁺*IG* II² 2452 line 10

*Adnotatiunculae*

### Agora I 6333

This is a rather puzzling piece. It may be the end of a list of officials similar to the two published in *Hesperia* 6 (1937) 457–61. The first three lines were inscribed by the Cutter of Agora I 6006 and mention the archon Andreas (144/3 or *ca.* 150). Lines 5–8 were inscribed by the present cutter a generation or more later as some sort of addendum. The last two lines are by another hand (not familiar) and probably therefore later still. The inscribed surface to the left is badly worn or perhaps, as Meritt thought, deliberately erased.

Line 6. There is a *vacat* of two letter-spaces after the word *hiereus*.

Line 9. Alpha and nu can be made out in the letter-spaces before the initial omikron. There are traces of more letters to the left all the way to the break, but I can read no certain or probable letter.

### *IG* II² 2452

This list of important men is rather worn in places and available to me at present in only one (not very good) squeeze. The names are inscribed close together with minimum interlines, as though the cutters, or someone in charge, knew that the number of names to be inscribed was likely to fill up the entire available vertical space. The lettering throughout is neat and professional-looking, despite the fact that numerous cutters inscribed it, obviously at different times. Except for the two lines (10, 42) which are by this cutter and one (56) by the Cutter of *FD* III 2 no. 26 (I), the writing is not familiar. The two known cutters were both at work right around 100. This fact, along with the neatness and uniformity of appearance in a list inscribed by so many different men, suggests that it was inscribed over a short period of time, not more than several years. I hope to devote a separate study to this text at a later date.

H. Mattingly (*Historia* 20 [1971] 33–34) reaches a similar conclusion using prosopographical arguments. However, one must also take into account the appearance in this list of three hierophants in lines 48, 53, and 59; on them, see Clinton, *Sacred Officials* 28. See also the article of S. Dow on *catalogi incerti generis* in *Ancient World* 8 (1983) page 104, where useful prosopographical references are collected.

# The Cutter of *IG* II² 1034

### Date: 103/2

## *General characteristics of the lettering* (fig. 38)

This lettering has a solid, reasonably neat appearance. The letter-strokes are quite thick and often have small serifs. This cutter leaves a distinct space between letters and between lines.

## *Peculiarities of individual letters*

| | |
|---|---|
| *Alpha* | This letter tends to be quite wide with a sharply broken or at least bent crossbar. |
| *Epsilon* | This is a wide letter. The top and bottom horizontals are as long as the vertical; the central horizontal is shorter. Serifs are usually attached to all three strokes in such a way that they extend downwards in a most idiosyncratic fashion. |
| *Theta* | This letter is distinctly larger than omikron and has a straight line in the center. |
| *Omikron* | This letter is usually small and in the middle to upper part of the letter-space. |
| *Rho* | The loop is quite large and round. |
| *Sigma* | This letter varies in size and shape. At times the top and bottom strokes are parallel and at times they slant perceptibly. The central v usually does not extend to the front of the letter. |
| *Upsilon* | This letter consists of two strokes; the right extends in a slanting curve from the bottom of the letter to its height. The left, a shorter straight stroke, joins it at, or slightly below, the mid-point of the letter. |
| *Omega* | This letter has long finials with serifs extending to right and left, making it an unusually wide letter. Occasionally one of the serifs is omitted. |

*Figure 38.* IG II² 1034a + b + c.

## List of Inscriptions

| | |
|---|---|
| ⁺IG II² 1034 | Archon [Theokl]es (103/2). |
| IG II² 1943 | Part of II² 1034, *q.v.* |
| IG II² 2327 | |

### IG II² 1034 and 1943

The hand(s), marble, and textual considerations make it clear that these fragments belong together. Fragments *a* and *b* of II² 1943 are to be inserted below fragments *a* + *b* + *c* of 1034 and above *d*. Fragment *b* of 1943 will come above 1943*a*. They do not go together or align, for their vertical spacing differs as do the hands. See more on this below. As for the vertical spacing, five lines on *b*, measuring from the top of line 18 to the top of line 23,[1] require 0.06 m.; five lines on *a*, from the top of line 2 to the

---

[1] The line numbers here are those as published in *IG* II².

top of line 7, take up 0.056 m. A similar lessening of vertical spacing can be observed on the fragments of II² 1034. Lines 8–12 occupy 0.065 m. while lines 15–19 (column I) take up 0.052 m. There was, in fact, a gradual diminution in vertical spacing from top to bottom of this stele. The decree was spaced out the most; the interline was reduced in the columns of names and made smaller towards the bottom of the stele.

With the new pieces added, the upper part of the register of names will be as follows:

[For the first 15 lines, see
IG II² 1034]

IG II² 1943b

                              2 or 3 lines lost
                              [Κεκροπίδος]

lacuna of about       [--- --]ην[----]
23 lines             [--- --]νος Με[λιτέως]
including the rubrics  4 [--- Σαρ]απίωνος Μ[ελιτέως]
of Erechtheis, Aigeis,    [--- --]νος Μελ[ιτέως]
and Pandionis         [--- ---] Αἰξωνέως
                      7 [--- --- Ἀλ]αιέως
                        [--- --- Συ]παληττ[ίου]
                        [--- --- Ἐπι]εικίδου
                     10 [--- --- Ἀλα]ιέως
                        [--- --- Μελι]τ[έ]ως
                        lacuna of 1 or 2 lines?

IG II² 1943a

                     14 [--- --- ---]
                        [--- --- ---]
                        [ Ἱπποθωντίδος]
                     17 [Θ]εοφ[ίλη --- ---]
                        Νικο[-- --- ---]
                        Λυσισ[τράτη --- ---]
                     20 Ἐρώτ[ι]ον [--- ---]
[Λεωντίδος]          Στρ[ατ-- --- ---]
[--- --- --- ἕ]ως      Σω[-- --- ---]
[--- --- ---]ς         23 Ἀμμω[νι- --- ---]
[--- --- ---ο]υ         Σωσ[-- --- ---]
[--- --- ---]έως       Νικω[-- --- ---]
[--- --- ---ο]υ       26 Εὐκο[λ- --- ---]

```
[___ ___ ___o]υ                    Λεον[τι_ ___ ___]
[___ ___ ____]                     'Αθην[__ ___ ___]
[___ ___ ____]                  30 Τι[__ ___ ___]
[___ ___ ____]                       [ 'Αιαντίδος]
[___ ___]ου Εὐπυρί[δου]              lacuna of 1 line?
    [Πτολεμαιί]δο[ς]                 Αἰν[___ _]ω[_ ___]
```

[For the continuation of the text, see *IG* II² 1034]

The second column of names, after the entries of Kekropis, is inscribed by a different (unfamiliar) hand. This cutter used serifs regularly and placed his letters more closely together than the principal cutter. His omega differs in shape, being more rounded (at times nearly closed at the bottom) and less wide. I have found no other examples of this writing.

The combined text allows us to determine with tolerable accuracy the enrollment of *ergastinai* in 103/2. There were about sixty-two lines originally in each column down to and including line 29 of II² 1034 (in Kirchner's numbering). This gives us 124 entries less twelve for the tribal rubrics. There are five more entries below line 29 in column II giving an enrollment of about 117. This is quite comparable to the ephebic enrollment in 102/1; it stood at 141, 101 citizens and forty foreigners.[2] The other partially preserved lists of *ergastinai*, *IG* II² 1036 of 108/7[3] and 1942 of *ca.* 100,[4] likewise suggest that each tribe tended to have eight to twelve representatives at this time. The enrollment in 103/2 seems then to have been typical of the late second century.

One striking fact about these three partial lists of *ergastinai* is that the same persons occur on more than one. Each list preserves entries for Akamantis in whole or in part. Three young women who served in 108/7 served again in 103/2; two Akamantids of 103/2 also appear in the list of *ca.* 100. There are no names common to the lists of 108/7 and *ca.* 100, presumably because the girls of the earlier list were all married or too old to be eligible. It was apparently customary before marriage for young women to serve Athena more than once. The five-year interval of the first two lists reveals that they started quite young, perhaps at seven or eight years of age.

---

[2] *IG* II² 1028 as republished in *Lettering* 32–48.
[3] C. A. Hutton, "Inscriptions in Petworth House," *ABSA* 21 (1914–16) 155–62. Hutton estimated the enrollment as "not less than one hundred and twelve" (p. 162).
[4] See *Lettering* 79–80.

# The Cutter of *FD* III 2 no 26, lines 1–24 (I)

*Date: 98/7*

### General characteristics of the lettering (fig. 39)

This cutter was the assistant to the master cutter charged with inscribing the record of the Pythaïs of 98/7 on the wall of the Athenian Treasury at Delphi (See *BCH* 93 [1969] 371–72 and 99 [1975] 212). He inscribed a plain alphabet which has a slightly ungainly appearance because some of the letters are outsized in relation to the others. Upsilon and sigma, for example, tend to be rather large. This cutter's lettering is very similar to that of the Cutter of *FD* III 2 no. 5.

### Peculiarities of individual letters

| | |
|---|---|
| *Alpha* | The crossbar is sharply broken. |
| *Zeta* | This letter is Z-shaped. |
| *Sigma* | The top and bottom strokes slant. The top one also curves quite frequently. |
| *Upsilon* | This letter is large, both in height and width. The vertical stroke is at least half as tall as the letter and usually more. |
| *Omega* | This letter is always open at the bottom and has a v-shaped finial turned on its side placed on each side. They tend to be about the same size. This letter is very idiosyncratic. |

### List of Inscriptions

| | |
|---|---|
| *IG* II² 995 | F. Sokolowski, *Lois sacrées des cités grecques* (1969) 79–80. The date in the *Corpus, med. s.* II, is a trifle early. |
| *IG* II² 2452, line 56 | See the discussion above under the Cutter of *FD* III 2 no. 5. |
| Agora I 4875 | *Hesperia* 29 (1960) 15. |

*Figure 39. FD* III 2 no. 26 lines 1–13 (I).

Record of the Pythaïs, *FD* III 2 no. 17, lines 11–13 (I), 16–17 (I), 4–7 (II), 10 (II), 16 (II); no. 26, lines 1–2, 3–24 (I), 3–10 (II); no. 48, lines 28–38, 44–61.   Archon Argeios (98/7). On these texts see *BCH* 93 (1969) 379–94.

# Discussion of Letter-Cutting and Cutters 229 to 86 B.C.

One of the most surprising results of this study, at least to the present writer, is that cutting activity over these years varied greatly and not just in quantity. This study has also revealed that a view which I had long held must be modified. Previous experience had influenced me to believe that learning the hand on any long decree of Hellenistic Athens was likely to repay study, because the men who cut such decrees were specialists who in all probability inscribed many texts. It is now clear that there is at least one period during which this expectation does not hold true. The odd single surviving example of a man's work one does, of course, expect to encounter from time to time. That is not surprising. But what is one to make of the fact, which this study has revealed for the first time, that a large number of major inscriptions beginning about 155 and continuing right down to 86 are apparently unique? There are no matches, no other examples of the writing among the inscriptions studied. This is a wholly unexpected discovery which demands an answer. It should not be the case, or so past experience suggested.

The bar graph (fig. 40, p. 224) presents the thirty-eight cutters identified during the course of this study. The bar covers the years each is known to have worked; the numbers in bold face at the right of each bar give the total number of inscriptions or parts of inscriptions attributed to each. This graph clearly reveals that after 160 there was a rapid decline both in the numbers of masons working and of texts inscribed. The work of only two, the Cutter of *IG* II² 3479 and the Cutter of Agora I 6006, spans the decade 148–138. Beginning in 135 B.C. a recovery of sorts takes place, with quite a few cutters being active, five in the decade 130–120 and seven in the next decade. But their careers, with one exception, the Cutter of *IG* II² 1028, are shorter and they inscribe fewer inscriptions by far in comparison with the cutters working in the years 229–160. The graph also reveals that only one of these cutters is known to have worked after the year 95 and none is attested after 90.

Indeed, a smaller number of inscriptions in general was inscribed in Athens after 150. One can see this simply by considering the numbers of

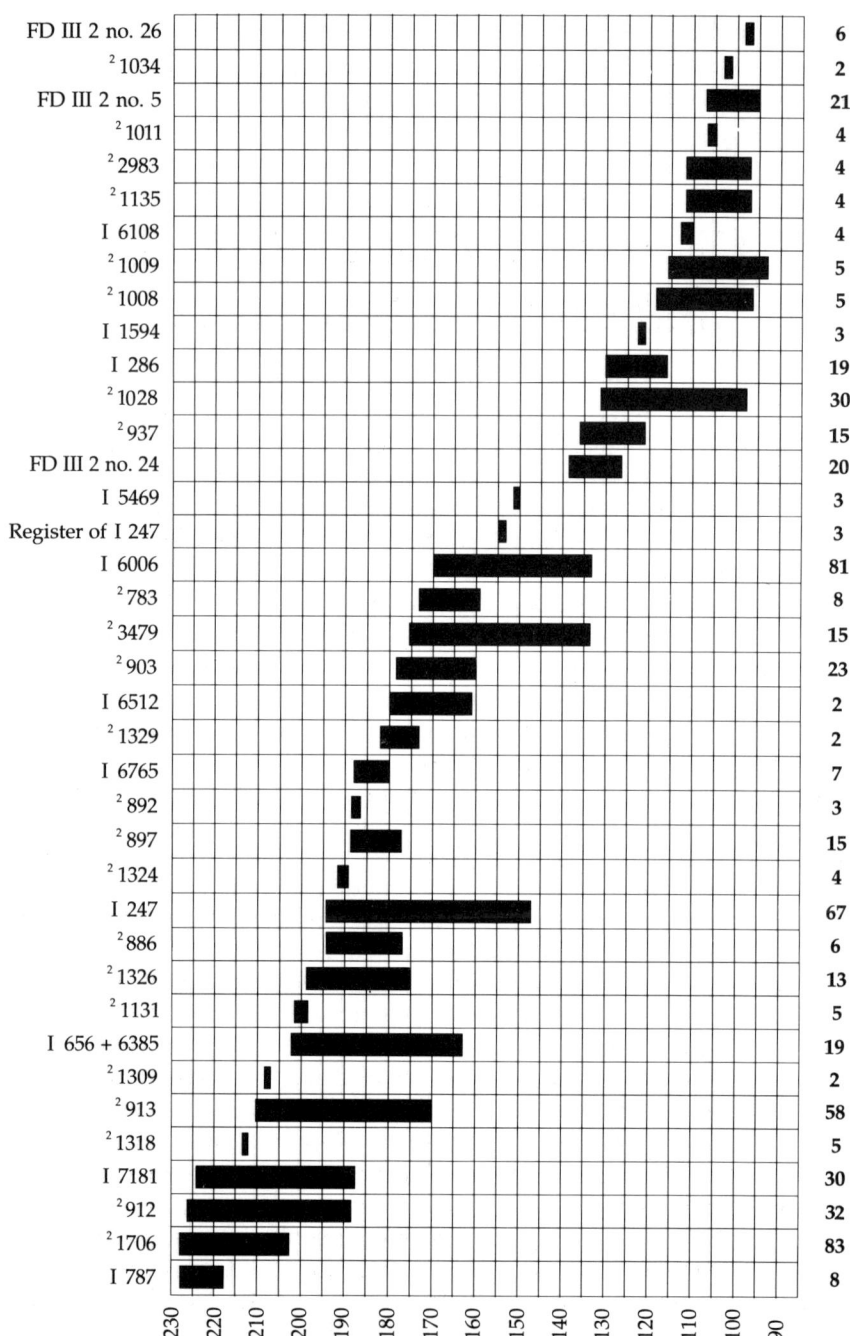

*Figure 40.* Careers of the cutters of 229–86 B.C.

known decrees. Of the decrees numbered 832–1038 in *IG* II², about 117 belong to the years 229–160 and about eighty-two to 160–86.[1] The prytany decrees recorded in *Agora* XV reveal an even sharper decline. About 105 can be assigned to the years 229–160 and only about thirty-eight to 160–86. Citizenship grants stopped being inscribed on stone completely around 140.[2] If it were a case of straightforward supply and demand, one would expect the graph to show after 160 fewer cutters each doing a fairly large number of inscriptions. But it does not. Not counting the two cutters who overlap the decades 160–140, there are twenty cutters working before 160 and sixteen after. The situation becomes even more puzzling when we consider the decrees and probable state decrees which have not been assigned (see Appendix D). Each unassigned inscription represents an individual cutter who cannot be identified with any other. There are a total of sixty-six, of which forty can be dated to the years 160–86 and twenty-two to 229–160. In short, with this added evidence from the decrees not assigned, we know of forty-two cutters at work during the years 229–160 and fifty-six during 160–86. Simply put, there were more different men inscribing long public decrees during a period in Athens when there was significantly less inscribing to be done. How could this be? There was not, the evidence suggests, sufficient work to keep them all busy. What were they doing? Where were they working? Surely the answer is, on Delos.[3]

The graph reveals that the period of change came in the decade 160–150; the near coincidence with the Athenian takeover of the administration of the island in 166 can scarcely be fortuitous.[4] The building program there[5] and the need for long temple accounts provided a whole new set of opportunities for cutters. These temple inventories, extremely long and elaborate documents, comprise an impressive series; there are fragments of more than seventy (*ID* nos. 1400–1479) beginning soon

---

[1] Joins and redatings account for the fact that the total is somewhat less than 207.

[2] See Osborne's collection, *Naturalization*.

[3] This must remain an hypothesis until such time as it is possible to study the hands on the Delian inscriptions of the years 166–86. These inscriptions are numerous and will be very profitable to study from this point of view. At the present time, however, the stones are stored in the *apotheke* in such a way that one cannot study them; the majority are placed leaning against one another like books on a bookshelf. Furthermore, I have not so far been able to ascertain the whereabouts of squeezes of these texts or even if they exist.

[4] On it in general, see P. Roussel, *Délos colonie Athénienne* (Paris 1916); W. A. Laidlaw, *A History of Delos* (Blackwell 1933) 169–95; on its economic impact, see M. Rostovtzeff, *The Social and Economic History of the Hellenistic World* II (Oxford 1941) 787–98 and J. Day, *An Economic History of Athens Under Roman Domination* (New York 1942) 50–61.

[5] See chapter IV of Roussel, *Délos colonie Athénienne*.

after the takeover and covering a period of about twenty-five years. There are also almost twenty-five decrees (*ID* 1497–1520) extant dating to the first fifteen years. This is a very substantial amount of cutting; the need for competent inscribers must have been great. And apparently so many men went to Delos to work in the first fifteen to twenty years that there was a real dearth of cutters in Athens. Demand for inscriptions did in time make a modest comeback in the city, but it appears that after 140 most cutters, the II² 1028 Cutter being an exception, either split their time or did most of their work on the island. The multiple hands on some major inscriptions, *IG* II² 2336, for example, also attest both to the surprising number of different workmen and the fact that the same ones were not always available to inscribe a few lines. In addition, there was apparently a conscious decision in the Athenian assembly (sparked by the exodus of cutters to the island?) to inscribe fewer of the routine honorary decrees. Simple limitations of space may also have contributed to this. The traditional places for setting up stelai on the Acropolis and in the Agora must have been filled to overflowing. Some corroboration for this view is to be found in the designation for the place of erection of prytany decrees. Throughout the period of this study down to the year 130, they were set up in the prytanikon. With *Agora* XV no. 246, passed in the seventh month of 131/0, that designation changes to οὗ ἂν εὔκαιρον ἦι, loosely translated, "wherever a good place could be found."[6] These observations and deductions account logically for the evidence which faces us.

The passing of a decree and setting it up was an extremely public action, surrounded no doubt on occasion by fierce partisanship and factionalism in the assembly. Not everyone will have wanted to honor this or that person or group. Surely in all periods the actions which created these now rather innocent-looking fragments were fraught with political controversy. It is not surprising, therefore, that this activity should reveal an unusual sensitivity to important changes in the political life of the city. A decided increase occurs in certain kinds of documents, namely those connected with religion and with the border forts, after the resumption of the democracy in 229 and a steady growth is observable in cutting activity; the reaction to the acquisition of Delos is rapid; and towards the year 95 there is a precipitous decline, almost cessation of decrees, as the Athenians faced the schism in world affairs created by the Romans and King Mithridates.

The thirty-eight workmen whose inscriptions are the real subject of

---

[6] Meritt and Traill, *Agora* XV p. 3 also discuss this and give evidence of some stones being removed after twenty-five to fifty years. These seem to be the exception.

this study came from that reasonably humble, but honorable, class of men who work with their hands. The task they were trained to do, no doubt through the apprentice system, was one needed by the city and various organizations of a religious and social character at all levels of society in Attica. They had a high degree of skill, at least most of them, and should be thought of as artisans. They took the place of what in today's society would be the newspaper or state printing press. There is no evidence, however, of an official group of cutters or shop always hired by the secretary of the assembly to inscribe state decrees. Nor did they specialize in one kind of document.[7] Rather each cutter whose dossier of extant inscriptions numbers more than a few did a cross-section of work for those organizations and groups which had need of long inscriptions. Very occasionally, it is now apparent, such a highly skilled cutter would even take on a gravestone.[8] There does seem to be a tendency for some cutters to inscribe more often for one group than another. For example, the Cutter of Agora I 247 inscribed a rather high percentage of prytany decrees and the Cutter of I 286 did quite a lot of work for the Dionysiac artists. There may be personal factors which lie behind this—a relative of the cutter might have held an important position in this or that group and been able to exercise a kind of patronage. Alternatively, these cutters may have simply built up a good relationship with their clients and earned the return business.

At any given time, there were a finite number of men at work who could produce long decrees efficiently, perhaps fifteen or twenty in any given year between 200 and 160 and twice that number between 140 and 100. They were in demand and routinely travelled to sites to do their work. Most inscriptions were inscribed, I think, not far from where they were to be set up. A makeshift workshop would do for the cutting. The cutter only needed to avoid eye strain caused by the direct glare of the sun to work. The tools required were few, a dozen or so chisels, a mallet, a sharpening stone, measuring devices, chalk, string, paint brush, paint, and the like. He could carry everything needed in a large toolbox. In any

---

[7] One or two of the honorary decrees for friends of Hellenistic kings have lettering so unique that one suspects that there might have been a specialist retained to cut honorary decrees in the entourage of the king or his follower. *IG* II² 922 and 945, each inscribed in a different unique lettering, fall into this class. Both, as it happens, honor friends of King Eumenes. II² 885, for Attalos I, is another inscription of this sort, but it may well come from Aegina.

[8] This is a small, but significant, modification of my view expressed in *GRBS* 11 (1970) 325 n. 35 and repeated in *Lettering* (1975) 85–86 and n. 3 and in *Hesperia* 47 (1978) 246 n. 7. I have not had the opportunity to search thoroughly among the gravestones, but I have checked enough to feel certain these cutters did not often inscribe ordinary gravestones.

case, most of these cutters regularly went to Piraeus and Eleusis, and, on occasion, they might also travel out to Sounion. They possessed a skill that was not available everywhere and it is not surprising to find that three of the most prolific of these men worked outside of Attica, two on the island of Kea (the Cutter of Agora I 7181, the Cutter of I 6006) and one in Corinth (the Cutter of Agora I 247).

Over against this, there is also evidence of local enclaves in Attica. Many people were used to working with marble and in any community there will have been persons able to inscribe letters, not always of the highest quality, but still acceptable. Local workmen clearly existed, a number right in Piraeus, *viz.* the Cutters of *IG* II² 1324 and II² 1329. There seems to have been a local group at Rhamnous who did all, or almost all, the inscribing there. The style is quite uniform and I think I have identified at least one cutter; see *IG* II² 1322 and EM 12694. There also appears at Sounion a very peculiar local style represented by three inscriptions, *IG* II² 1300, 1308, and 2857, which all date probably in the years 230–215. One might call it pointillist, for the *hastae* of letters are made with a punch in multiple dots. These three texts appear to be by more than one man. The crudest in execution is *IG* II² 1300, the most important inscription of the three, a garrison inscription honoring Eurykleides, the father of the new democracy, in his capacity as hoplite general. It probably belongs to about 229. *IG* II² 1308 cannot be dated precisely. The statue base for a general, *IG* II² 2857, is dated by archon to 220/19. Note in figure 41 that the first two lines exhibit the pointillist style in developed form, i.e. with the dots connected; by contrast the next two lines are inscribed in slightly larger lettering and, except for the round letters, seem to be done with a furrowing technique. These two lines were clearly added later in order to give the general's precise title and year of service. The same cutter may have inscribed them. If so, he used a different cutting technique from the first two lines.

Some of the cutters presented above were quite prolific, sixty to eighty extant fragments, and some worked forty years or more. Provided accident or illness did not take them away, long careers are not surprising, for they will have begun working in the shop quite young and could by their mid-teens be accomplished letterers.[9] They could have inscribed on the average one long inscription per month or about twelve a year if they worked steadily. Factoring in illness, holidays, and slack periods a cutter may have cut as many as four hundred long inscriptions over a full career. The most productive cutter of this study, the Cutter of *IG* II² 1706, worked for about thirty years, 229–*ca.* 203. Of three

---

[9] A. Burford, *Craftsmen in Greek and Roman Society* (Ithaca 1972) 90, lists some epitaphs of teenagers who were already at the time of their deaths recognized craftsmen.

## LETTER-CUTTING AND THE LETTER-CUTTERS

*Figure 41. IG II² 2857.*

hundred or more inscriptions which he probably inscribed we have parts of eighty-three or slightly more than twenty-five percent. This sounds like a good survival rate until we reflect that many of our fragments are just scraps. We possess in fact a very small percentage of his actual lettering, perhaps five percent.

Given this low rate of survival, it is surprising, on the face of it at least, that so many of the fragments which we happen to have relate to one another and often go together. It is in fact one of the great values of the study of hands that it enables one to bring all the fragments by an individual together and consequently often helps one to find joins and associations between them.[10] This happens because our inscriptions come mainly from central Athens and the excavations which have centered on the Agora and on the Acropolis. The inscriptions did tend to get broken up, but, unless they went into the lime kiln, they were used on the spot and did not wander too far afield. Thus separate fragments of the same inscription are often found.[11] Also the same types turn up again and again, because our excavations have been in the areas where they were customarily placed on view. Prytany and ephebic inscriptions, for example, were often set up in or near the Agora. Dedications, citizenship decrees, and other honorary decrees were often placed on

---

[10] See Appendix C for a list.

[11] Excellent examples of large inscriptions of which many fragments have been uncovered in the area of the Agora are the great archon list *IG* II² 1706 (*Hesperia* 2 [1933] 418–46 and 23 [1954] 266–68), an inscribed *kleroterion* (*Agora* XV no. 220), the long ephebic inscription Agora I 286 (*Hesperia* 24 [1955] 220–39 and 34 [1965] 22), and the important list of contributors for the Pythaïs (see Tracy, *IG* II² 2336).

the Acropolis. We are much less rich in deme decrees, though the excavations at Rhamnous and Eleusis show that quite a few were inscribed and presumably, therefore, more will be found.

The five cutters previously identified as the major ones of the period,[12] namely the Cutters of *IG* II² 1706, II² 912, II² 913, Agora I 247, and I 6006, continue to hold that status. Others who were also quite prolific and clearly important have emerged, for example, the Cutters of Agora I 7181, I 656 + 6355, II² 897, II² 903, and II² 937. No cutter or group appears to have dominated; rather the graph reveals that there were always rival cutters at work, as many as eleven identified ones in the decade 180–170. Similarly, there are twenty-six different cutters who work on *IG* II² 2336, a list of contributors dating 103/2–97/6.[13] Nor is there evidence of a large *atelier* controlling things. Rather, the individuality of the cutters suggests small independent shops staffed by a master cutter and an assistant or two. Though there must have been a fraternity of cutters, there is little compelling evidence for direct stylistic influence of one cutter on another.

The only valid criterion for calling one cutter the apprentice of another can be, it appears to me, a significant similarity, not merely in the shapes of the letters but in the personal, often trivial, idiosyncrasies that set one cutter off from another.[14] It is not possible to establish rigid criteria. Some of this, like the assignment of hands itself, must be subjective and a matter of instinct, based on long study of the cutters. It would be nice to weave a long essay connecting many of these cutters, constructing families and schools in marvelous ways; unfortunately, the evidence does not allow it. We simply have too little to go on. There are, however, four cases where similarities suggest a direct influence and I suppose a master and apprentice relationship to be likely. These are:

*IG* II² 1706 Cutter, apprentice of II² 788 Cutter

*IG* II² 897 Cutter, apprentice (?) of II² 1326 Cutter

*IG* II² 783 Cutter, apprentice (?) of II² 903 Cutter

I 6006 Cutter, apprentice of I 656 + 6355 Cutter

At first sight, there is little similarity between the rather hasty-looking lettering of the II² 1706 Cutter (*q.v.*) and the solid, neat lettering

---

[12] *Hesperia* 47 (1978) 244–68.

[13] On these hands, see Tracy, *IG II² 2336* 25–31.

[14] Here again there is a clear limitation in our method which must be acknowledged, namely that it is possible for an apprentice to study under a cutter extensively and still cultivate a style of lettering very different from that of the master. In that case we have no way of recognizing the relationship between them.

of the II² 788 Cutter.[15] On closer examination, they share some striking mannerisms, particularly the way they customarily make alpha, delta, and lambda with an opening at the apex. This opening, or failure to join the strokes neatly at the apex, is the origin of the name "disjointed" given to the style by S. Dow.[16] When the apex is open, the left slanting stroke is shorter and slants more; in addition, the crossbar slants and often bisects one of the diagonals. These mannerisms are exaggerated by the II² 1706 Cutter. Both cutters also at times place the horizontal of delta up a bit from the base of the letter, so that it can be difficult to distinguish delta from alpha. Each makes a very wide kappa with unusually long slanting strokes. They each make phi the same height as the other letters and produce a central element which is not round, but rather tends to have a straight bottom surmounted by an arcing stroke. One end or the other is "squared off." Both tend to place inverted-v serifs at the bottom of omega; the 788 Cutter does it quite neatly, the 1706 Cutter produces very large serifs and places them erratically. The cutting careers of these two men do not overlap. The working career of the II² 788 Cutter spans the period *ca.* 255–235/4. The II² 1706 Cutter did not apparently cut any decrees until 229/8, the year of freedom from the Macedonians. They were both major cutters, perhaps the dominant inscribers of their respective generations. Here we seem to have the true case of a very young man learning his trade from an established master and in the process absorbing some of his telltale mannerisms. The II² 1706 Cutter forsook the neatness of his mentor for a speedy, less exacting style which he presumably could inscribe much faster than the norm. He became, in any case, even with a style which can look *and be* rather sloppy, very successful; in fact, in terms of numbers of extant texts he is the all-time leader.

We encounter quite a different case with the Cutters of II² 1326 and II² 897; their lettering is so similar that, if they were not master and apprentice, they must have worked closely together. In fact their careers completely overlap; the II² 1326 Cutter spans the years 199–175, the II² 897 Cutter 189–177. The problem here is one of being able to distinguish them. There are subtle and consistent differences: the Cutter of II² 1326 leaves the apex of alpha open quite often and sometimes employs a curving crossbar. The II² 897 Cutter makes his alpha slightly wider, leaves it open at the top less frequently, and uses a curving crossbar only rarely. The II² 897 Cutter makes his epsilon with a central horizontal

---

[15] For a full description and illustration of his lettering, see *Hesperia* 57 (1988) 311–22 and plates 86–87.
[16] *AJA* 40 (1936) 58–60.

which is distinctly shorter than the other two horizontals or he omits it altogether. By contrast, the II² 1326 Cutter often makes all the horizontals about the same length. He does not omit strokes. Rho also differs. The 897 Cutter makes his loop from two curving segments; whereas the 1326 Cutter uses three strokes at least to make a rather square loop. The top and bottom of the loop are almost straight. Finally, the omega of the 1326 Cutter is more open at the bottom and less symmetrical than that of the 897 Cutter.

This same degree of similarity appears in the lettering of two other inscribers who were at work contemporaneously, namely the Cutter of *IG* II² 903 (179–160) and of II² 783 (173–160). Kappa and omega are the most helpful in telling them apart. The kappa of the II² 903 Cutter has slanting strokes of normal length which are placed so that they do not reach the top and bottom of the letter-space, thus the letter is fairly wide. The II² 783 Cutter creates a stubby, awkward-looking kappa by employing quite short slanting strokes which do not touch each other or the vertical; rather, they are placed so as to reach to the top and bottom of the letter-space. The omegas differ strikingly, but only in the serifs. Each cutter makes the letter large and round. The 903 Cutter attaches small neat serifs to both sides while the 783 Cutter uses rather large inverted-v serifs which are rarely attached in symmetrical fashion. The one on the left often does not quite touch the stroke which it is supposed to join.

The last case, that of the I 656 + 6355 Cutter and the I 6006 Cutter, also seems to be clearly one of master cutter and apprentice. The hands are easy to distinguish for the most part. Yet, when one examines closely the letter-shapes, there is a startling similarity between them. Theta with a large point or line in the center, a large and quite round omikron, phi with the central part made with a straight line surmounted by an arc, and omega of the horseshoe variety are identical in the writing of both cutters and idiosyncratic. The I 656 + 6355 Cutter began inscribing shortly before 200 and worked down to about 164. His protégé began work about 169 and became the dominant cutter in Athens at mid-century. He may in fact have been one of the few cutters in his generation to work primarily in Athens.

In addition to these eight closely related cutters, I think we can discern a group of cutters who share a mannerism. Omega, a frequently occurring letter, requires more time to inscribe because it traditionally has extra strokes to articulate the bottom. Around 200 an omega without these strokes, omega in the shape of a horseshoe, first appears and is popular with some cutters until about 150. The cutters who use it regularly are: the I 656 + 6355 Cutter (203–163), the II² 1326 Cutter (199–175), the I 247 Cutter (194–147), the II² 897 Cutter (189–177), the II² 892 Cutter

(188–186), and the I 6006 Cutter (169–134). It is first seen in the lettering of the I 656 + 6355 Cutter and, given his influence, it may be that he originated the shape. These cutters may constitute a school of some kind. Certainly, all but the I 247 Cutter cut in the same general style. In contrast, during the second half of the second century, there came into vogue a bold serifed style, often quite handsome; it is represented by the Cutter of *FD* III 2 no. 24 (138–127), the II² 937 Cutter (*ca.* 135–122), the II² 1028 Cutter (131–97), the I 286 Cutter (130–116), and the II² 1009 Cutter (116–93). Though there may be some mutual influence between these cutters, I rather suspect that this was one of the prevalent styles of the time and that what influence there was was merely casual.

There are a number of stones which have more than one cutter who worked on them. They fall into two groups: (1) texts which were inscribed at widely different times, i.e. years or months apart (*IG* II² 2323, Agora I 983, and I 6333) and (2) texts inscribed contemporaneously or virtually so (Agora I 247, 4933, and 6163). The first group tells us nothing about the relationship between the cutters who worked on them, for, once the first inscribing was completed, the stele was set up in a public place. All later inscribing was done on the stone as set up. *IG* II² 2336 falls into this class because, after the record of the first year was inscribed, the stele was set in place. *IG* II² 2443, and perhaps 2452, also fall into this category. The second group were clearly done in shop and, therefore, almost certainly provide a record of cutters who worked together in the same place. Two of these are decrees praising the prytaneis (Agora I 247 = *Agora* XV no. 225 and Agora I 6163 = *Agora* XV no. 141); in each case the list of names was done by a second cutter. I 247 was inscribed by the I 247 Cutter and by the Register of I 247 Cutter; I 6163 was inscribed by the I 7181 Cutter and by style of II² 1706. If this was in fact the II² 1706 Cutter, these two important cutters worked in the same shop at least for part of their careers. In the one other analogous document, Agora I 4933, the I 247 Cutter began an inscription listing the names of influential Athenians and Achaeans. He inscribed the Athenian names; the Achaean names were added by the II² 886 Cutter when they were supplied, presumably a few days later. It is, therefore, very likely that both the II² 886 Cutter and the Register of I 247 Cutter worked in the same shop with the I 247 Cutter, though not necessarily at the same time, since I 4933 dates to 178/7 and I 247 to 155/4.[17]

---

[17] It would be helpful to know *for certain* to which of these categories we ought to assign the Panathenaic victor list, *IG* II² 2314, for it was inscribed by two of the leading cutters, column I by the II² 913 Cutter and column II by the I 247 Cutter. I hesitate to claim them for the same workshop, for it does seem that the two columns represent different Panathenaic years.

Despite these interrelations and possible connections, one should not lose sight of the fact that the dominant impression of Attic lettering in this and all periods so far studied is of stubborn individuality. The lettering of each cutter, on close examination, reveals his distinctive stamp. As Kazantzakis said of his countrymen, speaking of a much later time, "they are pathological individualists." I suspect this was also true in antiquity. Such truly idiosyncratic writing as that of the II² 912 Cutter and the very prolific I 247 Cutter finds no obvious imitators. And, in the one case where we possess *prima facie* evidence for a master cutter and his assistant, namely the Cutter of *IG* II² 1028 and the man who assisted him at Delphi, the Cutter of *FD* III 2 no. 26,[18] it is salutary to keep in mind that they cut rather different styles, with no apparent influence of one on the other.[19] The former cuts rather ornate lettering with serifs, the latter a very plain style.

I have described in *Lettering* 85–122 the way one cutter went about his task. To summarize very briefly, the main points established are these. The cutters used a vertically directed technique for inscribing, in which the cutting edge of the blade is driven into the surface in such a way that the length of the blade determines the length of the letter stroke. Only lightly incised letters a centimeter or less in height can be inscribed in this way. The use of this technique accounts both for the dominant size of the lettering on Attic decrees (*viz.* 0.005–0.01 m.) and for the fact that the letters are, in conception, a sequence of straight lines, like "stick figures." These craftsmen inscribed from a working copy with only the minimal layout necessary to begin work. They blocked out the main sections of the text, determined where crowns would have to be inscribed, but left the final details to the actual inscribing. In short, they proceeded to inscribe after making these calculations and drawing guidelines; they did not lay out the letters one by one, for there was nothing to be gained in so doing. Errors could be corrected as work progressed. Centering did not play an important part in their approach to a text. They began with the first letter and ended with the last, rarely centering even the last line. The practice established by that study of one cutter has been borne out by this much broader study.

The present study allows us to infer more about the assignment and production of texts. At any given meeting of the assembly it is probable that two or three of the measures passed will ordinarily have been designated to be inscribed on stone. It has been the assumption that the secre-

---

[18] For more on them, see *BCH* 93 (1969) 371–95, especially 371–72.

[19] Note also the tremendous variety of letter-styles on *IG* II² 2336. On the various hands, see Tracy, *IG II² 2336* 25–31.

tary soon after the meeting contracted for the work and that he found cutters free to begin inscribing at once. A corollary of this is that he would probably not turn over all the work from one meeting to a single cutter, for otherwise it might be some time before the second or third decree could be worked on. It is possible to test this assumption. During the period of this study there are six instances of two decrees passed at the same session.[20] Were any inscribed by the same man? The answer, as the following reveals, is no.

The list (with attributions) is as follows:

| | | |
|---|---|---|
| 175/4 | *IG* II² 1328 third decree | unassignable/worn[21] |
| | *IG* II² 1329 | ²1329 Cutter |
| 173/2 | *IG* II² 996 | ²783 Cutter |
| | Agora I 5761 | I 247 Cutter |
| 169/8 | *IG* II² 911 | ²903 Cutter |
| | Agora I 164 | unassignable/worn[22] |
| 165/4 | *IG* II² 949 | not assigned |
| | *IG* II² 950 | not assigned |
| 122/1 | *IG* II² 1006 | not assigned |
| | *IG* II² 1004 | not assigned |
| 119/8 | *Kerameikos* III A3 | not assigned |
| | Agora I 560 and I 6127[23] | not assigned |

Moreover, in the one case where it had been thought that two decrees (*IG* II² 897 and 898, *q.v.*) which *were* inscribed by the same man had been passed on the same day, recent evidence (referred to above) reveals that they were passed in wholly different parts of the year. We can now add to this the case of the Cutter of Agora I 6765 (*q.v.*) who inscribed four inscriptions in one year, in fact in the last six months of 181/0. It appears to be meaningful that the dates of passage of these texts are sufficiently spread out that he could have finished each before the next was commissioned. The evidence in all strongly suggests that decrees were normally

---

[20] Ch. Habicht has aided significantly in the compilation of this list.
[21] The shape of sigma, see above, p. 126, reveals that the ²1329 Cutter did not inscribe this decree.
[22] The cutter of I 164 makes a rather small omikron and, so far as I can make out, a horseshoe-shaped omega. The hand is not identical with that of the ²903 Cutter.
[23] On the association of these two Agora texts and their synchronization with *Kerameikos* III A3, see *Hesperia* 57 (1988) 249–50.

inscribed very soon after their passage. This is what we would expect, for the decision to inscribe a decree on stone was a special one and, in the case of an honorary decree, an added honor. Most decisions passed in the assembly will not have been so treated. Part of the special treatment seems to have included the timely inscribing and setting up of the stone.

Such is the picture we reach, spotty and unclear to be sure, but not opaque. It is a definite gain to have evidence that the inscribing was ordinarily done quickly and to know that more than one major cutter worked at the same time in a particular shop. That the inscribing of decrees constitutes an important political act was perhaps something we all knew, at least intuitively. It has been something of a surprise to realize just how responsive the inscribing of decrees was to changing political conditions. The work of the cutters of 229–86 remains our single most important primary source for the history of the city in her last years of real independence. The establishment of these dossiers of work by individual cutters, the improvements in readings, and the resulting temporal implications will, I trust, help others in their studies of this important body of evidence.

# Inscriptions "Not Assigned"

This chapter will treat the inscriptions which I have not been able to assign to a cutter. Each is by the definition of this study a unique example of that particular writing, for, had I been able to isolate another example, the two together would have constituted the dossier for a separate cutter.

In any large group of inscriptions, even a self-contained group covering a relatively short period, there will naturally be the odd piece, the single example. It would, in fact, be highly suspect if one could neatly assign everything. How much more likely this will be for the present very large, heterogeneous group of inscriptions coming mainly, but not exclusively, from Athens and covering a time span of one hundred forty-four years! Add to this the following consideration. We have to deal with a region where marble is plentiful, in fact one of the usual building materials. In all probability there were lots of workmen in Athens at any given time accustomed to working with it and capable of inscribing passable lettering with hammer and chisel. Undoubtedly many gravestones and short inscriptions (fifty letters or less) were inscribed casually by such persons as the need arose. Thus it is that so many of these inscriptions appear to be the only extant text by that man. Undoubtedly too there were workmen who specialized in these short texts, though I have been able to identify only one (the Cutter of *IG* II² 3479); the reason for this is that the letters on such texts are usually large and few, with the consequence that the evidence for definitive study is severely limited.

In the case, however, of long inscriptions (hundreds or thousands of small letters), we are dealing with, it appears, a wholly different task. To inscribe such a text efficiently required special training, presumably some years working as an apprentice to a man who did such work. Such a man would in the normal course cut many inscriptions. Still, even among the decrees, there are quite a few single examples of a man's work. This is caused partly by the accidents of survival. Moreover, not all cutters, surely, were prolific or, even if proficient, successful; some certainly died young through illness or accident. Others may simply have given up and gone into some other line of work.

These single examples will be marked in the list which follows in one of two ways. If the lettering shows marked idiosyncrasies, such that it stands out among the inscriptions in this study, I label it "unique" and sometimes follow it with a slash and "school of X." This latter indication merely signifies that the writing is in the same general style, *with no implication intended of date or relation to that cutter, none at all.* If, on the other hand, the lettering is rather ordinary, I label it "unfamiliar" and occasionally add a slash and "school of" to indicate a general style.

For each of these texts, I indicate briefly the type of document and suggest a date based on my own study of Attic lettering. I also add references to substantive discussions or re-editions and, if necessary, offer new readings. Very occasionally I include here a comment on the style of lettering of a "worn" inscription. Furthermore, some of the texts in the category "not assigned" may well be erroneously dated and not belong to this period at all. I have added notes suggesting this where appropriate.

Finally, as an addendum of sorts, I offer here some rules of thumb for dating. But first a warning—dating by letter-style is very inexact. Cutters do not all adopt the same style at the same time. Some are way ahead of the times and some way behind. Even the best guess, and that is all it is when we date by style, may be off a century or more. Serifed lettering, for example, occurs as early as 220 and is not infrequent thereafter; broken-bar alpha and crowded lettering can occur as early as 180 or so, though one would normally place it after 150. With this warning, the following guidelines seem to me useful for this period, if not infallible, when one must resort to letter-style as the criterion for dating a text.

1. Spaced-out lettering and liberal interlines (¾ of the height of the letters or more) point to a date before 200. Conversely, very crowded lettering and minimal interlines suggest a date after 125.

2. Plain (without serifs) lettering especially characterizes the period 229–160 or so. Alpha with a sharply broken bar on lettering 0.008 m. high or less points to a date after 150. Sigma with parallel top and bottom strokes suggests a date near 100 or after.

3. Large, rather handsome, serifed lettering comes into vogue around 140 perhaps under the influence of Roman or island lettering. It is

typified by the Cutter of *FD* III 2 no. 24 and by the Cutter of *IG* II² 937. It flourishes down to 86 and after.

These are the most significant guides I can offer. To add more would suggest an exactitude which I do not think possible.

My dates frequently concur with those of J. Kirchner; in fact, I often adopt his dates, out of admiration rather than mere imitation. Kirchner was the master of dating by letter-style. He had an exquisite sense of style and, if that is possible, even better judgment. He was aware of the limitations of his criteria and never claimed too much. I have sought to follow his example.

## *IG* II²

837                                                            unfamiliar/school of I 787

Archon Theophilos (227/6). Part of a preamble.

862 Peçirka, *Enktesis* 116–17 & pl. 25       unfamiliar/school of ²1706

A date around 200 B.C. seems correct.

865                                                                  few and worn

Honorary decree of *fin. s.* III *a.*

More can be read at the end of line 2 as follows: Νικ[άν]ωρ Μ[ . . . ]-ν[ . . ]. A Nikanor son of Menander from Kedoi is attested on a grave monument dated *s.* III/II *a.* (*IG* II² 6382). It is possible that he is identical with the secretary here and worth noting that if he is restored, it gives us an archon's name of about ten letters. An archon with a name of this length and secretary from Kedoi are known from *IG* II² 917 (*Agora* XV no. 128)—but, *lacking further evidence, this must all remain conjecture.*

876                                                         unfamiliar/school of ²897

Citations from the bottom of a decree. *Ca. a.* 200 *a.*

884 Peçirka, *Enktesis* 117–18                                unique

This honorary decree for Heris of Byzantium seems on historical grounds to belong to about 200. If one were to date solely by the lettering, sigma with parallel top and bottom strokes would suggest a date of 150 or later.

885                                                                         unique

The lettering of this text honoring King Attalos I (241–197) is singularly well executed and elegant, with no real parallel at this early date. R. E. Allen (*ABSA* 66 [1971] 1–12, esp. 6–12, and pl. 1) provides a good photograph and argues that this text is from Aegina.

887 unfamiliar
Archon Dionysios [after Timarchid]es (135/4). For a new text of this preamble, see W. K. Pritchett in *Hesperia* 9 (1940) 132–33.

889 + 904 unfamiliar/school of I 7181
Archon Hippias (181/0). Osborne, *Naturalization* no. D99.

893 b,c unfamiliar/school of I 6006
Osborne (*Naturalization* no. D98) dates this fragmentary citizenship decree to around 200.

922 unique
Osborne (*Naturalization* no. D106 and pl. 15) dates this citizenship decree on prosopographical grounds to *ca.* 190–165.

945 unique
Archon Xenokles (168/7). Honorary decree for a friend of Eumenes II.

The letters lost at the ends of lines 5 and 6 can be determined to be at most four. The number lost may be three or even two. There are too many possibilities for the patronymic $[^{2-4}_{--}]$KOY in lines 6–7 to suggest a probable restoration. Of the names beginning Ἀρισ[τ$^{2-3}_{--}$] that suit the spacing, only Aristion is attested in the deme Semachidai. He is known as a councillor in 169/8 (*Agora* XV no. 212 line 110) and was almost certainly the proposer of the decree according to which this meeting was summoned on the last day of the following year (lines 5–6). When and where he proposed this psephism by which an *ekklesia synkletos* could be summoned, we do not have enough evidence to say. However, he did not, I think, carry the motion in the meeting of the boule just prior to this meeting of the ekklesia, for it is unlikely that he was also a member of the boule in 168/7. So far as our evidence allows us to see, men known to have served twice in the boule never did so in successive years. On this, see P. J. Rhodes, *ZPE* 57 (1984) 200–201 and the references there.

949 unfamiliar
Archon Pelops (165/4). Athenian decree honoring the demarch at Eleusis and set up at Eleusis.

950 unique
Archon Pelops (165/4). Honorary decree for a priest of Asklepios republished by R. O. Hubbe in *Hesperia* 28 (1959) 185–86 and plate 37.

957 unfamiliar
Archon Anthesterios (157/6). Honors the *agonothetes* of the Theseia.

958                                                           unfamiliar

Archon Phaidrias (149/8 or 153/2[1]). Honors the *agonothetes* of the Theseia. Kirchner-Klaffenbach, *Imagines* no. 104.

964                                                           unique

Catalog of victors at the Theseia. The hand is quite similar, though I do not think it identical, to the hand of *IG* II² 957. I think a date around 150 is preferable to *ca. a.* 130.

971                            unique/school of *FD* III 2 no. 5

Archon Hagnotheos (140/39). This citizenship decree in honor of Telesias of Troezen is probably a copy set up privately (Osborne, *Naturalization* no. D102; Kirchner-Klaffenbach, *Imagines* no. 106).

973                                unfamiliar/school of ²1131

Archon Apollodoros (204/3). Fragment of a preamble.

976                                                      unfamiliar

Hubbe (*Hesperia* 28 [1959] 199–200 and pl. 39) provides a new edition of this fragmentary decree honoring a priest of Asklepios and dates it to *post med. saec.* II *a.*

980                                                      unfamiliar

Osborne, *Naturalization* no. D112. *Ca. a.* 150 *a.*

982                                                      unfamiliar

*Ibid.* no. D113. The lettering suggests a date around 130. For a discussion of this now well-known Milesian family, see P. Herrmann, *Chiron* 17 (1987) 175–82; he follows Wilhelm in dating this decree to about 150 (177 n. 20).

985                                unfamiliar/school of ²1028

Fragment of an honorary decree. *Ca. a.* 130 *a.*

986                                                      unique

This honorary decree for Neokles of Messenia probably dates to about 130 or after.

1003                                                  unfamiliar

Archon Jason (125/4). *Agora* XV no. 250.

1004                                                  unfamiliar

Archon Nikodemos (122/1). *Agora* XV no. 252.

---

[1] On this latter date see Ch. Habicht, "The Eponymous Archons of Athens," *Hesperia* 57 (1988) 237–47.

1006                                                                      unfamiliar

Archon Nikodemos (122/1). There have been a number of additions and improvements to this ephebic inscription by Meritt (*Hesperia* 17 [1948] 23–25 and 26 [1957] 211), Mitsos (*ArchEph* 1950–51 45 and 1961 201–202), Reinmuth (*Hesperia* 30 [1961] 17 and 41 [1972] 185–91), and the present writer (*Hesperia* 57 [1988] 250–52).

1018                                                                      unfamiliar

The archon Eumachos of 120/19 has been restored in this preamble (Pritchett-Meritt, *Chronology* xxxiii); it is convenient but hardly certain. Based on the lettering this text could date anytime between 130 and 50.

1019                                          unique/school of ²1008

For notes on this decree concerning the cult of Asklepios, see R. O. Hubbe, *Hesperia* 28 (1959) 187–88. W. B. Dinsmoor's identification of the priest, thereby dating this fragment to 138/7 (*The Athenian Archon List in the Light of Recent Discoveries* [New York 1939] 194–95) is arbitrary. The small, crabbed lettering supports Kirchner's date of *fin. s.* II.

1022                                                                     unfamiliar

Fragment of a preamble—Kirchner's date, *fin. saec.* II (?), seems accurate. Below the final tau in line 2 the surface is preserved blank for 0.03 m., enough vertical space for two lines. The mention of the *symproedroi* continued into line 3, the end of which was left blank. The enactment clause, then, was placed by itself in line 4 with blank spaces on each side.

1038                                                                     unfamiliar

The letters of the first three lines are 0.012 m. in height; the rest are 0.008 m. This is well-made lettering with wide interlines. I would suggest a date for this honorary decree of *ca. a.* 130 *a.*

1055                                                                     unfamiliar

Osborne discusses this decree concerning citizenship in *Ancient Society* 7 (1976) 120–21 and concludes that it dates earlier than 100 B.C.

1056/7                                        unfamiliar/school of ²937

The lettering of this honorary decree suggests a date *ca. a.* 100 *a.* The remains of an incised crown appear just above line 1.

1130                                                                           unique

M. Guarducci includes this inscription in *ICreticae* II pp. 313–14. The honors were clearly granted in Crete, but the surviving text is perhaps a copy set up in Athens at the initiative of the Athenian honored. *Init. saec.* II seems a safe date.

1137 unique

The letter-strokes are thin and curve in an awkward manner. Kirchner's date of *fin. s.* II for this decree which deals with the Eleans seems as good as any.

1170 unfamiliar/school of ²1135

Citation from a tribal decree. *Ca. a.* 150 *a.*

1223 unfamiliar

Cleruchy decree. *Ca. a.* 150 *a.*

1300 unique

Garrison decree from Sounion of about 230.

1302 unfamiliar/school of I 787

Archon Menekrates (220/19). Garrison decree from Sounion.

1308 unfamiliar

Garrison decree from Sounion. *Fin. s.* III.

1310 unfamiliar

Pouilloux, *Rhamnonte* 132–34, offers a new text of this garrison decree from Rhamnous and suggests a date slightly before 229.

1311 unfamiliar

*Ibid.* 128–29. Prosopographical considerations suggest that this garrison decree belongs to *ca.* 235.

1312 unfamiliar

*Ibid.* 137–38. Decree of the deme. Pouilloux suggests a date in the second half of the third century. A councillor of 304/3 bears the same name as the speaker (*Hesperia* 47 [1978] 277–78).

1321 unique

Fragment of uncertain nature from Eleusis. *Ca. a.* 150 *a.*
Line 4. The left side of an omega is preserved following chi.
Line 11. ΕΠΙΓΡΑⱽ stands on the stone. See K. Clinton in L. L. Threatte, Jr., *The Grammar of Attic Inscriptions* I (Berlin 1980) 505.

1322 unfamiliar

This text from Rhamnous has been published by Pouilloux, *Rhamnonte* 145–47, who dates it to shortly after 229. Though very worn, it reveals lettering similar to *IG* II² 1311, another fragment from Rhamnous which is also quite worn. In particular, both preserve an omega which is rather small, occurs in the upper part of the letter-space, and has v-shaped finials. It is very probable that these two texts are by the same local cutter. See also EM 12694 below.

The proposer of this decree, Theotimos son of Theodoros of Rhamnous, is well known: he was an ephebe in 246/5, the archonship of Polyeuktos (*IG* II² 681, where his name, as Habicht points out to me, is to be restored in line 23 II), a general in 215/4 (Pouilloux, *Rhamnonte* 209); he was also praised at Rhamnous in ca. 205 for, among other things, serving as general ἐπὶ τὴν χώραν τὴν παραλίαν multiple times (*Praktika* 1979 24–25), and served as a member of the boule in the decade 200–190 (line 56 of Agora I 432 and 2965, *q.v.*).[2]

1335 lines 25–65　　　　　　　　　　　　　　　　　　　　unique
　　Archon Medeios (101/0). List of *sebaziastai*.

1337　　　　　　　　　　　　　　　　　　　　　　　　　unfamiliar
　　Archon Herakleitos (97/6). Decree of Orgeones.

1711　　　　　　　　　　　　　　unfamiliar/school of *FD* III 2 no. 24
　　The lettering of this catalog of officials varies considerably in height and in horizontal spacing. It dates to around 130 or later.

1712　　　　　　　　　　　　　　　　　　　　　　　　　unfamiliar
　　The lettering of this catalog is large, unadorned, and sloppy. *S.* II *a*.

1714　　　　　　　　　　　　　　　　　　　unique/school of ²1028
　　Dow re-edited this list of archons in *Hesperia* 3 (1934) 144–46 and dated it to 88/7. The marble is dark gray, not white (the photograph in *Hesperia* is misleading as to color). Ch. Habicht, *Chiron* 6 (1976) 127–35, suggests that King Mithridates was eponymous archon in this year. After Sulla's victory, for official purposes the year was considered as without an eponymous archon, thus the office is not listed on this inscription and was never listed. If this attractive suggestion is correct, this text was inscribed after Sulla's victory in 86.

1941　　　　　　　　　　　　　　　　　　　unfamiliar/school of I 6108
　　Catalog of pythaïsts of the year 106/5.

1944 lines 5–9　　　　　　　　　　　　　　　　　　　　unfamiliar
　　Archon Jason after Polykleitos (109/8). List of priests of Asklepios.

1958　　　　　　　　　　　　　　　　　　　unique/school of I 7181
　　Prosopographical considerations appear to place this text honoring the general Ekphantos Thriasios at Eleusis about 210. This same Ekphantos moved a decree (*IG* II² 848 = *Agora* XV no. 129) in the archonship of Archelaos, who should probably be dated with Habicht (*Studien* 176) to 212/1.

---

[2] On him, see also Habicht, *Studien* 82 note 20, 204–5.

## INSCRIPTIONS "NOT ASSIGNED"

2272                                         unfamiliar/school of *FD* III 2 no. 24
   List of names. Ca. a. 125 a.
   The lettering, vertical spacing, and the presence of incised guidelines suggest that this fragment and *IG* II² 2450 belong together. There is no obvious join and no way, seemingly, to establish their exact spatial relationship. For convenience, I present these two fragments one above the other and number the lines of each separately.

*IG* II² 2450

[Δημ]ήτριος [ _ _ _ _ _ _ _ ]
['Α]ρίστων 'Επι[ _ _ _ _ ]
Δωρόθεος Δωρο[θέου _ _ _ _ ]
Σωτέλης Νικοδ[ _ _ _ _ _ _ _ ]
5 Θεμιστοκλῆς Α[ _ _ _ _ _ _ _ ]
['Α]γαθοκλῆς 'Ασωπ[ _ _ _ _ _ _ ]
[Θρα]συκλῆς 'Απολλω[ _ _ _ _ _ ]

*IG* II² 2272

[ _ _ _ _ _ _ _ ]κι . . . ᴗ Ι
[ _ _ ca. 12 _ _ ]ρου Σουνιεύς, γόν[ωι 'Α]-
[ _ _ ca. 12 _ _ ]άνδρου Ἰωνίδης πο[λλωνί](ου)
[ _ _ ca. 12 _ _ ]ος 'Αλωπεκῆθεν
5 [ _ ca. 9 _ ]τρίδου Παλληνεύς
   [ _ ca. 9 _ ]ναίου 'Αλαιεύς
   ['Αγήνωρ 'Απο]λλωνίου 'Ερικεεύς
   [ _ ca. 9 _ ]ρος 'Αρτεμιδώρου Σουνιεύς
   [ _ ca. 10 _ ]νος Κολωνῆθεν                    18 Χαρίτω[ν]
10 [ _ ca. 10 _ ] Φρυνίσκου Σφήττιος                 'Ολυμπι[οδώ]-
    [ 'Εχεσθένης 'Εχ]εσθένου Κειριάδης          20 ρου
    [ _ ca. 11 _ ]οκλέους Θορίκιος                  Κοθωκ[ίδης]
    [ _ ca. 11 _ ] Διονυσίου Ἰφιστιάδης
    [ _ ca. 12 _ ]νος Σουνιεύς
15 [ _ _ _ ca. 17 _ _ _ ]ου Βατῆθεν
    [ _ _ _ _ _ _ _ _ _ _ Στ]ειριεύς
    [ _ _ _ _ _ _ _ _ _ _ _ _ _ ]ΤΟΓ

II² 2272 line 2. The letters to the right in this line and the next have been crowded into the margin in slightly smaller lettering by a different, *scil.* later, cutter. The two lines are to be taken together and identify the natural father of the man in line 2. For a parallel, see *FD* III 2 no. 8 line 7.

An Apollonios of Sounion is known as *kosmetes* of ephebes in 128/7 (*Hesperia* 24 [1955] 229 lines 81–82) and also perhaps as treasurer of the prytaneis in 131/0 (*Agora* XV no. 246 lines 23–24, 29–30).

II² 2272 line 7. For the restoration and a discussion of the family, see Clinton, *Sacred Officials* 92 n. 20.

II² 2272 line 8. Artemidoros of Sounion does not seem to be attested elsewhere.

II² 2272 line 10. As Kirchner noted, this man is probably identical with [Kallis]?tratos son of Phrynisskos of Sphettos who appears in a list of important persons around 100 B.C. (*IG* II² 2452 line 8).

II² 2272 line 11. Echesthenes of Keiriadai is known as a councillor in 135/4 (*Agora* XV no. 243 line 69). His brother Kallisthenes is attested in a list of *epimeletai* from Piraeus of about 140 (*IG* II² 1939 line 59). Kallisthenes could also be restored here.

N.B. The estimates of letters lost are based on the restoration of Echesthenes' name. This cutter crowds or spaces out letters as needed, so these estimates are rough at best.

II² 2272 lines 18–21. Olympiodoros son of Chariton, surely this man's son, is known from a text at Delphi as an ephebe in 106/5 (*FD* III 2 no. 25 line 13 III). These lines are crowded into the right margin by the same cutter who made the additions at lines 2 and 3.

2323 lines 144–204 (236–385)  unfamiliar/school of ²913

The numbers in parentheses are Ruck's line numbers (*Victors* 13–15) for this didaskaliai list covering the years 188/7 to 170/69.

2335  unfamiliar

*Epidosis* from Eleusis. *Med. saec.* II *a*.

2354  unfamiliar/school of I 787

Dedication by *eranistai*. *Fin. s.* II *a*.

2359  unfamiliar

List of *thiasotai* (?). *Ca. a.* 100 *a*.
See Peek, *AthMitt* 67 (1942) 29–30, for some new readings.

2445  unfamiliar

Crudely inscribed list of dedicators (?).
Prosopographical arguments fix the date around 140. Clinton, *Sacred Officials* 98 n. 31 suggests a valuable restoration for line 11.

2447  unfamiliar

The writing of this list is cursive and late in appearance. The final line, however, was added by a different cutter whose lettering is very close to the Cutter of I 6006. If it is by him, this text must date to about 150.

**2450**
See 2272, above.

**2451**                                                unfamiliar/school of ²1008
Catalog of names. *Ca. a.* 115 *a.*

**2455**                                                                unfamiliar
This opisthographic text is probably not from Athens but from Kea. The text on the back, published by Mitsos in *ArchEph* 1950–51 45–46, records a grant of citizenship made by the city of Karthaia.

**2458**                                                                unfamiliar
There are at least four different hands, none familiar, on this rather worn list of names. *Ca. a.* 100 *a.*

**2460**                                                                unfamiliar
The lettering of these names on a dedicatory base is well made; the date is probably about 100.

**2801**                                                                unfamiliar
The large lettering of this dedication is quite plain and has affinities with much of the lettering being done in the 180s.

**2864b**                                               unfamiliar/school of I 247
Inscription of *ca. a.* 180 *a.* on an allotment machine (Dow, *Prytaneis* 204–5).

**2864c**                                               unfamiliar/school of ²897
Inscription of *ca. a.* 180 *a.* on an allotment machine (*ibid.* 205).

**2864c′** (pub. in commentary *ad loc.*)     unfamiliar/school of I 247
Inscription of *ca. a.* 180 *a.* on allotment machine (*ibid.* 203–4).

**2865**                                                unfamiliar/school of ²937
Finely lettered small altar of about 150 B.C.

**2871**                                                                unfamiliar
The lettering and prosopography suggest a date after 86 for this dedication.

**2946**                                                                unfamiliar
The *koinon* of the Sidonians honors one of its members. Kirchner dated this text *s.* III/II *a.*, but the Phoenician text gives a date of 96 B.C.

The lettering, neat with small apices, suits this later date, which should be adopted.

2980                                unfamiliar/school of *FD* III 2 no. 5

The hand and prosopographical arguments (*NPA* 79) suggest a date for this dedication in the second half of the second century.

2981 lines 1–9                        unfamiliar/school of $^2$1324

Archon Tychandros (160/59). Dedication by ephebes.

    lines 10–16                                    unfamiliar

Archon De[ _ _ _ _ ]. The lettering indicates a date 130 or later.

2986                                             unfamiliar

Archon Theodotos (95/4). The text of this dedication to the Muses is arranged in three sections, each cut by a different man.

2988                                             unfamiliar

Archon Andronides (105/4?). Dedication to Hermes: the letters EPMEI *ca.* 0.15 m. high appear below line 3. The second epsilon appears under the interspace of pi and epsilon in the line above.

2989                                             unfamiliar

Dedication to Hermes. *S.* II/I *a.*

3216                                 unfamiliar/school of I 6108

Citation. *Ca. a.* 100 *a.*

3866                                             unfamiliar

Archon Philon (180/79). Commemorative column.

3879                                             unfamiliar

Fragment of a base. *Ca. a.* 100 *a.*

4033                                             unfamiliar

Honorary base. *Ca. a.* 100 *a.*

4276                                             unfamiliar

Artist's signature. Perhaps before 229.

4280                                             unfamiliar

Artist's signature. *Ca. a.* 200 *a.*

4286                                 unfamiliar/school of $^2$3479

Artist's signature. First half of second century.

4461                                 unfamiliar/school of $^2$1011

Dedication to Asklepios. *Ca. a.* 100 *a.*

## INSCRIPTIONS "NOT ASSIGNED"

4462     unfamiliar
     Poem accompanying dedication to Asklepios. *Ca. a.* 100 *a.*

4688     unfamiliar
     The lettering of this dedication to Artemis varies greatly in size. *S.* II *a.*

4693     unfamiliar
     Dedication to Dionysos of about 100.

4694     unfamiliar
     Dedication to Dionysos. *Ca. a.* 100 *a.*

4696     unique
     Dedication to Artemis of about 100.

4697     unfamiliar
     Dedication to Isis of about 100.

4698     unfamiliar
     Dedication, perhaps after 86.

4702     unfamiliar
     Dedication to Isis. *Ca. a.* 100 *a.*

## Agora I

73 H3 (1934) 28–29; 13 (1944) 266     worn/school of ²903
     Archon [Era]stos (163/2). Honorary decree for a *taxiarch*.

78 *Agora* XV no. 249     unique
     Archon Jas[on] (125/4).

113 H6 (1937) 460     unique
     This list of officials dates to about 150 B.C.

147 H15 (1946) 221     unique
     The lettering of this dedication is small and crude, almost amateurish; it has been dated to *ca.* 200 B.C. but could come from almost any period.

164 H5 (1936) 429     worn/school of I 247
     Archon Eunikos (169/8). Honorary decree.

176 H3 (1934) 68 = ²2980*a*     unfamiliar/school of ²1326
     This text records a dedication to Hermes made by ephebes; the lettering suggests a date in the first half of the second century.

243 *Agora* XV no. 155     unfamiliar
     The lettering of this prytany decree is quite worn. The letter-shapes,

particularly sigma and omega, seem to suggest a date in the second half of the second century. Meritt and Traill, however, date this fragment to *paullo post a. 200 a.*; they may well be correct.

260 H3 (1934) 11                                                          few/school of ²913
   Archon Euandr[os] (*ca. a.* 200 *a.*).³ Only the first few letters of the first line survive.

319 H3 (1934) 11                                                        unfamiliar/school of ²897
   This fragment is probably part of a decree dating to the first half of the second century.

456 H3 (1934) 37–38                                                                    unfamiliar
   Decree of a religious organization perhaps after 86 B.C.

560 H36 (1967) 65–66                                                                   unfamiliar
   Archon [Hipparchos] (119/8). Ephebic inscription.
   Agora I 6127 (H30 [1961] 224) forms part of this inscription (*Hesperia* 57 [1988] 249–50).

629 *Agora* XV no. 258                                                                 unfamiliar
   This prytany inscription appears to date to *ca. a.* 100 *a.*

706 *Agora* XV no. 226                                               unique/school of ²897
   A date around 150 B.C. or a bit earlier seems appropriate for this prytany inscription.

721 H15 (1946) 197                                                                     unfamiliar
   The letter-shapes of this text suggest a date around 100 B.C. Line 2 reads Ξενόφιλο[ς .3½. ]ξένου Οἰναῖος. To the right of lines 1–2 are two more lines of text unreported by Meritt.

$$\text{Ἑρμόδω[ρος}\ \_\_\_\ ]$$
$$\text{Αἰγιλ[ιεύς]}$$

This may be part of a dedication made by ephebes; it cannot, I think, be part of a roster from an ephebic stele.

746 H15 (1946) 222–24                                                                      unique
   Citations from a victor monument. Perhaps after 86 B.C.

813 *Agora* XV no. 239                                           unique/school of *FD* III 2 no. 24
   This prytany text appears to belong to the archonship of [Metrophanes] (145/4).

---

³On the date, see Ch. Habicht, *Studien* 159–60, 177.

933 H7 (1938) 126                                                unfamiliar
This decree recording the sale of confiscated properties has plain letters of a type characteristic of the mid-third century B.C.

1028 H36 (1967) 64                                               unfamiliar
I suspect that this fragment of an ephebe roster should be assigned to the mid-third century B.C. The lettering has some affinities in shape to that of the Cutter of *IG* II² 788.[4]

1220 *Agora* XV no. 152                                          unfamiliar
Saec. III/II a.

1250 H7 (1938) 127                              unique/school of ²1028
Decree concerning weights and measures. *Ca. a.* 120 a.

1299 H16 (1947) 160                        unfamiliar/school of ²897
This fragment of an honorary decree probably dates to the first half of the second century.

1460 H9 (1940) 355                                                   unique
This short dedicatory inscription dates to the archonship of Hippias (181/0). The writing is well made with small serifs. Alpha has a broken crossbar.

1466 H7 (1938) 468 = ²13124                                          unique
This sepulchral epigram is doubtless, like most grave markers, a private monument. The lettering is spidery, with very idiosyncratic shapes.

1559 H16 (1947) 160                                                  unique
Archon Theophilos (227/6). The lettering of this dedicatory inscription is quite crude. This is probably a private dedication by a group of councillors.

1921 H10 (1941) 62                                                   unique
Archon Dionysios. There are four men named Dionysios attested as archon in the second half of the second century alone, *viz.* in 141/0, 135/4, 128/7, and 112/1. The last three are usually characterized as "Dionysios after So and so," hence this is probably the archon of 141/0. The lettering of this text, a private dedication by *mellepheboi*, is crudely made with prominent straight-line serifs.

2165 H37 (1968) 273                          unfamiliar/school of ²783
This fragment honors a man who held office during the archonship of Epikrates (146/5).

---

[4] See *Hesperia* 57 (1988) 311–22.

2373 H29 (1960) 12                        unfamiliar/school of $^2$1318
    Fragment of an honorary decree. Perhaps before 229.

2453 H37 (1968) 273–74                    unique/school of $^2$1028
    The serifed letters of this honorary decree suggest a date around 120 B.C.

2701 H8 (1939) 44                                          unfamiliar
    The *stoichedon* pattern and liberal spacing suggest a date well before 229 for this fragmentary decree.

3804*b* H16 (1947) 191                                unique
    Archon Alexandros (174/3). Preamble of a decree.

3989 *Agora* XV no. 234                            unfamiliar
    This small fragment of a prytany inscription should probably be dated after 150 B.C.

4018 H23 (1954) 240                        unfamiliar/school of $^2$1318
    Fragment probably honoring ephebic instructors. *Ca.* 200 B.C.

4143 H29 (1960) 21                        unfamiliar/school of $^2$1028
    Decree of Orgeones of Bendis. *Ca. a.* 100 *a.*

4187 *Agora* XV no. 182                  unfamiliar/school of $^2$897
    Prytany decree of *ca. a.* 160 *a.*

4343 H29 (1960) 55                        unfamiliar/school of I 6006
    Dedication *post a.* 200 *a.*

4363 H52 (1983) 155                                    unfamiliar
    This is a dedication with relatively large letters (*ca.* 0.013 m.) which dates to *ca. a.* 115 *a.*

4377 H29 (1960) 20                                     unfamiliar
    This is an honorary decree; the letters have an occasional serif. The date *saec.* II *a.* is safe but it might be earlier.

4441 H26 (1957) 212                                      unique
    This is a dedication which names some generals. The lettering is very idiosyncratic and quite sloppy; the letters vary in size greatly. Carelessly incised guidelines occur which are neither parallel nor straight. Meritt cites as parallels the guidelines on *IG* II$^2$ 945, Agora I 6367 (H26 [1957] 47–51), and I 838 (*Agora* XV no. 209). But these guidelines are all carefully drawn and not persuasive parallels. Everything about this text suggests that it is a good deal later than 172/1. In fact Meritt's reading of the archon in line 5 as Σωσιγ[ε]- seems incorrect.

Σωσι is clear. Iota is dotted because only the lower half is visible. Only the top of the letter-space following it is preserved. One can make out the guidelines clearly at the top of this space (they are doubly incised, overstruck as it were) and also just the tip of a vertical stroke. If the letter were gamma, the horizontal too should be easily visible. The archon is probably Σωσικ[ρά]∥[τους] of 111/0. This cutter makes kappa and rho very thin so that there is just room for the proposed restoration.

4608 Osborne, *Naturalization* no. D94  worn/school of ²783
   Osborne's date, 225–202, for this decree seems a good one.

4609 Peçirka, *Enktesis* 133–34  unfamiliar
   This text, an honorary decree, is quite worn. The letters have small serifs. *Ca. a.* 130 *a.*

4791 H30 (1961) 269  unfamiliar/school of ²1009
   Small dedicatory base. *Ca. a.* 100 *a.*

4803 *Agora* XV no. 157  unique
   The letters of this decree are very neat despite being overstruck. It may well predate 229.

4991 *SEG* 17 no. 36  unfamiliar
   Archon Euandros (212/1 or *ca.* 200).⁵ This is perhaps a decree of orgeones; the lettering is quite large and worn.

5131 H30 (1961) 16  unique
   Reinmuth dated this ephebic text to *ca. a.* 184–171 *a.* The hand is very distinctive with serifs regularly employed, even on all three points of delta. This lettering cannot date much before 130 and it may well belong to after 86. I have as yet found no other examples of the writing.

5165 H11 (1942) 265  unique/school of I 247
   Deme decree in honor of a priestess. *Ca. a.* 180 *a.*

5400 H9 (1940) 355  unique/school of ²1324
   This fragment of a preamble of a decree apparently belongs to the archonship of Hippias (181/0). The shape of sigma (*viz.* compressed and with parallel top and bottom strokes) would otherwise suggest a date after 150 B.C.

5412 H30 (1961) 21  unfamiliar/school of ²1028
   Dedication to Hermes. *Ca. a.* 130 *a.*

---

⁵On this latter date, see Habicht, *Studien* 159–60 and 176.

5486 H26 (1957) 265–66            unfamiliar/school of *FD* III 2 no. 26
   This artist's signature appears to be properly dated as *fin. saec.* II *a.*

5887 H30 (1961) 227            unfamiliar/school of ²788
   This is a decree of an association from the year of Theophilos (227/6).

6020 *Agora* XV no. 118            unfamiliar
   The *stoichedon* order of this prytany text suggests a date before 229.

6155 H33 (1964) 193            unfamiliar
   Archon [D]iotimos (126/5). Only a few letters from the opening survive; they resemble in a general way the lettering of the Cutter of *IG* II² 1009 but I do not think they are his work.

6178 *Agora* XV no. 233            unfamiliar
   This fragment of a prytany text is quite worn and has relatively few letters well-preserved. The date, *med. saec.* II *a.*, seems a good one.

6253 H30 (1961) 268–69            unfamiliar
   The lettering on this small dedicatory base is crudely made. A date around 100 B.C. seems probable.
   Meritt read the first letter preserved in line 2, the final letter of the archon's name in the genitive, as sigma. The reading is incorrect. Before alpha there is a single stroke slanting down from left to right and no other stroke. This stroke runs exactly parallel to the right slanting stroke of alpha and seems to be a mis-stroke, i.e. part of an alpha which the cutter began before realizing that he wanted to leave a space between the archon's name and his title so as to fill the line more completely. In the letter-space before this mis-stroke appears a slanting stroke with serif; this is almost certainly upsilon, since this cutter makes sigma with virtually parallel top and bottom strokes.
   Line 2 should thus read

$$[\underline{\phantom{ca.6}}^{ca.\,6}\underline{\phantom{ca.6}}]\nu ~^{v} ~ ἄρχοντος ~^{v}$$

6299 *Agora* XV no. 236            unique
   This prytany decree seems correctly dated to *ca. a.* 150 *a.*

6372 Osborne, *Naturalization* no. D111            unfamiliar
   This citizenship decree does seem to belong to the first half of the second century B.C.

6413 H30 (1961) 251            unfamiliar
   This is probably a dedicatory plaque offered by ephebes; it could date almost anytime 150 B.C. or afterward.

6529 H32 (1963) 20–21            unfamiliar
   Fragment of an honorary decree. *Ante med. s.* II.

## INSCRIPTIONS "NOT ASSIGNED"

6575 H32 (1963) 42                                        unfamiliar

Part of a list of names—it may well date to after 86.

Meritt suggested that this might be part of an ephebe register. This seems unlikely, for such registers in this period (130–90) are usually quite crowded. The letters here are relatively large and well spaced. In addition, the stone is preserved to the left 0.054 m. and it is blank.

6595 H32 (1963) 46                                        unfamiliar

This votive base, a private dedication by *eranistai*, has large, very crudely inscribed letters. Sigma and epsilon are overstruck repeatedly as though by someone not accustomed to inscribing letters. The date, *init. saec.* II *a.*, is probably correct.

6906 H32 (1963) 43                                        unfamiliar

This fragment of a victor list has relatively large letters with intermittent use of serifs. A second century date is most probable.

6909 H32 (1963) 42–43                                  unfamiliar

This is a private dedication to Demeter and Kore. *Saec.* II/I *a.* is an appropriate date.

6934 H32 (1963) 42                   unfamiliar/school of I 656 + 6355

Archon Sosias (?).[6] Monument of uncertain nature belonging to the first half of the second century.

6965 *Agora* XV no. 244                      unique/school of I 6006

This is a prytany decree of 135/4.

6995 H36 (1967) 65                      unfamiliar/school of ²1009

Part of an honorary decree. *Fin. s.* II *a.* would appear to be a more likely date than *ante med. saec.* II *a.*

7030 H37 (1968) 73–76                                    unfamiliar

Archon Archelaos (212/1).[7]

This text set up by the *Metronomoi* has surprisingly uneven lettering. The shapes and size of the letters vary; serifs are used occasionally.

7042 *Agora* XV no. 130                      unique/school of I 787

This is a prytany decree dating to the archonship of Menekrates (220/19).

7111 H47 (1978) 284–85                                        unique

This is a list of names perhaps from a prytany inscription. It appears to date to the second half of the second century.

---

[6] Habicht, *Studien* 173 and 177, places him around 200 B.C.
[7] On the date, *ibid.* 176.

7345 H47 (1978) 285–86 unfamiliar
   Fragmentary citations from a prytany decree. *Saec.* II *a.*

## *Agora* XV

no. 251 unfamiliar/school of I 286
   Archon [Nikias] (124/3).

## *Deltion*

24B (1969) 89–90 H40 (1971) 109–10 unfamiliar
   Archon Hoplon (217/6 or 223/2).[8] This boundary stone from Sounion is almost certainly by a local cutter.

## EM

4694 H51 (1982) 203–4 unfamiliar
   The editor of the *editio princeps* dated this prytany text to the first half of the second century based on the lettering. The shapes, particularly the omega with a closed bottom, and the small and erratic interlines suggest a much later date, at least to my eye, say 120 B.C. or later.

12694 Pouilloux, *Rhamnonte* 134–35 unfamiliar
   Decree of the *paroikoi* at Rhamnous. *Ca. a.* 220 *a.*
   The lettering of this decree is very similar, probably identical with that of *IG* II² 1311 and 1322.[9]

13099 *ArchEph* 1953–54.1 130–36 unfamiliar
   = Pouilloux, *Rhamnonte* 134, 208
   Archon Niketes (225/4). Deme decree from Rhamnous.

13100 *ArchEph* 1953–54.1 126–29 unfamiliar
   = Pouilloux, *Rhamnonte* 135, 209
   Archon Diokles (215/4). Decree of the *paroikoi* at Rhamnous. Pouilloux gives the EM no., apparently incorrectly, as 13101.

13101 *ArchEph* 1953–54.1 122–25 unfamiliar
   = Pouilloux, *Rhamnonte* 129, 207

---

[8] S.B. Aleshire, "The Athenian Archon Hoplon," *Hesperia* 57 (1988) 253–55, argues for the earlier date.

[9] The decrees of Rhamnous have been available to me for the most part only in the published photographs, many of which are not very helpful for a detailed study of letterforms. A number of these inscriptions reveal, apparently, the same writing and are probably the work of one or more local cutters. They will repay study.

Garrison decree from Rhamnous. *Fin. s.* III *a*. Pouilloux gives (incorrectly?) the EM no. as 13102.

## *FD* III 2

No. 12 *BCH* 99 (1975) 190–91 fig. 13                             unique
    Archon Diony[sios after Lykiskos] 128/7. List of child pythaïsts.

## *Kerameikos* III

A2                                             unfamiliar/school of ²1131
    Honorary decree of a deme or tribe of the first half of the second century.

A3 H47 (1978) 286                                   unfamiliar
    Archon [Hi]pparchos (119/8). Prytany decree.

A7                                             unfamiliar/school of ²1028
    Decree of the *technitai*. *Ca. a.* 100 *a*.

## *Praktika*

1958 29–30 pl. 27                                     unfamiliar
    This is a decree of the *paroikoi* from Rhamnous; it appears to date to the first half of the second century.

# APPENDIX A

# *Inscriptions Erroneously Attributed to 229 to 86 B.C.*

**IG II²**

| | |
|---|---|
| 732 | Despite Peçirka (p. 104) this seems to date to before 229. |
| 806 | Osborne, *Naturalization* page 119 dates this to *ca.* 303/2. |
| 810 | Wilhelm in Peçirka (p. 114) dates this to before 230. |
| 845 | By the Cutter of *IG* II² 788 (*ca.* 250–235/4).[1] |
| 857 | By the Cutter of *IG* II² 788 (*ca.* 250–235/4). |
| 860 | By the Cutter of I 3238 (286/5–245/4). |
| 879 | By the Cutter of *IG* II² 788 (*ca.* 250–235/4). |
| 883 | Part of *IG* II² 43. |
| 928 | In the style of the II² 788 Cutter (*ca.* 250–235/4). |
| 1025 | Part of II² 1040; dated to 46/5. See *Hesperia* 34 (1965) 255–72 and *BCH* 90 (1966) 93–100. |
| 1035 | Dated to *ca.* 10 B.C. by G. R. Culley in *Hesperia* 44 (1975) 217–23; to 74/3–65/4 by von Freeden, *Oikia Kyrrestou: Studien zum Sogennanten Turm der Winde* (Rome 1983) 174. |
| 1058 | Part of II² 1051 of *post a.* 38 *a.* (*Hesperia* 36 [1967] 66–68). |
| 1059 = 1758 | Meritt and Traill, *Agora* XV no. 284 date this *ca. a.* 40–30 a. |
| 1273 | A. Oikonomides (*ZPE* 32 [1978] 85–86) restores Euxeinos as archon in line 1 and dates this text to 222/1. The restoration appears arbitrary; this inscription is best associated with one of the three archons named Nikias who are attested in the first half of the third century B.C. |
| 1304b | The archon Philinos is now dated by Meritt (*Historia* 26 [1977] 175) to 254/3 and somewhat earlier by Habicht (*Untersuchungen zur politischen Geschichte Athens im 3. Jahrhundert v. Chr.* [Munich 1979] 126–28). |
| 1316, 1317 | The archon Lysitheides is now dated to 272/1 (Meritt 173). |
| 1334 | The archon Zenion is now dated to 71/0 (*ibid.* 189). |
| 1705 | By the Cutter of II² 788 (*ca.* 250–235/4). |

---

[1] See the present writer's study of this cutter in *Hesperia* 57 (1988) 311–22.

APPENDIX A

| | |
|---|---|
| 1754 | Meritt and Traill, *Agora* XV no. 272, date this text to *ca. a.* 50 *a*. |
| 1755 | Meritt and Traill (*ibid.* no. 275) date this to *med. saec.* I *a*. |
| 2449 | After 86—S. Dow, "*Catalogi Generis Incerti*," *Ancient World* 8 (1983) 105, associates this with *IG* II² 2471a-d. |

**Agora I**

| | |
|---|---|
| 131 | H3 (1934) 60. By the Cutter of II² 788 (*ca.* 250–235/4). |
| 191 | H3 (1934) 69 = *IG* II² 2991*a*. The archon Philemon is now dated to 68/7 (Meritt, *Historia* 26 [1977] 189). |
| 2175 | H15 (1946) 226–28, but now dated after Sulla; see H33 (1964) 197. |
| 5882 | *Agora* XV no. 131. In the style of II² 788 Cutter (*ca.* 250–235/4). |

**EM**

| | |
|---|---|
| 12968 | This text was dated by Kent to *ca.* 190 in the *editio princeps* (*Hesperia* 10 [1941] 342–50). Pouilloux, *Rhamnonte* 135–37 dates it to about 236. |

# APPENDIX B

## *Inscriptions Redated*

(For each, see the List of Inscriptions Studied for page reference. I list here inscriptions which have been misdated by a generation or more and those which were dated correctly but too generally.)

| Number | Former date | New date |
|---|---|---|
| IG II² 443 | post a. 336/5 | ca. 225 |
| IG II² 701 | post a. 272 | ca. 205 |
| IG II² 702 | ante med. s. III | ca. 190 |
| IG II² 735 | ante med. s. III | ca. 225 |
| IG II² 736 | ante med. s. III | ca. 150 |
| IG II² 789 | med. s. III | ca. 190 |
| IG II² 807 | med. s. III | ca. 215 |
| IG II² 814 | med. s. III | ca. 170 |
| IG II² 822 | med. s. III | ca. 190 |
| IG II² 842 | med. s. II | 224/3 |
| IG II² 851 | (?) ca. 224 | ca. 190 |
| IG II² 854 | ca. 224–202 | ca. 190 |
| IG II² 856 | ca. 202/1 | ca. 185 |
| IG II² 867 | fin. s. III (?) | ca. 170 |
| IG II² 868 | fin. s. III ? | ca. 150 |
| IG II² 871 | fin. s. III (?) | ca. 215 |
| IG II² 877 | fin. s. III (?) | ca. 215 |
| IG II² 926 | c. init. s. II ? | ca. 150 |
| IG II² 927 | c. init. s. II | ca. 215 |
| IG II² 930 | c. init. s. II | ca. 150 |
| IG II² 937 | ca. a. 170 a. | ca. 135 |
| IG II² 946 | a. 166/5 | ca. 190 |
| IG II² 947 | ca. a. 166/5 a. | ca. 190 |
| IG II² 948 | ca. a. 166/5 a. | ca. 190 |
| IG II² 959 | c. a. 150 aut paullo post | 109/8 |
| IG II² 975 | saec. II a. | ca. 110 |
| IG II² 990 | med. s. II | ca. 170 |

## APPENDIX B

| Number | Former date | New date |
|---|---|---|
| IG II² 992 | s. II | ca. 170 |
| IG II² 994 | med. s. II | 224–200 |
| IG II² 995 | med. s. II | ca. 100 |
| IG II² 997 | med. s. II | ca. 170 |
| IG II² 998 | med. s. II | ca. 170 |
| IG II² 1024 | fin. s. II | ca. 205 |
| IG II² 1030 | post a. 94/3 | ca. 105 |
| IG II² 1037 | init. s. I | ca. 150 |
| IG II² 1045 | ante med. s. I | ca. 150 |
| IG II² 1131 | med. s. II | ca. 200 (?) |
| IG II² 1171 | s. II | ca. 125 |
| IG II² 1220 | c. 200–150 | ca. 205 |
| IG II² 1235 | ca. a. 274/3 | ca. 215 |
| IG II² 1236 | ante med. s. II | ca. 180 |
| IG II² 1243 | med. s. III | ca. 190 |
| IG II² 1281 | c. a. 266 | ca. 215 |
| IG II² 1296 | post med. s. III | ca. 190 |
| IG II² 1305 | fin. s. III ? | ca. 215 |
| IG II² 1306 | fin. s. III ? | ca. 215 |
| IG II² 1319 | fin. s. III ? | ca. 215 |
| IG II² 1341 | med. s. I | ca. 115 |
| IG II² 1536 | c. med. s. III | ca. 170 |
| IG II² 1552a | fere s. II a. | ca. 100 |
| IG II² 1934 | fin. s. IV a. | 170–150 |
| IG II² 1939 | a. 130–120 | ca. 150 |
| IG II² 1940 | a. 130–120 | ca. 150 |
| IG II² 2330 | fin. s. IV a. | ca. 150 |
| IG II² 2333a | ca. a. 180 a. | ca. 210 |
| IG II² 2353 | med. s. III a. | ca. 215 |
| IG II² 2357 | init. s. II a. | ca. 170 |
| IG II² 2404 | post med. s. IV a. | ca. 170 |
| IG II² 2435 | med. s. III a. | ca. 150 |
| IG II² 2436 | med. s. III a. | ca. 150 |
| IG II² 2440 | fin. saec. III a. | ca. 155 |
| IG II² 2448 | s. II a. | ca. 105 |
| IG II² 2452 | ca. a. 125 sqq. | ca. 105–95 |
| IG II² 2858 | fin. s. III a. | ca. 185 |
| IG II² 2944 | s. III a. | ca. 140 |
| IG II² 2993a | a. 50/49 | ca. 130 |
| IG II² 3058 | s. IV a. | ca. 175/4 |
| IG II² 3148 | s. II a. | ca. 170 |

## INSCRIPTIONS REDATED

| Number | Former date | New date |
|---|---|---|
| *IG* II² 3211 | s. III a. | ca. 190 |
| *IG* II² 3463 | s. III a. | ca. 150 |
| *IG* II² 3473 | med. s. II a. | ca. 210 |
| *IG* II² 3474 | s. II a. | ca. 125 |
| *IG* II² 3477 | post med. s. II a. | paullo post 138/7 |
| *IG* II² 3479 | 184/3 | ca. 155 |
| *IG* II² 3482 | s. II a. | ca. 155 |
| *IG* II² 3784 | init. s. I a. | ca. 130 |
| *IG* II² 3857 | post med. s. III | ca. 215 |
| *IG* II² 3874 | s. II a. | ca. 170 |
| *IG* II² 4459 | s. II a. | ca. 190 |
| *IG* II² 8494 | init. s. III a. | ca. 150 |
| *IG* XII.v 596B | undated | ca. 150 |
| *IG* XII.v 600 | undated | ca. 150 |
| *IG* XII.v 647 | init. s. III a. | 225–200 |
| Agora I 165 | a. 166/5 a. | ca. 190 |
| Agora I 178 | ca. a. 140 a. | ca. 205 |
| Agora I 388 + 719 | saec. IV a. | ca. 155 |
| Agora I 632 | a. 188/7 a. | ca. 210 |
| Agora I 642 | ca. a. 180 a. | ca. 210 |
| Agora I 684 | 190/89 | ca. 170 |
| Agora I 907 | saec. III/II a. | ca. 150 |
| Agora I 999 | med. saec. III a. | ca. 190 |
| Agora I 1013 | saec. II a. | ca. 205 |
| Agora I 1033 | second century B.C. | ca. 190 |
| Agora I 1312 | saec. II a. | ca. 150 |
| Agora I 1331 | ca. 158 B.C. | ca. 205 |
| Agora I 1680 | init. saec. II a. | ca. 150 |
| Agora I 1712 | paullo ante a. 178/7 a. | ca. 205 |
| Agora I 1813 | paullo ante a. 178/7 a. | ca. 205 |
| Agora I 1966 | ca. 225 B.C. (?) | ca. 190 |
| Agora I 2184 | ca. a. 225 a. | ca. 170 |
| Agora I 2264 | ca. a. 250 a. | ca. 150 |
| Agora I 2497 | post med. saec. II a. | ca. 200 (?) |
| Agora I 2943 | ca. a. 178/7 a. | ca. 150 |
| Agora I 2967 | post a. 225 a. | ca. 170 |
| Agora I 3028 | saec. II a. (?) | ca. 185 |
| Agora I 3142 | saec. III a. | ca. 190 |
| Agora I 3668 | saec. II/I a. | ca. 130 |
| Agora I 3675 | saec. III a. | ca. 190 |
| Agora I 3755 | fin. saec. III a. | ca. 165 |

## APPENDIX B

| Number | Former date | New date |
|---|---|---|
| Agora I 3777 | *saec.* II *a.* | *ca.* 170 |
| Agora I 3785 | *ante med. saec.* II *a.* | *ca.* 185 |
| Agora I 3939 | *a.* 150–100 *a.* | *ca.* 125 |
| Agora I 4246 | *ca.* 180 B.C. | *ca.* 155 |
| Agora I 4343 | *paullo ante a.* 200 *a.* | *post a.* 200 *a.* |
| Agora I 4605 | *ca. a.* 267/6 *a.* | *ca.* 210 |
| Agora I 4673 | *fin. saec.* III *a.* | *ca.* 185 |
| Agora I 4811 | *init. saec.* I *a.* | *ca.* 130 |
| Agora I 4875 | *init. saec.* II *a.* | *ca.* 100 |
| Agora I 4908 | *ca. a.* 200 *a.* | *ca.* 125 |
| Agora I 4917 | *a.* 190/89 *a.* | *ca.* 170 |
| Agora I 5016 | *ca. a.* 180 *a.* | *ca.* 215 |
| Agora I 5238 | *saec.* II/I *a.* | *ca.* 125 |
| Agora I 5414 | *ca. a.* 225 *a.* | *ca.* 150 |
| Agora I 5427 | *init. saec.* II *a.* | *ca.* 150 |
| Agora I 5912 | *ca. a.* 200 *a.* | *ca.* 170 |
| Agora I 5988 | *ca.* 200 B.C. (?) | *ca.* 150 |
| Agora I 5993 | *a.* 188/7 *a.* | *ca.* 210 |
| Agora I 6004 | *fin. saec.* II *a.* | *ca.* 150 |
| Agora I 6005 | *ante med. s.* III *a.* | 140/39 |
| Agora I 6035 | *ca.* 232 B.C. | 162/1 |
| Agora I 6053 | *a.* 95/4 *a.* | 143/2 |
| Agora I 6081 | *a.* 198/7 *a.* | *ca.* 170 |
| Agora I 6086 | *ca. a.* 95/4 *a.* | *ca.* 120 |
| Agora I 6097 + 6099 | *ca. a.* 130 *a.* | *ca.* 200 (?) |
| Agora I 6103 | *init. saec.* II *a.* | *ca.* 170 |
| Agora I 6190 | *init. s.* II *a.* | *ca.* 170 |
| Agora I 6234 | *saec.* II *a.* | *ca.* 200 |
| Agora I 6244 | *ca. med. saec.* II *a.* | *ca.* 185 |
| Agora I 6257 | *ca. med. saec.* II *a.* | *ca.* 170 |
| Agora I 6258 | *ca. a.* 250 *a.* | *ca.* 215 |
| Agora I 6461 | *ca. a.* 200–150 | *ca.* 215 |
| Agora I 6530 | *ca. a.* 250 *a.* | *ca.* 205 |
| Agora I 6545 | *a.* 224/3–200 *a.* | 162/1 |
| Agora I 6756 | *ca. a.* 230 *a.* | *ca.* 215 |
| Agora I 6819 | *a.* 97/6 *a.* | *ca.* 205 |
| Agora I 6843 | *init. saec.* II *a.* | *ca.* 170 |
| Agora I 7203 | *init. saec.* II *a.* | *ca.* 110 |
| Agora I 7226 | *fin. saec.* III *a.* | *ca.* 185 |
| ArchEph 1896 35 no. 18 | before 229 | *ca.* 170 |

## INSCRIPTIONS REDATED

| Number | Former date | New date |
|---|---|---|
| *ArchEph* 1897 45 no. 14 | second century B.C. | *ca.* 205 |
| *ArchEph* 1971 127–28 | *ca. med. s.* III? | *ca.* 215 |
| *AthMitt* 67 22 no. 25 | 200–150 | *ca.* 215 |
| *Corinth* VIII.1 no. 5 | third or second century | *ca.* 170 |

## APPENDIX C

# Joins and Associations Resulting from the Study of Hands: A Summary List

1. *IG* II$^2$ 760 associated with *IG* II$^2$ 662, H57 (1988) 308
2. Agora I 3370 joined to *IG* II$^2$ 665, H57 (1988) 306–7
3. Agora I 6801 associated with *IG* II$^2$ 665, H57 (1988) 306
4. *IG* II$^2$ 750 associated with *IG* II$^2$ 766, H57 (1988) 318
5. Agora I 3722 joined to *IG* II$^2$ 766, H57 (1988) 319
6. EM 12800 + 2463 joined to *IG* II$^2$ 766, H57 (1988) 318
7. *IG* II$^2$ 749 associated with *IG* II$^2$ 828, H57 (1988) 317
8. Agora I 5871 joined to *IG* II$^2$ 851, H47 (1978) 258
9. Agora I 2861 associated with *IG* II$^2$ 901, above p. 84
10. Agora I 3676 joined to *IG* II$^2$ 916, H39 (1970) 308–9
11. Agora I 4033 joined to *IG* II$^2$ 917, H47 (1978) 251–52
12. Agora I 2155 associated with *IG* II$^2$ 925, above p. 119
13. Unnumbered fragment X joined to *IG* II$^2$ 937, *GRBS* 29 (1988) 383–88
14. Agora I 2105 joined to *IG* II$^2$ 954a, H41 (1972) 46–49
15. EM 5588 + 6062 associated with *IG* II$^2$ 977, above p. 177
16. Agora I 6310 joined to *IG* II$^2$ 1006, H57 (1988) 250–52
17. *IG* II$^2$ 959 joined to *IG* II$^2$ 1014, above p. 183
18. Agora I 5225 associated with *IG* II$^2$ 1023, *Lettering* 77
19. Agora I 717 joined to *IG* II$^2$ 1028, H36 (1967) 244–45
20. Agora I 3810 joined to *IG* II$^2$ 1028, H36 (1967) 245
21. EM 8035 joined to *IG* II$^2$ 1028, *AJA* 75 (1971) 190
22. Fragment x joined to *IG* II$^2$ 1028, *AJA* 75 (1971) 190
23. Fragment y joined to *IG* II$^2$ 1028, *AJA* 75 (1971) 190
24. *IG* II$^2$ 1943 associated with *IG* II$^2$ 1034, above p. 217
25. Agora I 5679 associated with *IG* II$^2$ 1133, H39 (1970) 309–10
26. *ArchEph* 1897 45 no. 14 associated with *IG* II$^2$ 1307, above p. 67
27. Agora I 922 associated with *IG* II$^2$ 1705, H57 (1988) 314–15
28. Agora I 7496 associated with *IG* II$^2$ 1707, H53 (1984) 370–74
29. *IG* II$^2$ 1709, Agora I 1126, and *IG* II$^2$ 2863 joined, H41 (1972) 43–46

30. *IG* II² 2450 associated with *IG* II² 2272, above p. 245
31. Agora I 3318 joined to *IG* II² 2336, H39 (1970) 311
32. Agora I 4037 joined to *IG* II² 2336, H39 (1970) 312
33. Agora I 5045 joined to *IG* II² 2336, H36 (1967) 245–46
34. EM 144 rediscovered/rejoined to *IG* II² 2336, *AJA* 75 (1971) 189
35. Agora I 7361 joined to *IG* II² 2336, H51 (1982) 63–64
36. Agora I 6035 joined to Agora I 175, above p. 128
37. Agora I 6545 associated with Agora I 175, above p. 130
38. Agora I 1029 associated with Agora I 656 + 6355, above p. 86
39. Agora I 7492 joined to Agora I 984, H53 (1984) 374–77
40. Agora I 6459 joined to Agora I 5912, above p. 135
41. Agora I 6005 joined to Agora I 6006, above p. 159
42. Agora I 560 associated with Agora I 6127, H57 (1988) 249–50
43. Agora I 2499 associated with Agora I 6982, H47 (1978) 259–60
44. *IG* II² 944b joined to Agora I 7181, H Suppl. 19 (1982) 157–61
45. Agora I 7478 associated with *Agora* XV no. 248, H51 (1982) 63
46. Delphi inv. no. 4689 joined to *FD* III 2 no. 6, *BCH* 93 (1969) 373
47. Delphi inv. no. 6906 associated with *FD* III 2 no. 4, *BCH* 99 (1975) 196–97
48. Delphi inv. no. 4744 joined to *FD* III 2 no. 31, *Lettering* 54–55
49. Unnumbered Delphi fragment joined to *FD* III 2 no. 48, *BCH* 93 (1969) 387

# APPENDIX D

# A List of State Decrees, or Probable Decrees, Not Assigned

| Inscription | | Date | Inscription | | Date |
|---|---|---|---|---|---|
| IG II² | 837 | 227/6 | | 1018 | 130–50 |
| | 862 | ca. 200 | | 1019 | fin. s. II |
| | 865 | fin. s. III | | 1022 | fin. s. II |
| | 876 | ca. 200 | | 1038 | ca. 130 |
| | 884 | ca. 200 | | 1055 | before 100 |
| | 887 | 135/4 | | 1056/7 | ca. 100 |
| | 889 + 904 | 181/0 | | 1137 | fin. s. II |
| | 893b, c | ca. 200 | | 1714 | after 86 |
| | 922 | 190–165 | EM | 4694 | 120–100 |
| | 945 | 168/7 | Ker. III | A3 | 119/8 |
| | 949 | 165/4 | Agora I | 78 | 125/4 |
| | 950 | 165/4 | | 113 | ca. 150 |
| | 957 | 157/6 | | 243 | 200–100 |
| | 958 | 153/2 | | 260 | ca. 200 |
| | 964 | ca. 150 | | 319 | 200–150 |
| | 971 | 140/39 | | 560 | 119/8 |
| | 973 | 204/3 | | 629 | ca. 100 |
| | 976 | 150–100 | | 706 | ca. 150 |
| | 980 | ca. 150 | | 813 | 145/4 |
| | 982 | ca. 130 | | 933 | ca. 250 |
| | 985 | ca. 130 | | 1028 | ca. 250 |
| | 986 | 130–100 | | 1220 | ca. 200 |
| | 1003 | 125/4 | | 1250 | ca. 120 |
| | 1004 | 122/1 | | 1299 | 200–150 |
| | 1006 | 122/1 | | 2165 | ca. a. 146/5 |

## A LIST OF DECREES NOT ASSIGNED

| Inscription | Date | Inscription | Date |
|---|---|---|---|
| 2373 | paullo ante 229 | 5131 | ca. 110 |
| 2453 | ca. 120 | 5400 | 182/1 |
| 2701 | ca. 250 | 6020 | ante 229 |
| 3804b | 174/3 | 6155 | 126/5 |
| 3989 | 150–100 | 6372 | 200–150 |
| 4018 | 200–150 | 6965 | 135/4 |
| 4187 | ca. 160 | 6995 | fin. s. II |
| 4377 | 200–100 | 7030 | 212/1 |
| 4608 | ca. 215 | 7042 | 220/19 |
| 4609 | ca. 130 | 7111 | 150–100 |
| 4803 | ante 229? | 7345 | 200–100 |

Total: 73, of which 6 predate 229, 22 date 229–160, 1 dates ca. 160, 40 date 160 and after, 3 date 200–100, 1 postdates 86

# *Morphological Index of Characteristic Letters*

It is not possible to index every peculiarity of each cutter. However, I have sought to list here the most idiosyncratic letter-shapes of each so that others dealing with Attic inscriptions from this period can look up peculiar letters to see which of the cutters might be relevant. To make an attribution to a cutter is, it must be stressed, far more complicated than finding a single letter which matches; all the letters and their various peculiarities must match. To establish that this is the case obviously requires considerable study.

*Alpha* (N.B. Cutters usually also make delta and lambda the same way.)
    open at the top, left hasta shorter than right, crossbar slants and bisects right hasta: $^2$1706 Cutter
    thin, open at the top with the left hasta shorter than the right: $^2$913 Cutter
    thin, open at the top: I 6006 Cutter
    open at the top and relatively wide: $^2$912 Cutter
    slanting hastae curve, apex extends up a short distance: $^2$1309 Cutter
    with no crossbar: I 247 Cutter
    wide with a sharply broken crossbar: $^2$1329 Cutter, I 6512 Cutter, I 5469 Cutter, $^2$2983 Cutter, $^2$1034 Cutter
    thin with a sharply broken crossbar: $^2$937 Cutter
    thin and slightly taller with a broken or curved crossbar: $^2$1011 Cutter
    with a sharply broken crossbar: $^2$1009 Cutter, $^2$1135 Cutter, FD III 2 no. 26 Cutter

*Gamma*
    wide: I 7181 Cutter
    the crossbar extends back across the vertical a bit: $^2$937 Cutter

*Delta*
    open at top, horizontal placed up from bottom: $^2$1706 Cutter
    elongated to the left: $^2$1324 Cutter
    elongated to the right: I 286 Cutter

wide, compressed in height: ²1329 Cutter
wide, compressed in height with an extension of the apex: I 1594 Cutter

*Epsilon*
    wide: I 787 Cutter, Register of I 247 Cutter
    with curving top and bottom strokes and a very short central horizontal: ²912 Cutter
    very short central horizontal without a serif: I 7181 Cutter
    with all three horizontals slanting downwards: ²1326 Cutter
    with all three horizontals the same length and tapering to points: ²892 Cutter
    with rather short horizontals which tend to curve: I 286 Cutter
    with rather short horizontals which tend to curve and taper to points: *FD* III 2 no. 5 Cutter
    short central horizontal which does not touch the vertical: ²886 Cutter
    with no central horizontal: I 247 Cutter
    wide with short central horizontal placed closer to the top: ²897 Cutter
    with serifs that extend upwards on all three horizontals: ²1028 Cutter
    with serifs that extend downwards on all three horizontals: ²1034 Cutter

*Zeta*
    short, hangs from top of letter-space: I 787 Cutter, ²886 Cutter
    Z-shaped: I 286 Cutter, ²1009 Cutter, *FD* III 2 no. 26 Cutter

*Iota*
    serifs at both ends: ²1131 Cutter, ²3479 Cutter

*Kappa*
    wide: ²1706 Cutter
    thin with short diagonals which incline sharply: ²783 Cutter
    with short, lightly incised diagonals: I 5469 Cutter
    with a curving upper diagonal: *FD* III 2 no. 5 Cutter

*Lambda*
    thin, open at the apex with the left hasta shorter than the right: ²913 Cutter

*Mu*
    made with the outer strokes vertical and a v which extends down about one third of the way: ²1008 Cutter
    wide, two lambdas placed side-by-side: ²1009 Cutter

*Nu*
    the second vertical does not extend down to the base of the letter: I 7181 Cutter, ²3479 Cutter
    the second vertical extends down slightly more than halfway: ²1309 Cutter
    the initial vertical leans to the right: ²1318 Cutter

*Omikron*
    small, round, sits at or near the bottom of the letter-space: ²1309 Cutter
    small, tends to hang from top of letter-space: I 6765 Cutter, ²1329 Cutter, ²1011 Cutter
    large, incised slightly deeper than other letters: I 656 + 6355 Cutter
    large: ²2983 Cutter
    shaped like an "equals" sign: I 247 Cutter

*Pi*
    initial vertical extends up slightly beyond the crossbar: I 6006 Cutter
    with a serif only on the short right vertical: ²912 Cutter
    short right vertical curving or slanting out from the letter: ²1131 Cutter
    short right vertical perceptibly thickened at end: ²903 Cutter
    with verticals virtually the same length: I 5469 Cutter, ²1011 Cutter

*Rho*
    loop sweeps around back to the vertical in a nice curve: ²913 Cutter
    pennant-shaped: I 247 Cutter, ²1324 Cutter
    loop oblong or roughly pennant-shaped: ²897 Cutter
    with a sagging loop: ²3479 Cutter
    with a large and reasonably round loop: ²783 Cutter

*Sigma*
    with sharply curving top and bottom strokes: ²912 Cutter
    with slightly curved top and bottom strokes: ²892, FD III 2 no. 5 Cutter
    with a curving upper stroke which extends up above the other letters: Register of I 247 Cutter
    varies in size and leans backwards: ²1326 Cutter
    leans back with a short bottom stroke placed far up the slanting stroke to which it is attached: I 6765 Cutter
    leans back with the lower half larger than the upper: I 6006 Cutter
    with parallel top and bottom strokes: FD III 2 no. 24 Cutter, ²937 Cutter
    with parallel top and bottom strokes, top disproportionately large: I 1594 Cutter
    parallel top and bottom strokes with a short horizontal extending the central point: ²1008 Cutter
    with top and bottom strokes virtually horizontal; upper stroke bends downwards: I 6108 Cutter

*Tau*
    wide: I 7181 Cutter, ²1324 Cutter
    short and wide with the crossbar off-center to the left: ²1131 Cutter
    short and wide: FD III 2 no. 24 Cutter
    very wide with a serif at the bottom: I 6512 Cutter

with a short crossbar which is off-center to the right or left: ²886 Cutter
of ordinary size with crossbar off-center to left: ²903 Cutter, I 6006 Cutter

*Upsilon*
  made with three strokes, tall and wide: I 656 + 6355 Cutter, ²892 Cutter, *FD* III 2 no. 24 Cutter
  with an unusually wide and shallow v at the top: Register of I 247 Cutter
  with a short or non-existent vertical: ²1135 Cutter, *FD* III 2 no. 5 Cutter

*Phi*
  central part a straight horizontal topped by an arc: ²1706 Cutter
  central part a wide and compressed oval: ²1318 Cutter
  central part a short straight line with (sometimes) a small curving stroke attached underneath: ²1324 Cutter
  central part two rather flattened ovals: ²3479 Cutter
  central part two small complete circles: ²1028 Cutter, ²1135 Cutter
  vertical extends up into interline with the central part a small circle: I 6765 Cutter

*Omega*
  open with finials slanting upwards: I 787 Cutter
  open with serifed finials slanting downwards: I 6108 Cutter
  open with inverted-v serifs which are sometimes quite large: ²1706 Cutter
  open with small inverted-v serifs: ²783 Cutter
  large, open with straight-line serifs: ²886 Cutter
  large, open with inverted-v serifs turned on their sides: *FD* III 2 no. 26 Cutter
  large and round; horizontal strokes with serifs render it wide: *FD* III 2 no. 24 Cutter, ²1028 Cutter, ²2983 Cutter, ²1034 Cutter
  small, open with straight line or occasionally inverted-v serifs: ²903 Cutter
  horseshoe in shape with a short right side: I 656 + 6355 Cutter, ²1326 Cutter
  horseshoe in shape with a short left side: I 6006 Cutter
  horseshoe-shaped and relatively small: ²897 Cutter, ²892 Cutter

# Index to Greek Texts

*Persons*

['Α]γαθοκλῆς Ἀσωπ[ _ _ _ ], 245
['Αγήνωρ] Ἀπολλωνίου Ἐρικεεύς, 245
Ἀθην[ _ _ _ _ ] of Hippothontis, 219
Αἰν[ _ _ _ _ ] of Aiantis, 219
Ἀλέξα[νδρος], 76
Ἀμμω[νι _ _ _ ] of Hippothontis, 218
Ἀντιχάρης Ἐπιζήλου Ἀγγελῆθεν, 87
['Α]πο[λλώνιος] Σουνιεύς, 245, 246
['Α]ρίστων Ἐπι[ _ _ _ ], 245
Ἁρμόξενος, 178–79
Ἀρτεμίδωρος Σουνιεύς, 245
['Αφθ]όνητος, 153

[Γόργιλος Γοργίλου Ἀγγελῆ]θεν, 178

Δεξίχαρις Φι[ _ _ _ _ ], 184
[Δημ]ήτριος, 245
Δι[ _ _ ca.11 _ _ ]νος Αἰξωνεύς, 85
Διόδω[ρος], 153
Διοκλῆς of Ptolemaiïs, 85
Διον[υσ _ _ _ _ ] of Kekropis, 85
Διονύσιος Ἰφιστιάδης, 245
Διονύσιος [Ἑρ᾿]μίου Λευκ[ον]οεύς, 85
Δωρόθεος Δωρο[θέου], 245
Δωρόθεος Φυλάσ(ιος), 85

Ἐπιφάνης Ἐπιφάνου Λαμπτρεύς, 184
Ἑρμόδω[ρος _ _ _ ] Αἰγιλ[ιεύς], 250
Ἑρμόδωρος Ἀχαρνεύς, 85
Ἐρωτ[ι]ον of Hippothontis, 218
Εὔκο[λ _ _ _ ] of Hippothontis, 218

Εὐκτίμενος Εἰτεαῖος, 159
['Εχ]εσθένης Κειριάδης, 245, 246

Θεμιστοκλῆς Α[----], 245
[Θε]μιστοκλῆς 'Ολ[βίου Κηφισιεύς], 184–85
[Θ]εοφ[ίλη] of Hippothontis, 218
Θησεὺς 'Αρματίδου Τ[ῃι]ος, 51
[Θρα]συκλῆς 'Απολλω[---], 245

Καλλικράτης Στειριεύς, 184–85
Κλέαρ[χο]ς Σ[ωσι]στρά[του] Κ[υ]θήρρ(ιος), 85
Κλεόδωρος 'Αχαρνεύ[ς], 85

Λεον[τι ---] of Hippothontis, 219
Λυσισ[τράτη] of Hippothontis, 218

[Με]νεκράτης, 59

Νικο[----] of Hippothontis, 218
Νικω[----] of Hippothontis, 218

Ξενόφιλο[ς .³½.]ξένου Οἰναῖος, 250
Ξένων of Kekropis, 85
Ξέ[νων] Σφήττιος, 64

'Ονήσανδρος 'Ονήτορος Κυδαθηναιεύς, 87

[Παυσανία]ς Βιοτέλου Περιθοίδης, 87
Περσαῖος Κικυννεύς, 85

[Σαρ]απίων Με[λιτεύς], 218
Σιμάρ[ιστος] of Kekropis, 85
Στρ[ατ---] of Hippothontis, 218
[Στρά?]τιος Φηγαιεύς, 184
Σω[---] of Hippothontis, 218
Σωσ[---] of Hippothontis, 218
Σωσθένης [Σω]σθένου Κ[ρω]πίδης, 85
Σωτέλης Νικοδ[---], 245

Τι[----] of Hippothontis, 219
[Τιμοκλῆς Π]ολυκλέους Θορίκιο[ς], 85

276

Φί[λων?] archon, 76
Φίλων, 59
[Φ]ιλωτ[άδης], 51
Φίλωτας Θριάσιος, 154
Φρυνίσκος Σφήττιος, 245

Χαρίτω[ν] 'Ολυμπι[οδώ]ρου Κοθωκ[ίδης], 245

*Important Words*
ἀγωνο[θέτης], 76
'Απόλλων, 157
ἀρχαί, 153
ἄρχοντες, 154

Διόνυσος, 58

θύματα, 176

κλήρωσις, 153

νόμοι, 64–65

παννυχίς, 104

ταμίαι, 176
ταῦρος, 176

φιάλη, 76

# Index of Passages Cited

*Authors*

    Aelian, *Var. Hist.* 6.2, 51
    Aristotle, *Ath. Pol.* 55, 154

    Herodotos 7.227, 51

    Pausanias 1.2.5, 140
    Plutarch, *Thes.* 36, 185
    Polybios 5.93.8, 53 n. 7

*Inscriptions Mentioned*
*(For inscriptions studied, see pages 7–38.)*

    Agora I 131, 260
        191, 260
        2175, 260
        3625 (H7 [1938] 95), 154
        5882, 260

    *Agora* XV no. 151, 86
        194, 156
        206, 179
        212, 240
        220, 229 n. 11
        225, 86
        240, 159
        243, 155, 179, 246
        246, 226, 246
        261, 179 and n. 2

    *AthMitt* 66 (1941) 218, 142 n. 4

    EM 12968, 260

H6 (1937) 457–61, 214
H24 (1955) 229, 246
H35 (1966) 242–43, 155
H36 (1967) 89, 86
H47 (1978) 277–78, 243

*ID* 1400–1479, 225
    1497–1520, 226
    2589, 155
    2590, 199
    2591, 199
    2593, 199
    2598, 199

*IG* II$^2$ 43, 259
    334, 104
    661, 156
    663, 65
    681, 244
    704, 104
    707, 76
    732, 259
    775, 104
    780, 58
    788, 53
    806, 259
    808, 76
    809, 76
    810, 259
    845, 259
    857, 259
    860, 259
    879, 259
    883, 259
    928, 259
    1025, 259
    1035, 259
    1039, 140
    1051, 259
    1058, 259
    1059, 259
    1138, 86

1163, 154
1199, 104
1273, 259
1285, 160 n. 14
1299, 160 n. 14
1304b, 259
1316, 259
1317, 259
1334, 259
1705, 259
1754, 260
1755, 260
1758, 259
2449, 260
2471, 260
2991a, 260
3510, 142 n. 4
5380, 142 n. 4
6382, 239
7321, 108

*Praktika* 1979 24–25, 244

*REG* 91 (1978) 290–91, 106

*SB Berlin* 1904 917–31, 106

*SEG* 2 (1925) no. 12, 66
    31 (1981) no. 112, 52
    31 (1981) no. 120, 52

*SIG*[3] 976, 106

*Stud. D. Robinson* II (1953) 351 no. 9, 142 n. 4

# Index of Persons

*Eponymous Archons of Athens*
*(Texts in which they are named and, if applicable, pages where they are discussed.)*

Achaios: ²946, ²947, ²948, I 165, I 4241; xv, 57 n. 3
Agathokles ²1011, *FD* III 2 nos. 5, 25, 28
Aischron ²1304, ²1315
Alexandros I 2115, I 3804b, I 6162, I 6589
Alexis: ²996, I 5761, I 6671; 136
Andreas I 6333, Kerameikos I 10
Andronides ²2988
Ankylos: I 2334, I 2498; 53
Anthesterios ²957, ²2323
Antigenes I 166, I 171
Antiphilos ²842, ²1706
Apollodoros ²973
Archelaos: ²848, I 7030; 244
Argeios ²2336, *FD* III 2 nos. 2, 6, 17, 26, 32
Aristaichmos ²1027
Aristolas ²952, ²956, ²2323, I 984

Chairephon ²1706, I 79, I 5458
Charikles: ²785, I 605, I 4966, *BCH* 90 (1966) 727; 142 n. 5

De[___] ²2981
Demetrios (ca. 170): I 684, I 4917, I 6081; xv, 102 n. 4
Demetrios (123/2) I 25
Demochares ²1036
Demostratos ²1132
Diodotos ²2323, I 7181 + ²944b
Diodotos after Phanarchides ²916
Diokles ²846, ²847, ²1539, ²1706, EM 13100
Dionysios (194/3) ²850, ²888
Dionysios (141/0) I 1921

283

Dionysios after Lykiskos *FD* III 2 nos. 3, 8, 12, 24, 34, 35
Dionysios after Paramonos I 6282
Dionysios after Timarchides ²887, I 2145, I 6003
Diotimos I 6155

E[____]: ²2858; 94
Echekrates ²2336
Epikles ²977, ²1227
Epikrates I 2165
Erastos ²783, ²2323, I 73
Ergochares ²838, ²1706, I 918, I 3684
Euandros ²4441, I 260, I 4991
Euergetes ²2323, I 983, I 2539, I 5032, I 6675
Eumachos: ²1018; 242
Eunikos: ²910, ²911, ²2323, ²2944, I 164, I 6140; 94
Euphiletos ²1706, I 6625, I 7484
Eupolemos: ²897, ²898, ²899, ²900, ²1325, I 4003; 94
Euthykritos: ²978, I 1871; 94

Hagnias ²794, ²1706
Hagnotheos ²970, ²971, I 6006
Heliodoros ²832, ²833, ²1706
Herakleides ²989
Herakleitos (213/2) ²1314, ²1706
Herakleitos (137/6) ²974
Herakleitos (97/6) ²1337, ²2336, ²2990
Hermogenes ²1328, ²2323, ²2332, I 6771
Hippakos ²903, ²1326, I 4250, EM 454
Hipparchos I 560, *Kerameikos* III A3
Hippias ²889 + 904, ²920, I 1460, I 5344, I 5400, I 6765, I 7496
Hoplon *Deltion* 24B [1969] 89–90

Jason ²1003, ²1332, I 78
Jason after Polykleitos ²1014, ²1944

Kalli[__]: ²843, ²1303; 80
Kallias ²1033
Kallistratos (208/7): ²849, ²1309; 80
Kallistratos (156/5) ²1937, ²2323

Lenaios ²1008, I 6422
Leochares ²1706, I 787
Lysiades ²1938, I 4389, I 6977

INDEX OF PERSONS

Medeios of Piraeus: ²1028, ²1335, ²2336; 199
Menedemos I 6986
Menekrates ²1302, ²1706, I 4171, I 7042
Menoites I 7156
Metrophanes ²967, I 813
Mnesitheos ²979, ²2323, I 247

Niketes ²1706, EM 13099
Nikias *Agora* XV no. 251
Nikodemos ²1004, ²1006, I 1594
Nikosthenes ²951, I 3054

Pelops ²949, ²950
Phaidrias ²958
Phanarchides ²844, ²864, ²886
Philon ²1327, ²3866
Philon after Menedemos I 1025, I 4933, I 7453
Pleistainos: ²3479, I 4462, I 7188; xv, 141–42
Polyeuktos 244
Poseidonios ²2323, ²2864a, I 175
Prokles ²2336, I 6885
Proxenides ²915

Sarapion ²1009, ²1228
Sonikos ²1329, ²3088, I 656, I 4253
Sosias I 6934
Sosigenes ²2331, I 1938
Sosikrates: ²1135, ²2983, I 6108; 253
Sostratos ²1709, I 6982
Speusippos I 1057
Symmachos: ²891, ²892, ²893a, ²894, ²2323, I 4144; 160

Theaitetos ²968, ²2323
Theodorides I 286
Theodosios ²2336
Theodotos ²2986
Theokles ²1034, ²1335, ²2336
Theophilos ²837, ²1706, I 1559, I 5887
Theoxenos: ²2323, I 2155, Kerameikos I 1; 160
Thrasyphon ²839
Timarchos *AthMitt* 66 (1941) 228, *FD* III 2 nos. 7, 11
Timesianax ²902, ²2323, I 4267, I 4683
Timouchos I 6165

*285*

INDEX OF PERSONS

Tychandros ²953, ²2981

Xenokles ²945, ²2323

Zopyros ²896, ²2323, I 979

[_ _]ippos (199/8) I 1886, I 6100
[_ _]ippos (177/6) I 6166
[_ _]krates ²1029

*Athenians, Except for Eponymous Archons*
    Ammonios, s. of Ammonios, of Anaphlystos, 200
    Amynomachos, s. of Eukles, of Halai, 141
    Apelles of Sounion, 140
    Archo, 108
    Ariarathes of Sypalettos, 139
    Ariarathes, s. of King Ariobarzanes, of Sypalettos, 140
    Ariarathes, s. of Polemaios, of Sypalettos, 140
    Aristion of Semachidai, 240
    Aristokles, s. of Nouphrades, of Perithoidai, 155–56
    Artemon of Piraeus, 135
    Attalos of Sypalettos, 139

    Dionysios, s. of Agathokles, of Marathon, 112
    Dionysodoros, 123
    Dionysogenes, s. of Herakleitos, of Ikarion, 155

    Ekphantos of Thria, 244
    Euboulides III of Kropidai, 140, 190–91
    Eucheir II of Kropidai, 140, 180, 190–91
    Euelpis, 107
    Eukles of Trinemeia, 159
    Eurykleides I of Kephisia, 52, 53, 66, 228

    Habryllis, d. of Mikion IV, of Kephisia, 141, 179–80
    Herakleitos, s. of Dionysogenes, of Ikarion, 155
    Herakleitos, s. of Poseidippos, of Ikarion, 155, 160
    Hierophantes, s. of Nouphrades, of Perithoidai, 155–56

    Kallikratides, s. of Syndromos, of Steiria, 185
    Kallisthenes of Keiriadai, 246
    Kallistratos, s. of Phryniskos, of Sphettos, 246

## INDEX OF PERSONS

Kleon of Kikynna, 159
Ktesias of Thorikos, 43

Lakrates, s. of Mentor, of Perithoidai, 123
Leon, s. of Kichesias, of Aixone, 161
Leonides of Phlya, 142 n. 6

Menogenes, 108
Mikion of Kephisia, 52, 66
Miltiades, s. of Zoilos, of Marathon, 140, 160–61

Nikanor, s. of Menander, of Kedoi, 239

Olympiodoros, s. of Chariton, of Kothokidai, 246

Philiskos, s. of Krates, of Paiania, 159
Philon, 108
Philoxenides, 142 n. 4
Pollis of Sounion, 140

Simaristos of Trinemeia, 86
Sosikrateia, 156
Syndromos of Steiria,. 185

Theoboulos, s. of Theophanes, of Piraeus, 156
Theophilos, companion of Attalos, 140
Theorikos, s. of Syndromos, of Steiria, 185
Theotimos, s. of Theodoros, of Rhamnous, 244
Thymoteles of Paiania, 86

Xenokles, 179

*Kings, Their Retainers, and Others*
    Antiochos III, 120
    Antiochos IV, 135
    Antigonos, 52–53
    Ariobarzanes, 140
    Aristion, s. of Anaxandrides, archon at Delphi, 189
    Arrhidaios, 135
    Attalos I, 227 n. 7, 239
    Attalos II, 139, 140, 141

    Diodoros, friend of Eumenes, 135

**INDEX OF PERSONS**

Eukleides, archon at Delphi, 189
Eumenes, 135, 227 n. 7, 240

Karneades, 139
Kleomachides of Larisa, 168

Mithridates, 226, 244

Prytanis of Karystos, 52–53
Ptolemy IV, 66
Ptolemy V, 66

Seleukos IV, 120, 160
Sulla, 1, 244

Theophilos, companion of Attalos, 140

Xenokrates, archon at Delphi, 183

# General Index

Allotment of offices. *See* Sortition
Apollonia, 199
Artemis Phosphoros, 106
Asklepios, 104, 203
Association of fragments, definition of, 6
Athenian archons, xv, 2; dates, xv; lists, xv–xvi n. 1, 2, 159
Athenian treasury at Delphi, Pythaïs inscriptions on, 172, 183, 214, 220, 221
Athens, and the Seleucids, 120
Attaleia, the, 199
Attica, border forts, 52, 226

Corinth, 108–9
Crete, 91
Cutter of *IG* II² 788, 53, 230–31, 251, 259, 260
Cutters: began work young, 228; careers of, long, 228; in the entourage of kings and nobles, 227 n. 7; individuality of, marked and persistent, 234; local, 81, 228, 234, 256; master and apprentice, 82, 92, 161, 220, 230–32, 234, 237; mode of work, 227–28, 234; most productive, 228–29, 231; number at work in Athens, 227, 230; number of inscriptions cut by, 228–29; puzzling distribution of activity of, 223, 225; skilled artisans, 227; specialists at inscribing long decrees, 223, 227; training of, 237; travelling, 66, 108–9, 158, 162, 172, 228; unique examples of work of, 223, 237–38; who left Athens for Delos, 226; who share a style, 233; who share mannerisms, 232–33; who worked at Athens and on Delos, 226; who worked in the same shop, 233; worked in small shops, 230

Decrees: citizenship, 225, 229; deme, 230; inscribed soon after passage, 123–24, 235–36; passed on same day, 116, 126–27, 144 n. 1, 234–36; reflect political events, 226. *See also* Inscriptions
Dedications, 5, 229
Delos, recovery by Athens: effect on cutters, 162, 225–26

*289*

GENERAL INDEX

Democracy, renewal of in 229 B.C.: initial policies of, 53–54, 226; promotion of religious activity, 66, 226
Dionysiac artists, inscriptions recording activities of, 191

Eleusis: fort at, 52; mysteries, 54
Ephebeia, Attic, 54; enrollment, 86, 219
*Ergastinai* of 103/2: age of service, 219; number enrolled, 219
Eumeneia, 199

Gravestones, 1, 5, 161 and n. 15, 227 and n. 8, 237, 251

Hands: history of study, xv; purpose, xv; methodology for studying, 2–4; useful in joining and associating fragments, 229
Hieronymy, 155–56
Horoi, 5

Inscribing activity: casual, 237; decline in after 166 B.C., 223, 226; on Delos, 225–26; political nature of, 226; varied, 223–24, 226
Inscriptions: fewer in Athens after 150 B.C., 223–24, 226; honoring ephebes, 67, 116, 130, 131, 229; honoring important foreigners, 135; honoring prytaneis, 54 n. 10, 60, 109, 136, 225, 226, 229; inscribed by more than one cutter, 233; letter-height on, 5; long versus short, 1 n. 1, 5, 237; of which multiple fragments survive, 229 and n. 11; survival rate of, 229; with unique lettering, 223, 237–38. *See also* Decrees; Inscribing activity; Lists of names

Join, definition of, 6

Kea, 66, 158
Kirchner, J., 5, 60, 239

Letters: large, problems posed by, 5–6, 8, 237; techniques of cutting, 5, 228, 234. *See also* Serifs
Letter-styles, Attic, dating by, 5–6, 234, 238–39
Lists of names, multiple hands in, 158, 161, 185–86, 206, 214–15, 226, 233, 247, 248
Lyceum, 53

Macedonian control, end of, 1, 53–54, 231
Megalopolis, 53, 66

Panakton, fort at, 52
Paralia, 52

*290*

Photographs, limitations of, 7
Phyle, fort at, 52
Piraeus, local workmen from, 112, 127, 228

Rhamnous: fort at, 52; inscriptions from, 52 n. 5; 228, 243, 256 and n. 9

Serifs, 56, 61, 80, 89, 170, 173, 181, 187, 192, 197, 204, 207, 209, 212, 216, 233, 238
Sortition, 154
Sounion: fort at, 52; local style of cutting at, 228
Statue bases, 5
Stoa of Attalos at Athens, dedicatory inscription, 141
*Stoichedon* style, 61, 71 and n. 2

Theseia, 160, 179, 185
Tribal rotation, break in, xv, 159–60. *See also* Athenian archons

*Plates*

*Plate 1. Agora I 1731*

*Plate 2. Agora I 5997*

Plate 3. Agora I 5929

Plate 4. Agora I 6090

Plate 5. Agora I 918, crown

Plate 6. IG II² 443

*Plate 7. Agora I 5689*

*Plate 8. Agora I 6267*

*Plate 9. Agora I 1330*

*Plate 10. Agora I 4615*

Plate 11. Agora I 925

Plate 12. Agora I 3954

Plate 13. Agora I 5798

Plate 14. Agora I 4537

Plate 15. Agora I 896

Plate 16. Agora I 968

Plate 17. Agora I 2768

Plate 18. Agora I 4503

Plate 19. Agora I 4886

Plate 20. Join of Agora I 6035 and I 175

Plate 21. Agora I 6459

Plate 22. Agora I 2016

Plate 23. Agora I 6977 + 6980 + 6978

Plate 24. Join of Agora I 6005 and I 6006

*Plate 25. Agora I 750*

*Plate 26. Agora I 1912*

Plate 27. Join of EM 5588 and 6062

Plate 28. Join of IG II² 959 and 1014

Plate 29. Agora I 5782

| | |
|---:|:---|
| Designer: | Rick Chafian |
| Compositor: | G&S Typesetters, Inc. |
| Text: | 10/12 Palatino |
| Display: | Palatino |
| Printer: | Malloy Lithographing, Inc. |
| Binder: | Malloy Lithographing, Inc. |